BASIC
LOGIC

Richard L. Mendelsohn and Lewis M. Schwartz

Herbert Lehman College
The City University of New York

PRENTICE-HALL, INC., Englewood Cliffs, New Jersey 07632

Library of Congress Cataloging-in-Publication Data

Mendelsohn, Richard L.
    Basic logic.

    Includes index.
    1. Logic.   I. Schwartz, Lewis M.   II. Title.
BC71.M44 1987   160   86-12352
ISBN 0-13-062548-5

Editorial supervision and interior design: Serena Hoffman
Cover design: Ben Santora
Manufacturing buyer: Harry P. Baisley

PRINTED IN THE UNITED STATES OF AMERICA

10   9   8   7   6   5   4   3   2   1

ISBN 0-13-062548-5 01

PRENTICE-HALL INTERNATIONAL (UK) LIMITED, *London*
PRENTICE-HALL OF AUSTRALIA PTY. LIMITED, *Sydney*
PRENTICE-HALL CANADA INC., *Toronto*
PRENTICE-HALL HISPANOAMERICANA, S.A., *Mexico*
PRENTICE-HALL OF INDIA PRIVATE LIMITED, *New Delhi*
PRENTICE-HALL OF JAPAN, INC., *Tokyo*
PRENTICE-HALL OF SOUTHEAST ASIA PTE. LTD., *Singapore*
PRENTICE-HALL DO BRASIL, LTDA., *Rio de Janeiro*

To Marsha, Robin, and Joshua,
my reasons.

Richard L. Mendelsohn

To Eileen, Matthew, and Jennifer,
who know the depths of my
unreason.

Lewis M. Schwartz

CONTENTS

CHAPTER 7: THE CONDITIONAL 127

Part II

CHAPTER 8: ARGUMENTS 153

CHAPTER 9: ARGUMENT STRUCTURES 173

CHAPTER 10: NATURAL DEDUCTION 201

PREFACE

This book introduces you to basic, fundamental principles of logic, and it uses those principles to probe everyday language. When you have mastered this book, you will not only have sharpened your ability to reason well, but you will also have come to appreciate the integrity of what is said and the role of truth as a necessary condition of our ability to communicate with one another.

Throughout the text, you are going to be reasoning about reasoning. One of the nice things about studying this subject is that you already know it. You have been reasoning and figuring things out for years. "Why, then," you might ask, "study logic? If we already can reason, what is there to learn?" The answer is that there is a difference between reasoning and reasoning well, and studying the principles of correct reasoning helps you to reason well.

Consider an analogy. All of us can run, even though some of us can run faster than others. Almost all of us, however, could run faster than we now do by working with a track coach—an expert who has studied exactly how high our feet should be, where our toes should point, and when we should pump our arms to achieve maximum speed. In the same way, this book can help you improve your reasoning.

This book is divided into two parts. In the first part, we examine some of the most important logical relations that hold between statements. We will introduce symbolic notation and truth tables, devices that help us work out logical relations between statements and clarify their meaning. In the second part, we examine arguments. We identify the parts of an argument—premisses and conclusion—and we learn techniques for identifying them, especially as they may occur in passages we come across every day. We will learn techniques for interpreting difficult passages, among them natural-deduction techniques for re-creating the flow of reasoning in a passage. And finally, we will discuss the various sorts of problems you might run into in analyzing arguments: arguments that have suppressed premises, arguments that exhibit bad reasoning, informal fallacies, and last, the role of definition.

Logic is a large and growing discipline, and by the end of this book you will have only scratched its surface. But you will be fortified with logical principles that are deeply embedded in all languages, and tools that will serve you well in every aspect of your intellectual life.

ACKNOWLEDGMENTS

Our thanks to Eileen Abrahams, Stanley Bank, Martin Brown, Phyllis Cash, Michael Edwards, Barbara Geach, David Goldberg, Barbara Jacobson, Marsha Mendelsohn, Uday Naval, Jane Pollack, John Pittman, Victor Reed, and Mark Weinstein for their many helpful comments and criticisms of drafts of the book.

Our special thanks to Carol Springman, secretary to the Department of Philosophy at Lehman College, for her unflagging energy and devotion.

The National Endowment for the Humanities, the Exxon Education Foundation, and IBM have generously supported the basic logic program at Lehman College.

We would like to thank Lehman College for encouraging us to develop the text and for allowing us to experiment with it.

And, finally, we thank the authors of the many fine logic texts from which we have profited enormously, especially Irving Copi's *Introduction to Logic* and Stephen Thomas's *Practical Reasoning in Natural Language*.

Richard L. Mendelsohn
Lewis M. Schwartz

BASIC
LOGIC

1

STATEMENTS

"What is Truth?" asked Pontius Pilate, and he didn't wait around for an answer. Neither should you. Our question is a little more humble: "What is true or false?" The answer is: statements. And the fundamental principle of logic, that every statement is either true or false but not both, is the tool that helps us make our thoughts precise enough to begin to reason competently. The art of logic is the art of formulating our thoughts precisely.

1.1 WHAT IS A STATEMENT?

Each of the following sentences expresses a statement:

(1) The sun is 93 million miles from earth.
(2) New York City is the capital of New Jersey.
(3) There is life on Mars.
(4) Inflation will come down if the deficit is reduced.
(5) Clark Gable was handsome.

Each expresses a statement because each makes a *claim* about a subject matter. Each would ordinarily be used by someone to say something he or she thinks is true. Of course, people sometimes make mistakes and people sometimes lie. So, although each of these sentences is ordinarily used to say something the speaker thinks is true, each might nevertheless say something false. Each, in other words, says something that is true *or* false: true if the information is accurate, and false if the information is inaccurate.

The first claim is true. The sun *is* 93 million miles from earth. The second, however, is false. New York City is not the capital of New Jersey; Trenton is. But the fact that it's false does not mean that it's not a statement. On the contrary, something is said; a claim is put forward. It's just that the claim is mistaken: what is said is false. Since all we require of a sentence for it to make a statement is that it say something either true or false, (2) expresses a statement.

We don't even have to *know* which it is. The third claim, for example—that there is life on Mars—is one we are not sure about. We don't now know. We need more information before we can determine the answer. Nevertheless, (3) makes a statement, for a claim has been put forward. There either is life on Mars or there isn't. If there is, the claim is true, and if there isn't, the claim is false. So the claim is either true or false, even though we don't now (and might never) know which.

The fourth claim is one that economists and politicians often debate. It is highly controversial, even among informed people. But it is either true or false, so it is a statement.

The fifth, too, is a statement, even though it is hard to see how one could decide whether it is true, since people differ so much about who they think is handsome. Nevertheless, anyone who made this claim would be saying something he or she believed to be true.

A statement can be about anything whatsoever. Whatever we can talk about, we can make claims about. We can talk about numbers, about emotions, about feelings, about God, and about various moral issues. So, we can make claims about all of these things. Just as long as something has been said about something, just as long as some information has been presented that is either accurate or inaccurate, just as long as something has been put forward that could be believed, denied, doubted, or proved, a statement has been made.

Here are some more examples:

$2 + 2 = 4$.

James is hungry.

Everyone loves John.

I love Mary.

God exists.

Abraham Lincoln was a great president.

Slavery is immoral.

Each of these sentences expresses a claim that could be believed, denied, doubted, or proved. It is fairly obvious that $2 + 2 = 4$, and it is hardly likely that anyone would deny it. But some of the other claims in this list are more controversial. We can even imagine going to war over some of them—for example, the last. But whether everyone believes them or no one believes them, whether they are obviously true or not, they are all statements.

So you will be aware of the vast variety of statements one might make, consider some more sentences, each of which expresses a statement:

There is a 65 percent chance of rain tomorrow.

Columbus had a headache the day he discovered America.

Willie Mays was a better ballplayer than Mickey Mantle.

To every action there is an equal and opposite reaction.

If John had studied harder, he would have passed chemistry.

John doesn't want to go to the movies tonight.

If given the choice, I would choose chocolate chip cookies over chocolate chip ice cream, although I would never choose peanut butter crunch when I could have caramel crunch.

Our notion of a statement is a very broad one, then. It includes any claim or assertion a person might make about any subject matter whatsoever.

A sentence expresses a statement if (1) something has been claimed to be true, and (2) what has been said is either true or false.

(1) and (2) provide a test for determining whether a statement has been made. If a sentence passes this test, it expresses a statement.

EXERCISES

1.1:1 Give five examples of statements that you believe to be true.

1.1:2 Give five examples of statements that you believe to be false.

1.1:3 Give five examples of statements that you are unsure about.

Study Vocabulary: statement

1.2 KINDS OF SENTENCES

There are many different uses to which language is put. Making statements is only one such use. Among other things, we also use language to ask questions and to issue commands. These three uses—making statements, asking questions, and issuing commands—are so important to us in communicating with each other that we employ grammatical distinctions in our language to mark them. For the most part, we use

> INDICATIVE sentences to make STATEMENTS;
> INTERROGATIVE sentences to ask QUESTIONS;
> IMPERATIVE sentences to issue COMMANDS.

Indicative sentences are almost always used to make statements. In fact, all of the examples in Section 1.1 of sentences that express statements are also examples of indicative sentences.

Interrogative sentences are ordinarily used to ask **questions**. Here are some examples:

> Is it raining?
>
> How far is the sun from the earth?
>
> Why does oil float on water?
>
> Is New York City the capital of New Jersey?

None of these sentences would ordinarily be used to make a claim. In none of them is a person committing himself to the truth of something. The speaker is not giving information to another individual; rather, he is requesting information from another individual.

Imperative sentences are ordinarily used to issue **commands** (or requests), to tell (or request) someone to do something. Some examples of imperative sentences are:

> Make it rain!
>
> Place the sun 93 million miles from the earth!
>
> Boil the water!
>
> Please close the door!

Again, the speaker is not saying something that is either true or false. She is not committing herself to the accuracy of some piece of information. Nor is she requesting information. Rather, in each of these cases she is giving an order, telling someone to do something. No statement is made in any of these cases.

Here are some more examples. For each one, try to figure out whether a statement has been made.

> (1) Close the door!
>
> (2) Sign on the dotted line!
>
> (3) Does John love Mary?
>
> (4) Abortion is immoral.
>
> (5) Is it raining outside?
>
> (6) God exists.

We can see that (4) and (6) express statements. The others do not. (3) and (5) express questions. (1) and (2) express commands. Neither questions nor commands are true or false; therefore, neither questions nor commands are statements.

So, not every sentence expresses a statement. Just because a sentence has been produced, it does not follow that a claim has been made. Recall the test for statements from the last section: A sentence expresses a statement if (1) something has been claimed to be true, and (2) what has been said is either true or false. Indicative sentences pass this test.

EXERCISES

1.2:1   For each of the following sentences, determine whether a statement has been made, a question asked, or a command given.

a.   Should we continue to fight?

b.   Take me out to the ballgame!

c.   We are aiding rebellious citizens in Nicaragua.

d.   The United States expects to land a colony of explorers on the moon in 1997.

e.   Be careful with that umbrella!

f.   If John had been careful, he would not have been hurt.

1.2:2   Each of the following sentences lacks a final punctuation mark. Nevertheless, for each, determine whether a statement has been made, a question asked, or a command given.

a.   Abortion is just another name for murder

b.   Please answer as soon as possible

c.   Do you know the way to San Jose

d.   Little Boy Blue come blow your horn

e.   Does severing relations with Cuba promote the best interests of the United States

f.   Oh Father, why hast thou forsaken me

1.2:3   Read the following passage and follow the instructions.

I went to the movies last night and saw *Casablanca*. It was a bad movie. Have you ever seen a Bogart film? Well, don't ever go to see one.

a.   List the indicative sentences in this passage.

b.   List the interrogative sentences in this passage.

c.   List the imperative sentences in this passage.

1.2:4   Read the following passage and answer the questions.

So, you want to know where I was last night. Am I a suspect in the crime? Why are you holding me here? Do you think I did it? I don't have to tell you anything. I want to see my lawyer.

a.   What statements did the writer make?
b.   What questions did the writer ask?

1.2:5   In the following passage identify what statements were made and what commands were issued.

There are four men in the next room. One of those men is the greatest guitarist in the world. You can tell he is a guitarist because he has long fingernails. Go into the room, examine each man's fingernails, and tell me which one is the guitarist.

1.2:6   Read the passage *carefully* and answer the questions.

Read the next four sentences. The first sentence tells you to do something. The second and third sentences express statements. Is the fourth sentence a question? All the sentences in this passage express true statements.

a.   Do whatever you are told in this passage. (You should have done it before you got to this point.)
b.   Is there any difference between what you are told to do before you read the passage and what you are told to do in the passage?
c.   Identify the sentences in this passage that express true statements.
d.   Answer the question you are asked in this passage.
e.   Is the last sentence true?

Study Vocabulary: indicative sentence
                       interrogative sentence
                       question
                       imperative sentence
                       command

1.3   COMPLETING THE SENTENCE

In order to communicate successfully, we must make clear what thoughts we are presenting. To make our thoughts clear, we must ordinarily use complete sentences, for the sentence is the smallest unit of communication. An incomplete sentence, by itself, usually does not present a clear thought. However, sometimes the **context** in which the words are spoken—the surrounding circumstances (people, place, other words)—helps to complete the thought.

Consider a word standing by itself. For example, suppose someone says

Atlanta.

Has a claim been made? If so, what claim? What *about* Atlanta? To make a claim you must say something about something. But a word by itself doesn't do that; it expresses no thought, says nothing that is either true or false. Has a question been asked? If so, which question could it be? There are so many possible ways of completing the thought, we wouldn't know where to begin. Perhaps a command has been issued. But again, we are at a loss to determine which one.

The very same word, however, can be brought to life when a context is supplied. Suppose you overhear the following conversation:

John: Where are we?
Mary: Atlanta.

The word *Atlanta*—by itself—lacks purpose. The context, however, provides this purpose. In this context, we may be sure that Mary is making the statement

We are in Atlanta.

In the context of responding to John's question, Mary is able to make a statement, even though she uses an incomplete sentence. It is as though Mary were asked to fill the blank in

We are in _____

in order to create a complete, indicative sentence that expresses a statement.
Here is a similar example:

John: Are we in Atlanta?
Mary: Yes.

Although Mary has said only "Yes," which is not a complete sentence, she has made a claim that is either true or false. She has claimed that the two of them, John and Mary, are in Atlanta. Again, within the context of responding to John's question, Mary's single word "Yes" allows her to make the claim that she and John are in Atlanta. If Mary had said

We are in Atlanta,

this indicative sentence would express the same statement that the single word "Yes" does.

Here is a slightly different example:

John: I like olives.
Mary: Me too.

Mary's words do not constitute a sentence. Nevertheless, her message is perfectly clear. What she is claiming is that she, like John, likes olives. By saying "Me too" immediately after John's statement, Mary makes the same claim for herself. Again, if Mary had used the indicative sentence

I like olives too,

she would have made the same statement.

In each of the preceding examples, Mary is able to express a complete thought and make a claim even though she uses an incomplete sentence. Her words *by themselves* do not convey the thought, but in conjunction with other words that are said and the circumstances in which they are said, the thought is made evident. Of course, in each of these examples the thought could be made clear with a complete, indicative sentence that does not require knowledge of the context in order to be understood.

It is important to get into the habit of supplying all the relevant information in the words you use. For, whether you are reading or writing, all that is visible are the words. You cannot readily rely on nonverbal context. In logic, as you will see, you will be taking the words at their face value.

EXERCISES

1.3:1   Each of the following is an incomplete sentence. Complete each so that a *statement* is made.

a.   Ronald Reagan gave
b.   Although Africa has grown since World War II
c.   John either took French
d.   When the light turns yellow
e.   The orbiting telescope

1.3:2   Each of the following is an incomplete sentence. Complete each so that a *question* is asked.

a.   Ronald Reagan give
b.   The orbiting telescope
c.   is rich
d.   Was the king of France
e.   When the light turns yellow

1.3:3 Each of the following is an incomplete sentence. Complete each so that a *command* is given.

a. The orbiting telescope
b. Either do it
c. When the light turns yellow
d. Ronald Reagan, give
e. Be

1.3:4 In each of the following dialogues, Sam is able to make a statement even though he does not use an indicative sentence. In each case, write a complete sentence that expresses the statement Sam makes.

a. Harry: What movie do you want to see?
    Sam: *Bambi.*
b. Harry: Why did the chicken cross the road?
    Sam: To get to the other side.
c. Harry: John is a Republican.
    Sam: No, a Democrat.

1.3:5 In the text, we presented a dialogue in which Mary says the word "Atlanta" and succeeds in making the statement that she and John are in Atlanta. If John had said something else in that dialogue, Mary's words "Atlanta" might have expressed a different statement. Make up such a dialogue.

1.3:6 Find three passages in a newspaper or a magazine in which an incomplete sentence succeeds in making a statement. Identify the statement by expressing it as a complete indicative sentence.

Study Vocabulary: context

1.4 TRUE AND FALSE

We have already said that every statement is either true or false. There is, however, another principle governing statements: no statement is *both* true and false. Our two fundamental principles concerning statements are therefore:

> *(I) Every statement is either true or false.*

> *(II) No statement is both true and false.*

In fact, we can take these principles as defining what it means for something to be a statement: a statement is anything that is (I) either true or false and

(II) not both truth and false. There are only two truth values. Every statement has one, and only one, of them. There are no other possibilities.

The truth value a statement has is independent of whether anyone believes the statement. Just because I believe that a statement is true, it does not follow that the statement *is* true. I can be wrong. Even if everybody believes that a statement is true, that does not mean that it *is* true. Everybody can be wrong. Similarly, just because I believe that a statement is false, that does not mean that it *is* false. Finally, a statement is true or false even if we don't know which it is. It is highly unlikely, for example, that we will ever know whether the claim

Napoleon's last thought was of his dog

is true or whether it is false. But it must be one or the other: either Napoleon's last thought was of his dog or it wasn't.

The two truth values help us to uncover a structure of logical connections among statements. The truth value of one statement is linked with the truth value of others. These connections are also independent of our beliefs. Consider the statement

(1) Columbus had a headache the day he discovered America.

It is highly unlikely that anyone knows whether this statement is true or whether it is false. Nevertheless, if this statement is true, then it must also be true that

(2) Columbus discovered America.

Here are some other statements that would also have to be true:

(3) There is such a place as America.
(4) There is such a person as Columbus.
(5) Columbus was ill at least one day in his life.
(6) Columbus did not invent America.

If statement (1) is true, statements (3) through (6) must be true as well.

Knowing whether a statement is true is of the greatest importance to us. We all want to believe the truth—and only the truth. But the truth does not always stare us in the face; we often have to work hard to find out whether a claim is true. We have to ask questions to discover how it is connected with others. This will enable us to determine how the claim fits with what we see, what we hear, and what we believe. Logic is the science of "fit."

In logic, then, we ask "what if" questions. "What if the statement were true?" "What if the statement were false?" And we ask these questions in order to unfold the connection between the statement in question and other statements, to note other statements that would also have to be true (or false) if the original statement were true.

Our primary interest in logic is in what a sentence says, in the thought or information it contains. It is important that we distinguish carefully between what a statement says and whether we believe it. In doing logic, we are not interested in whether we believe that a statement is true; what is important is that we *understand* what we believe, that we recognize the connections between this belief and others. The notions of truth and falsity give us a structure that enables us to achieve these goals.

EXERCISES

1.4:1   In each of the following dialogues between Harry and Sam, Harry asks a question about what someone said. Sometimes Sam answers Harry's question, and sometimes he doesn't. Identify which cases are which.

a.   Harry: What did the president say last night?
        Sam: Something false.
b.   Harry: What did the president say last night?
        Sam: What do you care? He's a politician.
c.   Harry: Did you read the newspaper this morning?
        Sam: I don't believe that garbage.
d.   Harry: When did she say we make our turn?
        Sam: At the second light.

1.4:2   For each of the following, write at least three statements that would also have to be true if the statement were true.

a.   Gloria's mother is taller than her father.
b.   When Nelson won the Battle of Trafalgar, he was wounded.
c.   North Dakota is south of South Dakota.

Study Vocabulary: **truth value**
                              true
                              false

1.5   THE LOGICAL IDEAL

Our ideal in logic is to be precise and clear, to leave nothing to chance, to leave no room for being misunderstood. We want to make sure that everything is up front, so to speak, that nothing is left to guesswork or to context. We want to make sure that if something is being stated, then it is right there in the sentence that is being used to express that statement. There should be nothing hidden in the thought; there should be nothing assumed but not stated. Thus, we take each uttered sentence at its face value. We identify the statement made with the indicative sentence used to make it, in order to *force* ourselves to be as clear as possible about what statements we are making. And only when we reach this ideal do we mean what we say and say what we mean.

Our ideal in logic is to use only indicative sentences that conform to the same principles that govern statements:

(I)   Every statement is either true or false.

(II)   No statement is both true and false.

You can think of these two principles as a grindstone for sharpening thoughts, for eliminating the gap between the actual words we use and the statements we wish to make. A sentence that violates (I) is said to be **vague**; a sentence that violates (II) is said to be **ambiguous**.

Whenever a sentence has two or more *definite* meanings, it is ambiguous. Consider the following example:

John went to the bank.

Because the word *bank* has different meanings—a place where money is deposited, and the land at the edge of a river—the sentence "John went to the bank" can be used to express different statements. Which statement is being made? Without further information, we don't know. The very same sentence, then, can be used to say something true or false, depending upon the context. Our example might be true if we mean that John went to the river's edge, and false if we mean that he went to the savings bank.

Here is another example of ambiguity:

Sam is not a man.

What statement is being made? There would seem to be at least four possibilities:

Sam is not a man; he is only five years old.

Sam is not a man; she is a woman.

Sam is not a man; he ran away.

Sam is not a man; he is a dog.

Whenever we are inclined to answer a question by saying "Yes and no," we are confronting ambiguity. Suppose I am asked whether John is a good student. I might want to respond, "Yes and no." I think he is a good student in the sense that he attends all the classes and does all of his homework. But I might also think that he is not a good student in the sense that he never goes beyond the work assigned and takes no interest in the issues discussed. The question is ambiguous.

Ambiguities are often found in children's riddles. What's black and white and read all over? Answer: a newspaper. The word *read*, in its spoken context, can be ambiguous, though of course when written the riddle is less puzzling. Here is another one: What has four wheels and flies? Answer: a garbage truck.

Here is a somewhat different example of ambiguity:

I am hungry.

I is a pronoun referring to the one who is speaking. So, if John says "I am hungry," he will be making a statement different from the one Mary makes when she uses those very same words. John will be speaking about himself, and Mary will be speaking about herself. The very same sentence will thus express different statements in the different contexts. So, the very same sentence might express both a true statement and a false statement—true, say, when John says it and false when Mary says it. Of course, it is doubtful that this ambiguity will lead to trouble, since we are likely to know who is saying, "I am hungry." But think of what happens when you ask someone who has knocked on the door, "Who's there?" and you hear, "It's me."

If the very same sentence can be both true *and* false (at the same time), then we can conclude that it expresses different statements; the sentence is ambiguous. In such cases, some part of the thought we wish to convey is not being made explicit by the words we use, and so we have departed from our logical ideal. In such cases, we fail to say what we mean.

Consider now a different way in which sentences might fail the true/false test and so fail to make clear what statement is being made. A sentence might not be precise enough to enable us to assign it a truth value. It would violate (I), and so be vague.

Suppose I'm asked whether John is an old man. Well, how old is old? Or what if the host asks me how much sugar I want in my coffee, and I answer, "Not too much, please." How much is too much?

Of course, most words that we ordinarily use are vague to some degree. Suppose you're asked whether it is raining, and you see that it's damp and misty—a very light drizzle. Does this count as raining or not? Of course, if it were a matter of great importance, we might very well introduce, as scientists often do, a precise meaning. We might agree to apply the term *rain*, say, only to cases where there is precipitation of at least .05 inches per hour. Then, our saying that it is raining would commit us to a precise claim, though of course we might not know in a given case, unless we were able to use instruments, whether it's true.

For most purposes, we can tolerate the vagueness of most ordinary terms, for we know that we can, if it should become important, make the terms precise enough so that we can without question apply the true/false principles. Indeed, were we to insist on our logical ideal for most communication, things might become very dull.

On the other hand, vagueness can sometimes be of enormous importance. Consider a law that would permit trade only with democratic countries. Precisely what counts as a democratic country? Here, of course, there is occasion for considerable debate.

The logical ideal remains that of using only unambiguous, precise sentences, sentences that have only one interpretation. Such sentences would be indistinguishable from statements. They are either true or false, and they are never both true and false.

One more point. It is important not to be confused by the sense of clarity that we are interested in. Consider the following two sentences:

> The door is closed.
>
> The door is locked.

These two sentences express quite distinct statements. Neither is ambiguous or vague. The first sentence never *means* that the door is locked (though, of course, it is possible that it is locked), for if the door were closed and not locked, the sentence would express a truth. On the other hand, the claims expressed are logically connected. If it's true that the door is locked, then it must be true that the door is closed. Each sentence expresses a perfectly clear statement, though if the second is true, the first must be true as well.

Here, then, we have a good example of how our two true/false principles help us to understand what a sentence says. First, paying attention to the principles helps us uncover ambiguity and vagueness. Second, by enabling us to attend to the logical connection(s) between one statement and others, the principles help us to identify precisely what information is being conveyed.

In summary, a sentence is ambiguous if it violates principle (II), if it can be used to make statements having different truth values. An ambiguous sentence has two or more quite definite meanings. A sentence is vague, on the other hand, if it violates principle (I). A vague sentence lacks definite meaning, so that we are unable to assign it even one truth value.

EXERCISES

1.5:1   Each of the following sentences is ambiguous and can be understood in at least two ways. Identify the ambiguity in each case, and then write two sentences (for each) that express the different thoughts unambiguously.

a.   It's raining.
b.   I am happy.
c.   It's too hot to eat.
d.   The bird is free.
e.   John is cold.
f.   Flying planes can be dangerous.

1.5:2   Write three sentences that are ambiguous. For each sentence, identify the different statements that could be made by it.

1.5:3   Write three sentences that are vague. For each sentence, identify why you are unable to assign it a definite truth value.

1.5:4   The following passage contains an ambiguous sentence that is traded upon to produce a very strange result. Identify the ambiguous sentence and state the two interpretations.

> Before the big fight, Slugger Joe said that he could beat Killer Ken with his hands tied behind his back. After Killer Ken knocked him out in the third round, reporters asked Slugger Joe what went wrong. "They didn't tie my hands behind my back," Slugger said.

1.5:5   Read the following passage and answer the questions.

> It's not my fault. John told me to close the door. Those were his exact words: "Close the door!" He did not tell me to lock the door. So, it is not my fault that the door was left unlocked. It was not my negligence that resulted in the apartment being robbed.

a.   What were John's exact words?
b.   Did John tell the writer to lock the door?
c.   What reason do you give for your answer to (b)?
d.   Who is responsible for the apartment's having been left unlocked? Explain your answer.

1.5:6   Read the following passage and answer the questions.

> The homework instructions are as follows: Read the following passage, underline all statements in the passage, and then answer any questions at the end.

a.   Were you told to write the passage out?
b.   Were you told to respond to any commands made at the end?

1.5:7   Read the following passage and answer the questions.

> The landlord said, "I won't give you a new refrigerator. And, if I give you a new sink, then I will have to raise your rent."

a.   Did the landlord say he would give you a new refrigerator?
b.   Did the landlord say he would give you a new sink?
c.   Did the landlord say he would not give you a new sink?
d.   Did the landlord say he will have to raise your rent?

Study Vocabulary: vague
                      ambiguous

REVIEW

1.   Statements are the basic building blocks of logic and reasoning. A statement is a claim someone puts forward, a commitment he or she makes to the truth of something. Every statement is either true or false, but not both. For someone to have made a statement, both of the following tests must be satisfied:

(1) something has been claimed to be true, and

(2) what has been said is either true or false.

2.   Indicative sentences are, with few exceptions, used to make statements; interrogative sentences are used to ask questions; imperative sentences are used to issue commands. Each of these types of sentences contains a complete thought, but only in an indicative sentence is one claiming the thought to be true.

3.   Although indicative sentences are almost always used to make statements, we do succeed in making statements in other ways. Just as long as a complete thought is present, communication is successful. We can even use incomplete sentences: we rely on the context to complete the thought so that a statement is made. Every statement can be expressed with an indicative sentence.

4.   There are only two truth values—true and false. Every statement is either true or false; no statement is both true and false. Statements have logical connections with one another: the truth value of one statement often determines the truth values of others. In logic we examine the sorts of connections that hold among statements. So, in logic we are interested not so much in whether a statement is true as in what else would have to be true *if* it were true.

5.   In logic, our interest is in the statement expressed by a sentence— what the sentence says. To be clear about what a sentence says, we take it as an ideal that a statement be identified with an unambiguous, complete, indicative sentence. This assures us that there is no room for interpretation of the words used: all the information necessary for determining a unique truth value is in the sentence, and nothing is hidden.

2

NEGATION

Basic to our understanding of what a person claims is true is our understanding of what he does not claim is true and what he claims is not true. If you already understand the statement we have just made, then you are well on your way to understanding negation. Puzzle over it a while. What is the significance of the placement of the two "nots" in the statement? By the end of this chapter, you will be able to answer this question easily, and you will be able to explain the difference in placement and why you must pay attention to it.

2.1 WHAT IS A NEGATION?

Any statement a person can make can also be denied. To deny a statement is to say that the statement is false, that it's not true, or that it's not so. A statement that denies what an original statement asserts is called the **negation** of the original.

The surest way of forming the negation of a statement is to put *It is not the case that* in front of it. If you want to deny

John is happy,

all you need do is say

It is not the case that John is happy.

Usually, however, we form the negation of a statement by putting *not* inside it at the appropriate place. To negate "John is happy," for example, we would most likely say

John is not happy.

In many cases, however, as in negating

John walks with a limp,

we also require the help of the verb *to do* to form the negation:

John does not walk with a limp.

Putting *It is not the case that* in front of a statement always yields the negation of that statement. Inserting *not* inside the statement often gets us the negation—but not always. We will discuss some of these complications in later sections of this chapter.

The negation of a statement is itself a statement, one that denies exactly what the original asserts. A statement and its negation must therefore have exactly opposite truth values. If the statement is true, then its negation is false; conversely, if the statement is false, then its negation is true.

Let us use P to represent any statement you like, and let us use *not* P to represent the negation of that statement. For example, if we suppose that P is the statement "John is happy," then *not* P is the statement "It is not the case that John is happy." Using this notation, we can summarize the properties of negation concisely by means of what is known as a **truth table**. Using T to abbreviate *true* and F to abbreviate *false*, we have the following truth-table definition of negation:

P	*Not P*
T	F
F	T

In the first column, we list the two possible truth values for P: P will be either T or F. In the second column, we list the corresponding truth values for *not* P. Now, read across the rows. In the top row, when P is T, we find that *not* P is F. In the bottom row, when P is F, we find that *not* P is T.

This truth table gives us the **truth conditions** of the negation of a statement: it shows the conditions under which the negation is true and the conditions under which it is false. Since a statement and its negation always have opposite truth values, the truth conditions for *not* P are as follows: *not* P is true when P is false, and it is false when P is true.

We are actually going to make our notation even more concise by eliminating the word *not* and introducing a special symbol, '$-$', for negation. $-P$ will represent the negation of P; that is, it will stand for "it is not the case that P." Our truth table now becomes:

P	$-P$
T	F
F	T

What do you think $--P$ would be? Such a statement is called *the double negation of* P. If P were the statement "John is happy," then $--P$ would be, literally,

It is not the case that it is not the case that John is happy,

or, more colloquially,

It is not the case that John is not happy.

We can represent the truth conditions for $--P$ with our truth table. Let us add a column for $--P$:

P	$-P$	$--P$
T	F	
F	T	

Now, $--P$ is the negation of $-P$, so it must have the opposite truth value of $-P$. Working across the top row of our truth table, we find that $-P$ is F; $--P$ must therefore be T:

P	$-P$	$--P$
T	F	T
F	T	

Next, working across the bottom row of our truth table, we find that $-P$ is T; $--P$, its negation, must therefore be F. Our completed truth table looks like this:

P	$-P$	$--P$
T	F	T
F	T	F

You can see from the table that P and $--P$ are **logically equivalent**; that is, they are true together and false together. They have the same truth conditions. And this is precisely the result we would have expected.

EXERCISES

2.1:1   Write the negation of each of the following statements in two ways: first, by putting *It is not the case that* in front, and second, by inserting *not* in the appropriate place.

a.   The class started late today.

b.   The president was very forceful last night.

c. John is not playing in this game.
d. John likes everyone.
e. Happiness is an illusion.
f. Freud was a metaphysician.
g. Birth-control pills are not immoral.

2.1:2 Assume that each of the following statements may be represented as
$-P$. Write out, for each case, the statement represented by P.

a. Lenin was not a Menshevik.
b. It's not true that God is dead.
c. John was not unhappy with his grade.
d. Mary does not think highly of her teacher.
e. Sally did not say that she loves Harry.

2.1:3 Work out a truth table for $---P$. What is it logically equivalent
to?

Study Vocabulary: negation
truth table
truth conditions
logically equivalent

2.2 CONTRADICTORY STATEMENTS

Two statements that *must* have opposite truth values are called **contradictory** statements, or simply contradictories.

> *Two statements are contradictory if (1) they cannot both be
> true, and (2) they cannot both be false.*

Since a statement and its negation must have opposite truth values, they
are contradictories.

Contradictory statements give exactly opposite information. We can
see this most clearly in the case of a statement and its negation: whatever
a statement asserts is explicitly rejected by its negation. If Jones says that
it's raining and Smith says that it's not raining, Smith is in effect saying:
the weather conditions are anything other than what Jones claims them to
be.

The following diagram will help us see the relation between this pair
of contradictory statements. Let the horizontal line represent all possible
weather conditions. We divide the line into those conditions that count as
rain and those conditions that do not count as rain.

---	drizzle	hurricane	downpour	snow	sleet	sun	hail	---

It is raining. | It is not raining.

You can see from the diagram that all possible weather conditions must fall into one, and only one, of the two categories. Either it's raining or it's not raining.

Consider what happens when Smith denies Jones's claim by saying that it's not raining. Smith is not claiming that it's snowing; he is not claiming that the sun is shining; he is not claiming that it is cloudy. To be sure, if any of these were to hold, then it would not be raining, and Smith would be right. But he is not claiming any one of these *in particular*. He is simply denying Jones's claim that it is raining. Thus, Smith's denial will be true as long as the weather is anything other than rain.

Here is a different example:

John is very rich.

John is very poor.

Are these statements contradictory? The answer is no. They are opposites, but not *exact* opposites. We can see the relation between the two statements if we construct a diagram representing all the different levels of wealth:

very poor	poor	middle-income	rich	very rich

A person cannot fall into more than one category. So, if John were in the *very rich* category, he could not also be in the *very poor* category. In this sense, the two statements are opposites: they cannot both be true. On the other hand, a person might fall in one of the other categories. John might, for example, be middle-income. So, the two claims could both be false. They are therefore not *exact* opposites.

For the same reason, "John is poor" would not contradict the original statement. Neither would "John is middle-income" or "John is rich." In each of these cases, we would have a pair of statements that are opposites, but not exact opposites. Although they could not both be true, they *could* both be false.

To contradict the claim that John is very rich, we need to say something that will be exactly opposed to that claim. So, we want to claim not that John is *specifically* in this or that category, but that he is in one of the other categories, without specifying which one:

John is either very poor or poor or middle-income or rich.

The simplest way of saying this is,

John is *not* very rich,

because this takes up all the other possibilities:

not very rich				
very poor	poor	middle-income	rich	very rich

A statement and its negation, then, like all pairs of contradictory statements, have exactly opposite truth values. They cannot both be true, and they cannot both be false. The very conditions that make one of them true make the other of them false.

Just to make this clearer, let's consider the case of a horse race. Suppose that Jones bets ten dollars that

Horse 1 will win the race.

And suppose Smith bets ten dollars that

Horse 1 will not win the race.

Jones and Smith have placed exactly opposite bets. One of them must win the bet and one of them must lose, since horse 1 either wins the race or doesn't.

What if the race ends in a dead heat—a tie? In horse racing, when there is a tie for first, both horses are declared winners. So if, for example, horses 1 and 2 tie for first, then both are winners. Horse 1 would be declared a winner, and Jones would collect on his bet. Smith, on the other hand, would lose her bet.

In some other sports, ties are treated differently. In ice hockey, for example, a tie does not count as a win. So, if you bet ten dollars that, say, the Bruins will beat the Maple Leafs, and the game ends in a tie, then you lose your bet. Interestingly, if you had bet ten dollars that the Bruins would lose the game, and the game ends in a tie, then you would also lose your bet, since ties are also distinguished from losses.

In horse racing, the two statements

Horse 1 wins the race

Horse 1 loses the race

are contradictory. In ice hockey, however, where ties are distinguished from both wins and losses, the two statements

The Bruins win the game

The Bruins lose the game

are not contradictories, since both might be false. On the other hand, both of the following pairs of statements are contradictories:

Horse 1 wins the race.

Horse 1 does not win the race.

The Bruins win the game.

The Bruins do not win the game.

One will always get the contradictory of a statement by negating it.

In summary, to deny a statement is to assert its contradictory. A statement and its negation always have exactly opposite truth values. If a statement is true, its negation is false; if the statement is false, its negation is true.

EXERCISES

2.2:1   Which of the following pairs of statements are contradictories and which are not? (Remember the test for contradictories. There are two parts. Can they both be true? Can they both be false? Only if the answer is *no* to both questions are they contradictories.)

a.	John is happy.	John is sad.
b.	The sky is blue.	The sky is red.
c.	The sky is blue.	The sky is not blue.
d.	Rome was built in a day.	Rome was not built in a day.
e.	John is exactly four feet tall.	John is exactly three feet tall.
f.	John is more than four feet tall.	John is less than four feet tall.
g.	John is a human being.	John is a man.
h.	Mary is a doctor.	Mary is a mother.
i.	John took the train to school.	John took the bus to school.
j.	John is four feet tall.	John is not four feet tall.
k.	John is four feet tall or more.	John is not four feet tall.
l.	The cup is half empty.	The cup is half full.
m.	John is a Democrat.	John is a Republican.
n.	Harry went to college.	Harry did not go to college.
o.	Sam went to private school.	Sam went to public school.
p.	John took physics in high school.	John did not take physics in college.

Study Vocabulary: **contradictory**

2.3 LOGICAL RELATIONS

Two statements are **logically related** to each other if the truth value of one can determine the truth value of the other. We want to say more about this notion of a logical relation, using what we have already learned about contradictory statements.

Let us review the definition of contradictory statements. Two statements are contradictory if (1) they cannot both be true, and (2) they cannot both be false.

There are two parts to this definition. (1) says that the statements are **exclusive**, or **inconsistent**. The truth of one excludes the truth of the other; if one is true, the other *must* be false. (2) says that the statements are **exhaustive**. One or the other of the two statements *must* be true—they exhaust all possibilities—so that if one is false, the other *has to* be true.

To appreciate what we mean by a logical relation, we must understand the strength of the word *cannot* in (1) and (2), and of words such as *must* and *has to* in our discussion of exclusive and exhaustive statements.

Consider the following two statements:

Ronald Reagan is the president of the United States.

Valéry Giscard d'Estaing is the president of France.

It happens to be the case at the time of our writing this example that one of these statements is true and the other is false. Nevertheless, the two are not logically related. Suppose, as is the case now, that Ronald Reagan is the president of the United States. What effect does the truth of that statement have on the truth value of the other statement? The answer, of course, is none. Now suppose it is false that Ronald Reagan is the president of the United States. Would that affect the truth or falsity of the other statement? Again, the answer is no.

These two statements are **logically independent** of each other. The truth (or falsity) of one does not determine the truth (or falsity) of the other. If we were to discover that the first statement is true, we would still have to inquire independently about the truth of the second. It is, after all, possible that both statements are true. Similarly, if we were to discover that the first statement is false, we would have to inquire independently about the truth or falsity of the other.

When two statements are logically related, the truth or falsity of one will enable us to determine the truth or falsity of the other without further inquiry. Consider, for example:

Ronald Reagan is the president of the United States.

Ronald Reagan is the vice-president of the United States.

These two statements are logically related, for once you know the first to be true, you know the second must be false. No one can be both president and vice-president of the United States at the same time.

In short, just because we have two statements, one of which happens to be true and the other of which happens to be false, it does not follow that they are logically related. For, even if *as a matter of fact* they have opposite truth values, it might not be that they *have to have* opposite truth values. And it is what would *have to be* that determines the logical relation.

Let us consider another example:

The United States is the largest importer of automobiles.

The United States ranks third in importing automobiles.

Clearly, these two statements cannot both be true. If we learn that the first is true, then we do not have to undertake a separate investigation to determine whether the second is true; we know that the second is false. And if we learn that the second is true, then we know that the first is false. They are therefore logically related: they are *exclusive*.

These same two statements are not, however, *exhaustive*: they could both be false. This means that if one were false, we could not immediately figure out the truth value of the other; we would need further research.

When two statements are contradictory, we can always determine the truth value of one from the truth value of the other; contradictory statements always have opposite truth values.

But we can have logical relations that are weaker than contradiction. Two statements might be exclusive but not exhaustive, as in our last example. So, if one is true, the other must be false, but if one is false, we cannot yet determine the truth value of the other. It might be true or it might be false. We can also have a case where two statements are exhaustive but not exclusive—for example:

Some of the hostages were injured.

Some of the hostages were not injured.

These two statements are not exclusive. After all, both might be true. But they are exhaustive. If we were to learn that one of them is false, we would need no further inquiry to determine that the other is true. In this case, if one were false, the other would have to be true, but if one were true, the other might be true or might be false.

The idea that some statements *must* be true (or *must* be false) can be made clearer by considering the following examples. Suppose you hear a weather forecast saying that it is raining. You hadn't expected it to rain, so you look out the window to check, and you see the sun shining. You conclude that the statement

It is raining

is false. But, although it is false, the statement might have been true. It is not impossible that it is true. It might have been raining. That is why you checked—to discover whether the statement is true.

Now suppose you were to hear a weather forecast saying

It is raining and it is not raining.

At the same time. At the same place. No fudges here. Do you need to look out the window to discover the truth value of this statement? No. This statement is false. But it is not merely false; it *cannot* be true. You do not have to look outside to determine that it is false. Without looking, you *know* that it is false. To assert both P and −P is to contradict oneself. Even though we don't know which part of the statement is false, we know that one part *must* be false.

Similarly, if a statement *has to be* true, then it is true, but also, it couldn't be false. Consider the same example: you look out the window and you see the sun shining. So, the statement

The sun is shining

is true. But, although true, it does not have to be true. It might have been false, for the sun might not have been shining. On the other hand, the statement

Either the sun is shining or the sun is not shining

has to be true. We don't have to look outside to determine that this statement is true. Look back at our truth table for negation. As you go down each line of the table you will find that either P turns out to be true or −P turns out to be true. There is no possible circumstance in which both are false.

When a logical relation holds between two statements, we are able to answer certain questions about the connection between the truth value of one and the truth value of the other. Let's review.

When two statements are *exclusive* (or *inconsistent*), then if one is true, the other must be false. What happens if one is false? If all we know is that they are exclusive, the answer is indeterminate—the other might be true or false.

When two statements are *exhaustive*, then if one is false, the other must be true. What happens if one is true? If all we know is that they are exhaustive, the answer is indeterminate—the other might be true or false.

When two statements are *contradictory*, then if one is true, the other is false; and if one is false, the other is true. We can always determine the truth value of one if we know the truth value of the other.

When two statements are *logically equivalent*, they always have the same truth value: if one is true the other is true, and if one is false the other is false.

EXERCISES

2.3:1 Consider this pair of statements:

(a) Mary went to the movies.

(b) Mary did not go to the movies.

a. Suppose (a) is true. Is (b) true, false, or indeterminate?
b. Suppose (a) is false. Is (b) true, false, or indeterminate?
c. Suppose (b) is true. Is (a) true, false, or indeterminate?
d. Suppose (b) is false. Is (a) true, false, or indeterminate?

Are the two statements contradictory? Exclusive? Exhaustive?

2.3:2 Consider this pair of statements:

(a) John is extremely happy.

(b) John is extremely sad.

a. Suppose (a) is true. Is (b) true, false, or indeterminate?
b. Suppose (a) is false. Is (b) true, false, or indeterminate?
c. Suppose (b) is true. Is (a) true, false, or indeterminate?
d. Suppose (b) is false. Is (a) true, false, or indeterminate?

Are the two statements contradictory? Exclusive? Exhaustive?

2.3:3 Consider this pair of statements:

(a) John is six feet tall or more.

(b) John is six feet tall or less.

a. Suppose (a) is true. Is (b) true, false, or indeterminate?
b. Suppose (a) is false. Is (b) true, false, or indeterminate?
c. Suppose (b) is true. Is (a) true, false, or indeterminate?
d. Suppose (b) is false. Is (a) true, false, or indeterminate?

Are the two statements contradictory? Exclusive? Exhaustive?

2.3:4 Consider this pair of statements:

(a) The train from Chicago gets in at 6:00 P.M.

(b) The train to Chicago departs at 7:00 P.M.

a. Suppose (a) is true. Is (b) true, false, or indeterminate?
b. Suppose (a) is false. Is (b) true, false, or indeterminate?
c. Suppose (b) is true. Is (a) true, false, or indeterminate?
d. Suppose (b) is false. Is (a) true, false, or indeterminate?

Are the two sentences contradictory? Exclusive? Exhaustive?

2.3:5 You will be given a statement that Harry has made. Then you will be given a list of statements. Supposing Harry's statement to be true, answer which statements in the list would have to be true, which would have to be false, and which would be indeterminate.

a. Harry: Mickey Mantle was the greatest center fielder.

    1. Willie Mays was the greatest center fielder.
    2. Mickey Mantle was the greatest switch-hitter.
    3. Willie Mays was greater than Mickey Mantle as a center fielder.
    4. Mickey Mantle had less style than Willie Mays.
    5. Mickey Mantle was not the greatest first baseman.

b. Harry: There is no life on Venus.

    1. There is life on Earth.
    2. There are no animals on Venus.
    3. There is no life on Mars.
    4. Venus has no oxygen in its atmosphere.
    5. There is life on all nine planets.

c. Harry: Logic is a hard subject.

    1. Logic is not the hardest subject.
    2. Logic is not harder than French.
    3. Logic is an easy subject.
    4. Logic is not a hard subject.
    5. Logic is harder than mathematics.

2.3:6 In which of the following passages is the speaker inconsistent? Identify the inconsistency.

a. Even though the Rangers won, it was a great game. I had a terrific time. It ended in a tie.

b. John told me that Mary is starting a new job today. But Sam told me that Mary wasn't starting a new job today.

c. I don't ever approve of capital punishment. We shouldn't take the matter of life and death into our own hands. Still, what he did was really terrible. He should have been executed.

Study Vocabulary: **logically related**
                       exclusive
                       exhaustive
                       inconsistent
                       logically independent

2.4 CONTRARY STATEMENTS

One of the most common errors in logic and reasoning is to confuse contradictory statements with **contrary** statements.

Two statements are contrary if (1) they cannot both be true, but (2) they can both be false.

When two statements are contrary, they are opposites of a sort, but they are not *exact* opposites. They are opposites because they are exclusive; they cannot both be true. But they are not *exact* opposites because they are not exhaustive; they *can* both be false.

To determine whether two statements are contradictories, contraries, or neither, we must therefore ask *two* questions:

(1)   Can they both be true?

This test determines whether the statements are exclusive. If the answer is yes, they are neither contradictories nor contraries. If the answer is no, then they are either contradictories or contraries. To decide which, we must ask a second question:

(2)   Can they both be false?

This test determines whether the statements are exhaustive. If the answer is yes, they are contraries. If the answer is no, they are contradictories, since they cannot both be true *and* they cannot both be false.

Let's use this procedure to test whether the following statements are contradictories or contraries:

John likes everybody he meets.

John likes nobody he meets.

At first glance, you might think that these are contradictories. Perhaps you think that the *nobody* in the second sentence negates the *everybody* in the first. But these two statements are contraries. To be sure, they cannot both be true. If John likes everybody he meets, then it must be false that he likes nobody he meets. The answer to the first question is no. But the answer to the second question is yes. They *can* both be false. For it might turn out that John likes some people he meets and doesn't like others. In that case, the statements would both be false.

Here is another example of a pair of statements that are contraries:

John is rich.

John is poor.

If John is rich, then he cannot be poor; if he's poor, then he cannot be rich.

The two statements cannot both be true. But they can both be false, for John might be, say, middle-income. Recall the diagram we used earlier to represent the different levels of wealth:

very poor	poor	middle-income	rich	very rich

These categories are exclusive: no person can be in more than one category. If a person is poor, then he cannot be rich. You can see from the diagram that the statements are exclusive. But the diagram also shows that the statements are not exhaustive: it is not the case that John *must* be in one or the other of these two categories. It needn't be that he is rich or poor. He might be middle-income, or he might be very rich, or he might be very poor. Rich and poor do not exhaust the possibilities. Our two statements are exclusive but not exhaustive; they are contraries.

Using the diagram, you can see that each of the following pairs are also contraries:

John is very poor.
John is middle-income.

John is poor.
John is very rich.

Although they are exclusive, they are not exhaustive.
Here is another pair of contrary statements:

John is four feet tall or less.
John is six feet tall or more.

Let us draw a diagram to represent all possible heights:

1 ft	2 ft	3 ft	4 ft	5 ft	6 ft	7 ft	etc.

John has to be somewhere on this line. And since he can have only one height, he can fall on only one place on the line. Now, if we divide the line into the two categories *four feet tall or less* and *six feet tall or more*, it would look like this:

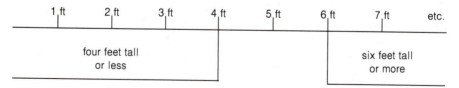

It's clear from the diagram that if John fits into one of these categories, then he cannot fit into the other. He cannot occupy more than one place on the line. The two statements, then, are exclusive. But they are not exhaustive. John doesn't *have* to be in one or the other of the two categories. There is a large open space on the line that does not fall into either of the categories. If John is five feet tall, for example, then both claims would be false.

Now consider the following pair:

John is six feet tall or less.

John is more than six feet tall.

You can see from the diagram that if John falls in one category, then he cannot fall in the other. The two statements cannot both be true, so they are exclusive. But these statements are also exhaustive. For John has to be somewhere on this line, and he will therefore fall into one or the other of the two categories. If he's four feet tall, then he is six feet tall or less. If he's six feet tall, then he's six feet tall or less. If he's seven feet tall, he is more than six feet tall. So, one of these two statements has to be true: either John is six feet tall or less, or, on the other hand, he is more than six feet tall. The statements are therefore contradictory, just like a statement and its negation. If you think about it, you can see that the following two statements are logically equivalent. They say the same thing.

John is six feet tall or less.

John is not more than six feet tall.

So, when two statements are exclusive, we know that if one is true, the other must be false. If, moreover, the two statements are contradictory (exclusive and exhaustive), then if one is false, the other is true. If, however, the two statements are contrary (exclusive but not exhaustive), then if one is false, we cannot conclude that the other is true. We would need more information to determine the truth value of the other.

EXERCISES

2.4:1   Which of the following pairs of statements are contraries and which are contradictories?

a.   The book is completely red.   The book is completely blue.

b.   John is president.   Harry is president.

c.   Pam will go home.   Pam will not go home.

d.   Everyone is happy.   Everyone is sad.

2.4:2 For each of the following pairs of statements, identify whether the statements are exclusive, exhaustive, contradictory, contrary, or neither contradictory nor contrary. (Note that more than one of these terms may apply.)

a. John is happy.   John is sad.
b. The sky is blue.   The sky is red.
c. The sky is blue.   The sky is not blue.
d. Rome was built in a day.   Rome was not built in a day.
e. John is exactly four feet tall.   John is exactly three feet tall.
f. John is more than four feet tall. John is less than four feet tall.
g. John is a human being.   John is a man.
h. Mary is a doctor.   Mary is a mother.
i. John took the train to school.   John took the bus to school.
j. John is four feet tall.   John is not four feet tall.
k. John is four feet tall or more.   John is less than four feet tall.
l. The cup is half empty.   The cup is half full.
m. John is a Democrat.   John is a Republican.
n. Harry went to college.   Harry did not go to college.
o. Sam went to public school.   Sam went to private school.

2.4:3 Which of the following sets of categories are exclusive?

a. Men, women, people, children
b. even number, odd number
c. even number, number greater than 2
d. animal, vegetable, mineral

2.4:4 Which of the sets of categories in 2.4:3 are exhaustive?

2.4:5 Provide a categorization of the people in your class that is both exclusive and exhaustive. Provide a categorization of the people in your class that is exclusive but not exhaustive. Provide a categorization of the people in your class that is exhaustive but not exclusive.

Study Vocabulary: **contrary**

2.5 THE SQUARE OF OPPOSITION

The surest way of forming the negation of a statement is to put *It is not the case that* in front of it. To negate

John is happy,

all we need say is

It is not the case that John is happy.

Most commonly, however, we would negate the statement by placing a *not* inside, as follows:

John is not happy.

Either way of negating the original statement is acceptable. But whereas the first way *always* gives us the negation, the second does not. In the next few sections, we shall discuss some cases where placing a *not* inside a statement does not yield the negation, and we shall have to use our knowledge of the logical relations we have studied to find this out. In this section, we will be discussing statements that involve the words *all, no,* or *some.*

Our procedure will be as follows. We know that a statement and its negation are contradictories. So, if placing a *not* inside the statement does not yield the contradictory of the original statement, then we know that we have not formed its negation.

Consider the following statement:

All books are novels.

How can we form its negation? One way, of course, is by using our mechanical procedure:

It is not the case that all books are novels.

But suppose we wanted to place a *not* inside. Where should we place it? There would seem to be two choices:

Not all books are novels.

All books are not novels.

The first choice, like our mechanical procedure, explicitly negates the original claim. Instead of saying *It is not the case that,* we say *Not.* But the second presents problems in interpretation. One could emphasize the words in such a way that they say the same thing as the first statement. But the literal reading of the statement, and the one we find most natural, is this:

Each and every book fails to be a novel.

In other words, no book is a novel. But the two statements

All books are novels

No books are novels

are not contradictories. Because of the *No,* one might think we have the negation of *All.* But this is a mistake. The statements are contraries. To be sure, they are inconsistent: they cannot both be true. But they *can* both be false. It is possible, after all, that some books are novels and some books are not novels.

So, either of the following will serve as a negation of the claim that all books are novels:

It is not the case that all books are novels.
Not all books are novels.

Both explicitly deny the original. On the other hand,

All books are not novels

is not a good choice because it literally means

No books are novels,

and this is not the contradictory of the original claim, but the contrary.

There is, however, another way to contradict the statement that all books are novels. We may say

Some books are not novels.

In logic, we use the word 'some' to mean 'at least one—possibly all'. You can see that the statements

All books are novels
Some books are not novels

cannot both be true and cannot both be false. If it is true that all books are novels, then it must be false that some books are not novels, and if it is false that all books are novels, then it must be true that some books (at least one) are not novels.

Note that

Some books are not novels

is *not* the negation of

Some books are novels.

Don't let the *not* inside fool you. These two statements can both be true, so they are not exclusive. However, they are exhaustive, for any book you consider either is a novel or is not. Two statements that are exhaustive but not exclusive are called **subcontraries.**

The contradictory of "Some books are novels" is "No books are novels."

We can sum up the logical relations between the statements we have been discussing by what has come to be called the **square of opposition.** This is a useful pictorial device for remembering the relations:

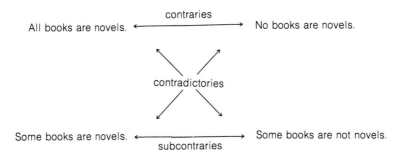

The statements diagonally opposite each other are contradictories (exclusive and exhaustive). The two top statements are contraries (exclusive but not exhaustive): they cannot both be true, although they can both be false. The two bottom statements are subcontraries (exhaustive but not exclusive): they can both be true, but they cannot both be false.

EXERCISES

2.5:1   Which of the following pairs of statements are contradictories? Which are contraries? Which are neither? *Explain your answer.*

a.   All sportscasters are rude.
     All sportscasters are not rude.
b.   All sportscasters are rude.
     No sportscasters are rude.
c.   Some sportscasters are rude.
     Some sportscasters are not rude.
d.   No sportscasters are rude.
     Some sportscasters are rude.
e.   All sportscasters are rude.
     Some sportscasters are not rude.
f.   No sportscasters are rude.
     Some sportscasters are not rude.

2.5:2   Write the negation of each of the following statements.

a.   Everyone is happy.
b.   Everyone is sad.
c.   We all scream for ice cream.
d.   Wars will never end.
e.   All good things must come to an end.

2.5:3   The following statements may each be represented by $-P$. Write out, for each case, the statement that is represented by P.

a.   Some boys do not like baseball.
b.   It never rains in California.
c.   John doesn't like anybody he meets.
d.   Not everyone is at the meeting.

2.5:4   For each of the pairs of statements below, explain the difference between the two sentences.

a.   The president is not always smiling.
    The president is always not smiling.
b.   He didn't tell us everything.
    He told us nothing.
c.   Not everything he said is true.
    Everything he said is not true.
d.   Everyone is not here.
    Not everyone is here.
e.   She is not especially tactful.
    She is especially not tactful.

Study Vocabulary: subcontraries
                      square of opposition

2.6   COUNTEREXAMPLES

The claim

All dancers are thin

is a **generalization.** The claim is about *all* dancers. This means all types of dancers: disco dancers, ballroom dancers, tap dancers, ballet dancers, and any other type you might think of. This means dancers from everywhere in the world: from the United States, from Europe, Asia, Africa, anywhere. And this means all the dancers that there have been in the past, as well as all the dancers that there will be in the future. The claim is an extremely *general* one.

What evidence would show this generalization to be true? It would be an extremely difficult, if not impossible, task to check out all these people to determine if they are thin. The best you can do is study a representative sample of dancers and generalize from the cases you have actually examined—mindful that you haven't examined all dancers and that there might well be a dancer you have not checked who is not thin. You cannot be certain of your answer. You can see immediately how suspicious you must be of the truth of such a generalization—and of anyone who claims to know this generalization to be true. The scope of the claim is so vast.

What evidence would it take to show that this generalization is false? All you need is one case—*one case*—of a dancer who is not thin. Such a case is called a **counterexample** to the original claim. Once you have found such a counterexample, you can stop the search. You have found a dancer who is not thin, and so it must be false that *all* dancers are thin.

Attempting to show that a generalization is true comes to the same thing as attempting to show that it is false. The procedure is the same. In each case, you search for a counterexample. If after considerable investigation you cannot come up with a counterexample, then you would have reason to believe that the generalization is true; if, on the other hand, you do find a counterexample, then you know that it is false.

This might make it look as though it is easier to show that a generalization is false than to show that it is true. For it would seem that all you need is one case to show that it is false, whereas you would need indefinitely many cases to show that it is true. But this is not quite accurate. For if the generalization is true, then you will never find a counterexample; so you will have to check an indefinite number of cases. But if the generalization is false, you might be able to find a single case and complete the task. So, it is easier to show that a generalization is false only if it happens to be false. Or rather, if it is false, your search comes to an end as soon as you find a counterexample, but if it is a true generalization that you are checking, your search can come to an end only when you have considered all the cases, assuming that's possible.

The search for counterexamples comes into play whenever you have a generalization, the truth of which depends on the truth of a host of **instances**—that is, specific claims. The truth of "All dancers are thin," for example, depends on the truth of all these individual claims:

Al is thin.
Sam is thin.
Sarah is thin.
Jean is thin.

and so on, where Al, Sam, Sarah, and Jean are all dancers. The claim

No dancers are thin

is also a generalization. In order for this to be true, each of the following instances would have to be true:

Al is not thin.
Sam is not thin.
Sarah is not thin.
Jean is not thin.

and so on. In order to determine that the statement "No dancers are thin" is true, each and every dancer would have to be checked out. You will have a counterexample to the generalization if you come across an individual—all you need is one—who is a dancer and is thin. If you find such a counterexample, the generalization is false; otherwise it is true.

Let's suppose that someone claims to have discovered a counterexample to the claim that all dancers are thin. Let's suppose that she claims that she's found a dancer—call him Al—who is not thin. What is the logical relationship between the original generalization,

All dancers are thin,

and

Al is not thin?

These two statements cannot both be true. If we have established the truth of the second statement, then we know that the first must be false. Alternatively, if we have established the truth of the first statement, then we know that the second must be false. But the two statements are not contradictories, for they could both be false. That is, it is entirely possible that not all dancers are thin, even though Al, it turns out, is thin. For it might be the case that some *other* dancer is not thin. These two statements are therefore contraries. The contradictory of "All dancers are thin" is

Some dancers are not thin.

There are many different possible ways in which this statement might be true; Al's not being thin is only one particular way.

In short, the two statements

All dancers are thin

Some dancers are not thin

are *contradictory*. On the other hand, the two statements

All dancers are thin

Al is not thin

are *contrary*. For the two statements

Al is not thin

Some dancers are not thin

are *not* logically equivalent; they do not say the same thing. To be sure, they are logically related in that if it's true that Al is not thin, then it must be true that some dancers are not thin. But they don't always have to have the same truth value. If it is false that Al is not thin, it does not have to be false that some dancers are not thin. Some other dancer might not be thin.

It is just this sort of example that leads some to think (mistakenly, of course) that contraries are exact opposites. They are not. They are opposites, but not exact opposites. Someone who maintains that all dancers are thin will be opposed by someone who maintains that Al is not thin. These two people hold conflicting views—conflicting in the sense that they cannot both be correct. But, although they are conflicting views, they are not the only ones someone might hold. They do not exhaust all of the possibilities.

You will be surprised to find how many different types of statements turn out to be generalizations. Here are some examples:

(1) It never rains in sunny California.

(2) A rose by any other name would smell as sweet.

(3) Gas expands when heated.

(4) Idle hands are the devil's playground.

Consider in each case what you would need to show the statement to be false. For (1), you need an instance where it rains in sunny California. For (2), you need an instance in which a rose, called by a name other than *rose*, does not smell as sweet as when it is called by the name *rose*. For (3), you need an instance of a gas that doesn't expand when heated. And for (4), you need an instance in which an individual who, while not kept busy, nevertheless does not fall into mischief. Each of these would be a counterexample to the generalization in question.

EXERCISES

2.6:1   For each of the following generalizations, say what would constitute a counterexample. Explain your answer.

a.   All men are mortal.

b.   All men seek the Good.

c.   Alexander's is closed on Sundays.

d.   Wheaties is the breakfast of champions.

e.   Jerry Lewis makes funny movies.

2.6:2   In which of the following cases has Sam produced a counterexample to Harry's claim? Explain your answer.

a.   Harry: Balsa wood floats in the bathtub.
     Sam: Well, I floated an oak wood boat in my bathtub.

b.   Harry: People are basically kind.
     Sam: Well, Tom is a person and he's vicious.

c.   Harry: Democrats are for the people.
      Sam: Well, Tom is a Republican and he's for the people.
d.   Harry: No one liked the movie last night.
      Sam: That's not true. Tom did.

2.6:3   Are the following pairs of statements contradictories, contraries, or neither? Explain your answers.

a.   All sportscasters are rude.
      Howard Cosell is not rude.

b.   No sportscasters are rude.
      Howard Cosell is rude.

c.   No sportscasters are rude.
      Howard Cosell is not rude.

Study Vocabulary: **generalization**
                      counterexample
                      instance

2.7   FINDING THE NEGATION

It is very important to have the notion of negation and the more general notion of contradiction firmly in mind. For even though we can provide mechanical formulas for forming the negation of a given statement, these formulas are not always helpful, since people don't always speak in this way. People use all kinds of short cuts when they speak, and we must come to understand and apply logic to these typical, everyday situations. To sharpen our understanding of negation, we will consider some more complicated examples.

Consider the statement

(1)   John has the right to watch television on Sunday.

For the most part, we believe this statement to be true: we all have the right to watch television on Sunday. Of course, this is not a right that is explicitly written into the Constitution, and it is, on the other hand, a right that could be taken away, as when a parent, say, forbids a child to watch television on Sunday until he brings his grades up in school. But for all practical purposes, the statement is true.

What is the negation of this statement? We can always use our foolproof mechanical formula, in which case we get

It is not the case that John has the right to watch television on Sunday.

This is certainly the negation of the original. But this is a rather stilted way of speaking. How can we deny the original claim a bit more concisely and colloquially? Let's try putting *not* inside the statement, as we did earlier. But there is a problem here that we have not faced before. There are two verbs in this statement:

John *has* the right *to watch* television on Sunday.

So, there are two places in which we might try to insert the *not*. We would then get either

(2) John *does not have* the right to watch television on Sunday

or

(3) John has the right *not to watch* television on Sunday.

There is, of course, a third possibility—namely, to insert *not* in *both* places:

(4) John *does not have* the right *not to watch* television on Sunday.

You should try to figure out (4) when you have completed this section.

Which, if either, is the negation of the original? Let's consider (3) first. The original statement, (1), says that John has a certain right, the right to watch television on Sunday. (3) also says that John has a certain right. Which right? The right not to watch television on Sunday. To be sure, John is said to have different rights in each case:

the right to watch television on Sunday, and

the right not to watch television on Sunday.

The rights John is said to have are exactly opposite to each other. But does the fact that the rights are exact opposites mean that the two statements we are interested in are exact opposites? No. Clearly, John can have both of these rights; indeed, it is quite likely that he does have both of them. Surely, we may, for the most part, do whatever we like on Sunday. We may watch television or not watch television. We are under no obligation either way. (3), then, cannot be the negation of the original statement because it does not have the proper logical relation to the original; both (1) and (3) could be true. Hence, they are not contradictory statements.

Now consider (2). It *is* the contradictory of the original claim. Originally we claimed that John has a certain right, the right to watch television on Sunday. But (2) denies that John has that right. The very same right John is claimed to have by (1) is denied to him by (2). Either he has that right or he doesn't; he cannot both have that right and not have it. So, (2) is our negation.

There are many other examples of statements that we have to be careful about when forming the negation. One in particular that we ought to look at concerns the notion of belief. For example, consider the claim.

(5)   John believes that Grant was a good president.

Here, someone is claiming that John has a certain belief. Now, if we wish to deny this claim, we can easily do so by using our mechanical formula:

It is not the case that John believes that Grant was a good president.

But can we say this more concisely? The same three choices come to mind, depending upon where we place the *not* in the statement, for again we have two verbs:

(6)   John *does not* believe that Grant was a good president.

(7)   John believes that Grant was *not* a good president.

(8)   John *does not* believe that Grant was *not* a good president.

Which, if any, is the contradictory of the original? Which asserts the exact opposite of the original? Let's look at (7) first. (7) says that John has a certain belief. Which belief? John believes that Grant was not a good president. So, the difference between this claim and the original lies in the belief John is said to hold. Now the two beliefs

Grant was a good president

Grant was not a good president

are contradictory. No rational person would want to hold both beliefs. Since they are contradictory, one must be false. However, sometimes people do hold contradictory beliefs, and it must sometimes be pointed out to them that they are doing so. So, (5) and (7) might both be true.

More important is to note that (5) and (7) could both be false. John might hold neither of these two beliefs, not believing that Grant was a good president and not believing that Grant was not a good president. Does he have to believe one of these? What if he doesn't know who Grant was? What if John were only three years old? A three-year old knows nothing about politics. What if John knows little or nothing of American history? In any of these cases, John probably wouldn't hold either of these two beliefs. So, it *is* possible that both claims are false.

Actually, we don't need to imagine a case as special as a three-year-old to make the point. People often *suspend judgment* about a given claim. Is the prisoner guilty or not guilty? You might not know. Do you have to believe that she is guilty or believe that she is not guilty? You might hold no belief about the matter. You might think that in order to form any judgment about the situation, you have to know more about the case. So, (7) is not the contradictory of (5).

Let's now consider (6). (6) denies that John has the belief he is claimed to have in the original statement. (6) thus explicitly denies what (5) claims. Either John holds the specified belief or he does not. Similarly, you either believe the prisoner is guilty or you do not believe that she is guilty. If you have suspended judgment, waiting for more evidence, then you do not believe that she is guilty. But this is *not* to say that you believe she is not guilty.

To summarize, when there are two verbs in the sentence, we must negate the *main* verb in order to negate the sentence.

EXERCISES

2.7:1   Negate each of the following by inserting *not* at the appropriate place in the statement (and, if necessary, changing the verb form).

a.   It is possible that John was caught in traffic.
b.   John eats at McDonald's every Friday night.
c.   Sally learned to tango in Paris.
d.   Sam hoped that Harry would not be late again.
e.   Perry Mason challenged the prosecution to produce its witness.

2.7:2   Consider the following two statements:

(1)   John believes that Santa Claus does not exist.

(2)   John does not believe that Santa Claus exists.

a.   What evidence about John might lead you to conclude that (2) is true but (1) is false? Explain your answer.
b.   What evidence about John might lead you to conclude that (1) is true?

2.7:3   Consider the following two statements:

(1)   Sally tried not to fix the car.

(2)   Sally did not try to fix the car.

a.   What evidence about Sally might lead you to conclude that (2) is true but (1) is false? Explain your answer.
b.   What evidence about Sally might lead you to conclude that (1) is true? Explain your answer.

2.8   DOUBLE NEGATION

Any statement can be negated. And since the negation of a statement is itself a statement, it too can be negated. The negation of

(1)   Mary loves the Chicago Zoo

is

(2) It is not the case that Mary loves the Chicago Zoo.

And the negation of this statement is

(3) It is not the case that it is not the case that Mary loves the Chicago Zoo.

(3) is an example of a **double negation**. Two negatives make a positive, or so it is said. Logically, this means that the two negations *cancel each other out*: (1) and (3) are logically equivalent. For since (2) is the negation of (1), (2) must have the opposite truth value of (1). And since (3) is the negation of (2), it must have the opposite truth value of (2). Therefore, (3) must have the same truth value as (1). The opposite of the opposite is the same as the original.

The argument could be put in a different way. If (1) is true, its negation, (2), must be false. And if (2) is false, then its negation, (3), must be true. So, if (1) is true, (3) is true. On the other hand, if (1) is false, then its negation, (2), must be true. And if (2) is true, then its negation, (3), must be false. So, if (1) is false, then (3) is false. (1) and (3) must therefore always have the same truth value: they are either both true or both false.

If you go back to Section 2.1, you will see this very argument laid out in much simpler form on the truth table. We showed there that P and $--P$ are logically equivalent.

Of course, we could continue indefinitely creating new statements by placing *It is not the case that* in front of those we have already constructed. Negating (3), for example, yields

(4) It is not the case that it is not the case that it is not the case that Mary loves the Chicago Zoo.

And so on. But we have no longer succeeded in saying anything new. Rather we are saying in a convoluted way something that can be said much more simply. (4), after all, is logically equivalent to (2).

But it's fun to consider how inserting *not* in a statement can change its meaning in surprising ways. Consider, for example, the following:

John favors raising the speed limit above 55 mph.

Now let's consider what we get when we place one or more *nots* in various places in the statement. Here are some possibilities:

(1) John does not favor raising the speed limit above 55 mph.
(2) John does not favor not raising the speed limit above 55 mph.
(3) John favors not raising the speed limit above 55 mph.
(4) It is not the case that John does not favor raising the speed limit above 55 mph.

(5) It is not the case that John does not favor not raising the speed limit above 55 mph.

(6) It is not the case that John favors not raising the speed limit above 55 mph.

Clearly, (1) is the negation of the original. And, since (4) is the negation of (1), (4) is logically equivalent to our original. (4) is a case of double negation. How about (2)? Is (2) also a double negation of our original statement? One might think so because of the two occurrences of *not* in (2). But appearances are deceiving. (2) is the negation of (3), and since (3) is a contrary (not the contradictory) of our original statement, (2) cannot be logically equivalent to our original statement. (5) is a double negation: it is the negation of (2) and (2) is the negation of (3). So, (5) is logically equivalent to (3). (6) is not a double negation. It is simply the negation of (3); it is logically equivalent to (2).

EXERCISES

2.8:1 Consider the statements in the following list and determine which are double negations of the following statement:

Mary hopes that John will call her.

a. It is not the case that Mary hopes that John will not call her.
b. It is not the case that Mary does not hope that John will call her.
c. Mary hopes that John will not call her.
d. Mary does not hope that John will not call her.
e. It is not the case that Mary does not hope that John will not call her.
f. Mary does not hope that John will call her.

2.8:2 Suppose that John is not in favor of raising the speed limit above 55 mph. Does it follow that he favors not raising the speed limit above 55 mph? Explain your answer.

2.8:3 Suppose that John is in favor of not raising the speed limit above 55 mph. Does it follow that he doesn't favor raising the speed limit above 55 mph? Explain your answer.

2.8:4 Consider the following statement:

The enemy of my enemy is my friend.

Is this true or false? Defend your answer.

2.8:5   For each of the following, state whether you think it is correct or incorrect, and then defend your answer.

a.   If P and Q are contradictories and R is logically equivalent to P, then R and Q are contradictories.

b.   If P and Q are contraries and R is logically equivalent to P, then R and Q are contraries.

c.   If P and Q are contradictories and Q and R are contradictories, then P and R are contradictories.

d.   If P and Q are contraries and Q and R are contraries, then P and R are contraries.

Study Vocabulary: **double negation**

REVIEW

1.   Any statement can be denied by asserting its negation. To form the negation, either put *It is not the case that* in front of the statement or insert *not* at the appropriate place. The logical relation between a statement, P, and its negation, $-P$, is summarized by a truth table:

P	$-P$
T	F
F	T

2.   A statement and its negation are contradictory. Two statements are contradictory if

(1)   they cannot both be true, and
(2)   they cannot both be false.

Two statements that cannot both be true are exclusive. Two statements that cannot both be false are exhaustive. So, contradictory statements are exclusive and exhaustive. Statements that cannot both be true are also called inconsistent. Statements that can both be true are called consistent.

3.   Contradictory statements must be carefully distinguished from contrary statements. Contrary statements are exclusive but not exhaustive. That is, contrary statements

(1)   cannot both be true, but
(2)   can both be false.

4.   Statements involving *all*, *some*, and *no* are tricky. The logical relations between such statements are summarized in the square of opposition:

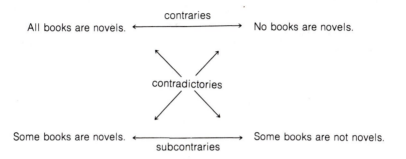

5.   To form the negation of a statement that contains more than one verb, insert the *not* so that it attaches to the main verb.

3

CONJUNCTION

Harold McLoud was never allowed to eat both chicken and rice. So he never ate chicken, and just to be sure, he never would eat any rice. His doctor then told him, for a very small price, to eat plenty of chicken but never touch rice. What reason he had was never precise, but McLoud thought the doctor was just being nice. Believing his doctor's was sound advice, McLoud ate chicken without any rice. He died the next day, and to be concise, his wife sued the doctor in less than a trice. McLoud couldn't eat both chicken and rice, and the doctor knew it when he tried to entice poor McLoud to eat chicken without any rice.

Do you think McLoud's wife should win her suit?

3.1 WHAT IS A CONJUNCTION?

When two statements are joined by the word *and*, the result is another statement, called a **conjunction**. Each of the following is a conjunction:

John ate dinner, and Mary had lunch.

Kennedy was the president, and Johnson was the vice-president.

The dancers are from Montreal, and the singers are from St. Louis.

The two statements making up a conjunction are called **conjuncts**. In the first statement, for example, "John ate dinner" is the *left conjunct* and "Mary had lunch" is the *right conjunct*.

Frequently, however, we find the word *and* connecting names or even sentence fragments. For example:

John and Tom both take piano lessons.

What are our two constituent statements here? Could "John" be the left conjunct? No. "John" is a name, not a statement. Could "Tom both take piano lessons" be the right conjunct? No. "Tom both take piano lessons" is a sentence fragment, and so it expresses no statement. On reflection, it should be apparent that this is an abbreviated version of

John takes piano lessons and Tom takes piano lessons.

In this unabbreviated form the two conjuncts are immediately evident. "John takes piano lessons," is one conjunct, and "Tom takes piano lessons" is the other. Such cases occur very often. For example:

You must take both physics and chemistry.

She's tall and mean.

You can easily rephrase these statements so that *and* connects their constituent statements.

When you claim that a conjunction is true, you commit yourself to the truth of both conjuncts. When you claim

Granny Smiths are green, and McIntoshes are red,

you claim that *both* constituent statements are true. If you want to claim simply that Granny Smiths are green, then you would say "Granny Smiths are green" and stop right there. Similarly, if all you want to claim is that McIntoshes are red, then you would say "McIntoshes are red" and go no further. But you are claiming that Granny Smiths are green *and* McIntoshes are red. You are committing yourself to the truth of both constituents. You are making a much stronger claim by conjoining statements than you would if you were to commit yourself to the truth of only one of the conjuncts.

You can see this clearly in the case of a bet. Consider the following three bets:

The Democrats will win in New York.

The Republicans will win in California.

The Democrats will win in New York, *and* the Republicans will win in California.

The first bet concerns only the Democrats in New York. If the Democrats win, you collect; if they lose, you don't collect. What the Republicans do in California is irrelevant. The second bet concerns the Republicans in California only. If the Republicans win, you collect; if they lose, you don't collect. What the Democrats do in New York is irrelevant. The third bet, however, concerns both elections and it is clearly a harder bet to win than either of the first two. For in order to win the last bet, *both* have to happen: the Democrats have to win the election in New York, and the Republicans have to win the election in California. If only one happens, you fail to win your bet. (Clearly, you should get better odds on the last bet than on either of the first two.)

Under what conditions is a conjunction true? Under what conditions is a conjunction false? Let's examine a concrete case. Imagine that you are on the witness stand in a trial, and the prosecutor asks you the whereabouts of John and Mary the night of the crime. You respond:

John went to dinner, and Mary went to the movies.

Remember that you are under oath and that you risk perjuring yourself if your statement is false. Under what circumstances would you have told the truth?

To answer this question, we need to consider the following four possibilities:

Case 1:   John went to dinner, and Mary went to the movies.
Case 2:   John went to dinner, but Mary didn't go to the movies.
Case 3:   John didn't go to dinner, but Mary went to the movies.
Case 4:   John didn't go to dinner, and Mary didn't go to the movies.

That is, both did what you said (case 1), or one did and the other didn't (cases 2 and 3), or neither of them did what you said (case 4). These are *all* the possibilities.

The claim you made under oath is that both went out. If they both did go out, as is described in case 1, your statement would turn out to be true. Now let's consider case 2. John went to dinner, but Mary did not go the movies. Did *both* do what you claimed? Clearly not. It is not the case that both conjuncts are true, and so the conjunction is false. The same reasoning applies to case 3. If John didn't go to dinner, then even though Mary went to the movies, they didn't both do what you said they did. Your statement is false. Finally, in case 4, if neither went out, then it must be false that *both* went out. So, in case 4, the statement is false. If neither conjunct is true, the conjunction is false.

We can summarize the logical properties of conjunction by means of a truth table, just as we did for negation in the previous chapter. The only difference is that in the case of a conjunction, we have two constituent statements; in the case of a negation, we have only one. So, whereas we needed only two rows in the negation table, we need four rows in the conjunction table.

P	*Q*	*P and Q*
T	T	T
T	F	F
F	T	F
F	F	F

Here, *P* and *Q* are any two statements you like. Each statement can be either T or F, so there are four possible ways of assigning truth values to *P* and *Q*: both are T (top case), or one is T and the other F (two middle cases), or both are F (bottom case). Each row of the truth table represents a possible case. Reading across each row, we assign a T to the conjunction when both conjuncts are T; we assign an F when one or the other or both of the conjuncts is F.

As in the case of negation, we can introduce a special symbol for conjunction; we will symbolize *and* by '&'. Instead of writing *P and Q*, we will write *P & Q*. Our truth table, then, becomes:

P	*Q*	*P & Q*
T	T	T
T	F	F
F	T	F
F	F	F

A conjunction is true when and only when both conjuncts are true; otherwise it is false.

(We say "when and only when" in order to indicate not only that a conjunction is true when both of its conjuncts are true, but also that that is the only condition under which it is true.)

Alternatively, we can say:

A conjunction is false when and only when at least one conjunct is false; otherwise it is true.

If you study these two definitions, you will see that they come to the same thing.

EXERCISES

3.1:1   Identify the two conjuncts in each of the following conjunctions.

a.   The Democrats won California and Oregon.

b.   There are huge copper mines in Arizona and Utah.

c.   Mary and I will visit relatives in Texas.

3.2:1   Based on your own knowledge, state whether the following conjunctions are true or false.

a.   Harrisburg is the capital of Pennsylvania, and Trenton is the capital of New Jersey.

b. Harrisburg is the capital of Pennsylvania, and Newark is the capital of New Jersey.
c. Pittsburgh is the capital of Pennsylvania, and Newark is the capital of New Jersey.
d. Pittsburgh is the capital of Pennsylvania, and Trenton is the capital of New Jersey.

Study Vocabulary: conjunction
                        conjunct

3.2   THE NEGATION OF A CONJUNCTION

Whatever can be asserted can also be denied. For any statement, *P*, its negation, *not P*, will be true when and only when *P* is false, and it will be false when and only when *P* is true. A conjunction is a statement like any other; it too can be negated. In this section we examine how we negate a conjunction.

Consider the conjunction

(1)   John went to dinner and the movies.

This is certainly a claim someone might make; it is also a claim someone might wish to deny. And the surest way of forming the negation would be to say

(2)   It is not the case both that John went to dinner and the movies.

This is, of course, just to use our mechanical procedure of placing *It is not the case that* in front of the statement we wish to deny. Our problem is: Can we negate (1) in a more colloquial and comfortable way?

The usual way we do this is by inserting *not* in the statement we wish to deny. However, because there are two constituent statements in the conjunction, there are two distinct places we might insert the *not*. This creates three distinct possibilities we have to consider:

(3)   John went to dinner, but he did not go to the movies.

(4)   John *did not* go to dinner, but he did go to the movies.

(5)   John *did not* go to dinner, and John *did not* go to the movies.

Let's go down the possibilities, starting with (3). Is (3) the negation of (1)? Remember, in order for (3) to be the negation of (1), (3) must be the contradictory of (1). And, for (3) to be the contradictory of (1), the two statements must have exactly opposite truth values. So we have to test two things: whether they can both be true, and whether they both can be false.

Can (1) and (3) both be true? (1) says that John went both to dinner and to the movies; (3) says that he went to dinner but not to the movies. In order for (1) to be true, John must have gone to the movies; and in order for (3) to be true, John must not have gone to the movies. He couldn't have both gone and not gone to the movies. So, (1) and (3) could not both be true. They are exclusive.

But are they also exhaustive? The answer is no. (1) and (3) would both be false if John did not go to dinner. For if he did not go to dinner, then it would be false that he went *both* to dinner and the movies, as (1) claims; and it would be false that he went to dinner and not to the movies, as (3) claims. (1) and (3) are contraries. We can therefore eliminate (3); it is not the negation of (1).

Our next candidate is (4). Can (1) and (4) both be true? In order for John to have gone to both places, as (1) claims, he must have gone to dinner. And in order for John to have gone to the movies but not to dinner, as (4) claims, he couldn't have gone to dinner. But the statement that he went to dinner cannot be both true and false. So, (1) and (4) cannot both be true. Can they both be false? Yes. They would both be false if it were false that John went to the movies. This case is entirely analogous to the previous one. So, (1) and (4) are also contraries. (4) is not the negation of (1).

This leaves (5) to consider. Can (1) and (5) both be true? (1) says that John went to two places—dinner and the movies. (5) says that John went to neither of those two places; he didn't go to dinner and he didn't go to the movies. He couldn't have gone to both places and also to neither of the two places. So, they cannot both be true. Can (1) and (5) both be false? Yes. They would both be false if John went to one place but not the other. If, for example, John went to dinner but not to the movies, it would be false that he went to both places (because he didn't go to the movies), and it would also be false that he went to neither place (because he did go to dinner). So, (1) and (5) are also contrary statements. (5) is not the negation of (1).

It turns out that none of the three statements is the negation of (1). Each of them is a contrary of (1). If (1) is true, then none of the others can also be true. But both (1) and any of the others might be false simultaneously.

We cannot, then, negate our original statement by inserting *not* in the statement. We are, for the most part, stuck with our mechanical formulation, (2). Let us see why this is so. To assert a conjunction is to assert that *both* of its conjuncts are true. So, to negate a conjunction is to deny that *both* of its conjuncts are true. But to deny that both are true is *not* the same thing as to deny the conjuncts individually. Rather, to deny that both are true is to claim that *at least one* conjunct is false (and possibly both are false), without specifying which is false.

Imagine, for example, that I know that John is unable to afford both dinner and the movies. He sometimes goes to one, he sometimes goes to the other, and he sometimes goes to neither, but he never goes to both. Now if you tell me that he went to both, I might very well want to deny this, even though I don't know whether he went to one, to the other, or to neither. So we sometimes deny a conjunction even though we do not know which of the conjuncts is false.

There is, then, a significant difference between saying that two statements are *both not true* and saying that they are *not both true*. The first commits us to the denial of both statements: it is equivalent to saying *neither* is true. The other commits us only to denying at least one.

There are a lot of everyday situations where we are very careful to make this distinction. For example, a child asks a parent to buy him a lollipop and bubble gum. The parent says no, the child cannot have both. Is the parent saying that the child can have neither? That is, is the parent saying that the child cannot have a lollipop and also cannot have bubble gum? No, the parent is simply saying that he cannot have *both* of these candies. At most, he can have one of them. Or, taking another example, a student asks his adviser whether he has to take both math and science in order to graduate. The adviser says, "No. Not both." Is she saying that the student must take neither of these in order to graduate? No, she is saying that the student does not have to take both of them.

To summarize, we cannot negate a conjunction by placing *not* in front of either of the conjuncts. We must use our mechanical formula. We would say *It is not the case both that P and Q*, or, for short, *not both P and Q*. It is important, however, to distinguish this from *both not P and not Q*. The latter is the same as saying *neither P nor Q*.

EXERCISES

3.2:1 Write the negation of each of the following statements.

a. New York is shrinking.

b. California is growing.

c. New York is shrinking, and California is growing.

d. Computers are sweeping the country, and typewriters are dying out.

e. Computers are not sweeping the country, and typewriters are not dying out.

3.2:2 For each of the following conjunctions, state three different circumstances that would make it false.

a. Oil is expensive, and air is free.

b.   Tom was not here, and Mary was here.

c.   School was closed today, and the auditorium was empty.

3.2:3   For each of the following, state a circumstance under which the statement comes out true.

a.   It is not the case that France conquered both Italy and Germany.

b.   She is both not tall and not beautiful.

c.   She is both not tall and beautiful.

d.   It is not the case that she is both not tall and not beautiful.

e.   The wine is not both fruity and dry.

f.   The wine is both not fruity and not dry.

g.   The wine is not both not fruity and not dry.

3.3   CONJUNCTION AND NEGATION

In this section, we are going to see how to symbolize the statements we analyzed in the previous section.

Let us adopt the following abbreviations:

P: John went to dinner.

Q: John went to the movies.

Then our original conjunction,

(1)   John went to dinner and the movies,

is symbolized as

(1') $P \& Q$.

Next, consider the three statements we constructed by trying to place *not* inside the conjunction:

(3)   John went to dinner, but he did not go to the movies.

(4)   John did not go to dinner, but he did go to the movies.

(5)   John did not go to dinner, and John did not go to the movies.

These would be symbolized, respectively, as

(3') $P \& -Q$

(4') $-P \& Q$

(5') $-P \& -Q$.

The interesting problem, however, is to determine how to symbolize the negation of the conjunction:

(2)   It is not the case both that John went to dinner and the movies.

Remember, we want to deny the conjunction without denying any of the conjuncts. We can do so using **parentheses**:

(2') $-(P \,\&\, Q)$

We do not use parentheses in English to group. Instead, we use the word *both*. It might be somewhat surprising that the word *both* operates in English in the same way the parentheses operate in our symbolism. But it should not be too surprising that we have some method of grouping in English. After all, we use parentheses all the time in mathematics, and all mathematical notation can be written in English. So there must be some devices in English that do the same job that parentheses do in mathematics. *Both* is just such a device.

> *Both not P and not Q is symbolized as $-P \,\&\, -Q$.*
> *Not both P and Q is symbolized as $-(P \,\&\, Q)$.*

When an expression occurs inside parentheses, we take it as a unit. So, to determine the truth value of $-(P \,\&\, Q)$, first figure out the truth value of the parenthesized expression, $P \,\&\, Q$, and then figure out the truth value of the negation of that expression.

Using the truth table will clarify the matter. Let us add a new column— the negation of a conjunction—to our truth table. Since a statement and its negation have opposite truth values, it will simply be a column whose truth values are exactly opposite those of the conjunction itself:

P	*Q*	*P & Q*	$-(P \,\&\, Q)$
T	T	T	F
T	F	F	T
F	T	F	T
F	F	F	T

You can see plainly that the conjunction, $P \,\&\, Q$, and its negation, $-(P \,\&\, Q)$, always have opposite truth values: whenever one is T the other is F, and conversely. And you can also see that the negation of a conjunction is true whenever at least one conjunct is false.

Now let's expand our truth table to show the truth conditions of (3')–(5'):

P	*Q*	*-P*	*-Q*	*P & Q*	(2') $-(P \,\&\, Q)$	(3') *P & -Q*	(4') *-P & Q*	(5') *-P & -Q*
T	T	F	F	T	F	F	F	F
T	F	F	T	F	T	T	F	F
F	T	T	F	F	T	F	T	F
F	F	T	T	F	T	F	F	T

Look at the P & Q column. There is a T in this column when and only when there is a T in both the P column and the Q column. $-(P$ & $Q)$ is the negation of $(P$ & $Q)$; whichever truth value appears in the $(P$ & $Q)$ column, the opposite appears in the $-(P$ & $Q)$ column. (3′) is the conjunction of P *and* $-Q$; there is a T in this column when and only when there is a T in both the P column and the $-Q$ column. For (4′) we have to look at the $-P$ column and the Q column. (4′) is T when and only when there is a T in both these columns. Finally, for (5′) we look to the $-P$ column and the $-Q$ column. The conjunction of $-P$ and $-Q$ is T when and only when we find a T in both these columns.

But none of (3′)–(5′) is the exact opposite of the original conjunction, P & Q. When P & Q is F, one of (3′)–(5′) has to be T, but there is no commitment which *specifically* is T.

EXERCISES

3.3:1   Let P abbreviate "Harry likes classical music," and let Q abbreviate "John likes classical music." Symbolize each of the following.

a.   Harry and John don't both like classical music.
b.   Harry and John both don't like classical music.
c.   Neither Harry nor John likes classical music.

3.3:2   Symbolize each of the following. (Let W abbreviate "Water mixes with oil," and let V abbreviate "Vinegar mixes with oil.")

a.   Water mixes with oil.
b.   Water does not mix with oil.
c.   Water mixes with oil, and vinegar mixes with oil.
d.   Water mixes with oil, and vinegar does not mix with oil.
e.   Water doesn't mix with oil, and vinegar does mix with oil.
f.   Water doesn't mix with oil, and vinegar doesn't mix with oil.
g.   It is not the case both that water mixes with oil and that vinegar mixes with oil.

Which of (a)–(f) are contradictory to (g)?

Which of (a)–(f) are contrary to (g)?

3.3:3   Construct a truth table for the negation of each of the following conjunctions.

a.   Rock music is dangerous to your health, and classical music is not.
b.   Classical music is dangerous to your health, and rock music is not.
c.   Both classical and rock music are dangerous to your health.

3.3:4 Write two grammatically correct English sentences for each of the following symbolic abbreviations.

a. $P \& Q$
b. $-P \& Q$
c. $-(P \& Q)$

Study Vocabulary: parentheses

3.4 LOGICAL EQUIVALENTS OF AND

Frequently we find more than two conjuncts in a conjunction. Consider, for example:

> The car is expensive, big, comfortable, and poor on mileage.
> Ted and Alice are hungry and thirsty.

Each of these is an example of a conjunction—but one in which more than two statements are being conjoined. The last is especially complicated. There are four claims contained in it:

> Ted is hungry.
> Ted is thirsty.
> Alice is hungry.
> Alice is thirsty.

It is equivalent, therefore, to

> Ted is hungry and Ted is thirsty and Alice is hungry and Alice is thirsty.

In order for this conjunction to be true, *each* conjunct would have to be true. If any one of them is false, the statement is false.

We can therefore generalize the truth conditions of a conjunction:

A conjunction with n conjuncts will be true when and only when all n conjuncts are true. Otherwise it is false.

Here, n is a variable that enables us to say generally when a conjunction with any number of conjuncts—two, three, four, or whatever—will be true. A conjunction with two conjuncts will be true when and only when both conjuncts are true. A conjunction with three conjuncts will be true when and only when all three conjuncts are true. And so on. Generally, then, to claim that a conjunction with n conjuncts is true is to claim that all n of its conjuncts are true. If even one is false, then they are not all true, and the conjunction is false.

From a logical point of view, it is helpful to think of a generalization as a large conjunction. Recall the example we used in our discussion of counterexamples in Chapter 2:

All dancers are thin.

This could be understood as the claim

Dancer 1 is thin and dancer 2 is thin and dancer 3 is thin and dancer 4 is thin and . . . .

This helps to explain why it takes only a single case to disprove a generalization. Since a generalization is a conjunction, someone who makes a generalization claims that each and every one of its conjuncts is true. A single counterexample is enough to disprove the claim, since if a single conjunct is false, the entire conjunction is false.

One further point. In English, there are many words that frequently have the same logical force as *and*. They too serve to form conjunctions. Examples are:

however

nevertheless

yet

moreover

In fact, many of the so-called *transition words* have the same logical force as *and*. It should be noted, however, that these are not necessarily interchangeable, because other elements of their meaning can differ. Consider the statement

John went to the store and Mary went to the movies.

That statement will be true when and only when both of its constituent statements are true. Each of the following statements has exactly the same truth conditions:

John went to the store, *yet* Mary went to the movies.

John went to the store; *however*, Mary went to the movies.

John went to the store; *nevertheless*, Mary went to the movies.

John went to the store, *but* Mary went to the movies.

These statements differ in *tone*. Nevertheless, each will be true when and only when both of its constituent statements are true. Take the first statement. *Yet* injects a comment on the two constituent statements. Perhaps it is odd, or surprising, or annoying that Mary went to the movies while John went to the store. The speaker is marking the two of them off in some way that would no doubt be understood in the context in which the statement is made. *However* is doing a similar job in the second statement, and *nevertheless* in the third. All of them have the same force as *and* with respect to their function in determining truth values.

Here are some more examples:

I studied harder than he did, *but* he did better than I.

England won the battle; *however,* it lost the war.

She made the noise; *nevertheless,* we got punished.

Even though I want to go, I'm going to stay.

She did a good job as governor; *moreover,* she was popular.

Tom is thirsty *but* not hungry, and Alice is hungry *but* not thirsty.

Even though these statements are perhaps slightly different in tone from conjunctions formed by the word *and,* they too will be true when each of their constituent statements is true. It is in this sense that we say that these transition words have the same *logical force as and.* Statements in which they occur are to be treated logically as conjunctions.

But is a particularly interesting connective. Contrast the following two statements:

He was rich and honest.

He was rich but honest.

Whereas the first is a straightforward conjunction, the second appears to add something. We might characterize this additional element as one of surprise or contrast. The second statement seems to suggest that he—whoever is referred to—is different from the general run of rich people, that he is an exception to what the speaker takes to be the general rule—namely, that rich people are generally not honest. The word *but* is often used to indicate surprise that two specific characteristics are found together. But if we ask ourselves what conditions would make each of the statements true, we can clearly see that the sole condition is the truth of each conjunct—that he is rich, and that he is honest. If both of those conditions are satisfied, then both statements are true.

But is also helpful in making the meaning of a statement clear, especially when there is a *not* in the statement. Consider, for example, the statement

John went to dinner and not to the movies.

This statement is more naturally formulated as

John went to dinner but not to the movies.

Thus, *but* has the same logical force as *and* although it differs in *rhetorical* force.

It is rather interesting that we should have different words that have the same logical force but differ in other aspects of their meaning. Language is very rich; operating within it are many different levels of meaning. Logic captures only one of them, but a very important one.

EXERCISES

3.4:1   Formulate the negation of each of the following conjunctions. State for each of them a circumstance under which the negation would be true.

a.   Tom is sneaky, and Mary is sneaky.
b.   Sally is not tall, but she was accepted anyway.
c.   Some lawyers are wise, and some lawyers are wise guys.
d.   Even though he thinks he's boss, he's not.

3.4:2   Identify the constituent conjuncts of each of the following conjunctions.

a.   Richard and Lewis can't read and write.
b.   Richard can read and write, but Lewis can't do either.
c.   Lewis can write, but he doesn't know what to say, and Richard can't read, but he writes every day.
d.   The movie had a good plot and good characters, and it was set in an interesting locale, but I didn't like it, and you shouldn't see it.

3.4:3   For each of the conjunctions in 3.4:1, state at least two circumstances that would make the conjunction false.

3.4:4   State each of the following generalizations as a conjunction.

a.   All football players take steroids.
b.   No drugstore sells newspapers.
c.   Cats climb trees.
d.   A sucker is born every day.
e.   A rose by any other name would smell as sweet.

REVIEW

1.   When two statements are joined by *and*, the resulting statement is a conjunction. The constituent statements are conjuncts. A conjunction is true when and only when both conjuncts are true. Otherwise it is false. We introduce '&' to abbreviate *and*, and give the following truth-table definition of conjunction:

P	*Q*	*P & Q*
T	T	T
T	F	F
F	T	F
F	F	F

2.   In order to negate a conjunction, we must place *It is not the case both that* in front of it. We cannot negate the conjunction by negating each conjunct. In logic, we use parentheses to help group phrases. We express *not both P and Q* as $-(P \& Q)$. We express *both not P and Q* by $-P \& Q$. We express *both not P and not Q* by $-P \& -Q$. *Neither P nor Q* is also expressed by $-P \& -Q$.

3.   A conjunction can have more than 2 conjuncts. A conjunction with *n* conjuncts is true when, and only when, all *n* conjuncts are true. Otherwise it is false.

4.   There are a number of English words that have the same logical force as *and*, mainly transition words: *however, nevertheless, but, even though, however, yet.*

4

IMPLICATION

You infer what I imply only if you know the consequences of what I say. If you don't infer what I imply, then you do not know the consequences of what I say. And if you infer what I don't imply, then you have mistaken the consequences of what I say. So if you infer that I imply that your inferences are the consequences of what I say, then you must believe that I believe you know what I am talking about. Right? Stay tuned.

4.1 WHAT IS IMPLICATION?

In Chapter 2, we introduced a number of logical relations. We discussed what it means for statements to be contradictory, contrary, exclusive, and exhaustive. In this chapter, we are going to examine what it means for one statement (or group of statements) to *imply* another.

We will define **implication** as follows:

P implies Q if whenever P is true, Q must also be true.

When one statement implies another, if the first is true, the second *has to be* true. It is therefore impossible for the first to be true and the second false. This gives us another way of defining the notion of implication:

P implies Q if it is impossible for P and not Q both to be true.

Make sure you understand that these two definitions are logically equivalent.

Each of the following says the same thing:

P implies Q.
Q follows from P.
Q may be *inferred* from *P.*

For example, John's being a freshman *implies* that he is a student. From the fact that he is a freshman, *it follows* that he is a student; if we know that he is a freshman, we may **infer** that he is a student. On the other hand, John's being a student *does not imply* that he is a freshman. From the fact that he is a student, *it does not follow* that he is a freshman, and we *may not infer* that he is—for he might be a junior. (Be careful about the ordering of *P* and *Q* in these expressions.)

Here are some examples to help secure the notion of implication. The statement

John read a novel

implies the statement

John read a book.

Since a novel is a book, John couldn't have read a novel without having read a book. The two statements

John read a novel

John did not read a book

are inconsistent: they cannot both be true.

This implication, however, does not work the other way. The statement

John read a book

does *not* imply the statement

John read a novel.

Although all novels are books, not all books are novels. John might have read a history textbook. So, even though the second statement *might* be true when the first is, it also *might* be false. The two statements

John read a book

John did not read a novel

are *not* inconsistent.

Here are some more examples. The statement

All men are taller than ten feet

implies

> John (who is a man) is taller than ten feet.

The statement

> This table is completely blue

implies

> This table is not red.

On the other hand, the statement

> John has the right to watch television

does not imply

> John does not have the right not to watch television.

Having the right to watch television does not rule out having the right not to watch television.

We have already used the notion of implication throughout this textbook, even though we have not yet formally introduced it. When we talked about the truth conditions of statements, using truth tables, we frequently called your attention to the implications of statements. For example, to say that P is a circumstance that would make Q true is to say P implies Q. And to say that P is a circumstance that would make Q false is to say P implies $-Q$. Similarly, to say that P must be true *in order for* Q to be true is to say Q implies P. This follows from our definition: if P must be true in order for Q to be true, then Q couldn't be true without P's being true.

Recall what we learned about negation. We know that if a statement is true, then its negation is false. So the truth of a statement implies the falsity of its negation. Also, the falsity of a statement implies the truth of its negation. The same can be said, of course, about a statement and its contradictory. But this is not the case with contraries. Though the truth of a statement implies the falsity of its contraries, the falsity of a statement does not imply the truth of any of its contraries.

> *If P and Q are contradictories, then P implies not Q, and not P implies Q.*
> *If P and Q are contraries, then P implies not Q, but not P does not imply Q.*
> *P implies not not P, and not not P implies P.*

There are several important facts about implication that should be mentioned here. First, every statement implies itself:

> *For any statement P, P implies P.*

The statement "John is tall," for example, implies the statement "John is tall." This is an immediate application of the definition we gave. For if the first statement is true, then the second statement—which is exactly the same as the first—must also be true.

From the fact that P implies Q, it does not follow that Q implies P.

For example, the statement

This table is completely blue

implies

This table is not red.

But the implication does not work the other way. The statement

This table is not red

does not imply

This table is completely blue.

Just because the table is not red, it doesn't have to be blue; it could be any of a number of colors.

Sometimes the implication does work both ways. When it does work both ways, however, the two statements have the same truth conditions—they are logically equivalent. For example,

John is a parent

implies

John has a child.

The implication works the other way too. If John has a child, then he must be a parent. The implication works both ways because to be a parent is to have a child. The two statements say the same thing in different words. But although implication can work both ways, as in this case, it need not always work both ways.

Note that if P implies Q, then if P is true, Q must be true. What if P is false? Can we infer anything about Q? No. John's being a freshman implies his being a student. So if it's true that he is a freshman, then it must be true that he is a student. But if it's false that he's a freshman, we cannot infer that it's false that he's a student (for he might be a junior), and we cannot infer that it's true that he's a student (for he might be neither a freshman nor a student).

Finally, implication is **transitive**. This means:

If P implies Q and Q implies R, then P implies R.

For example,

> (1)   John is a college junior

implies

> (2)   John is a college student.

And (2), in turn, implies

> (3)   John has a high school diploma (or its equivalent).

If (1) is true then (2) must be true, and if (2) is true then (3) must be true. So if (1) is true then (3) must true: (1) implies (3).

EXERCISES

4.1:1   For each of the following, determine whether the implication holds. Explain your reasoning.

a.   John took the subway to school *implies* John took the train to school.
b.   John took the train to school *implies* John took the subway to school.
c.   John graduated from college *implies* John passed all his required courses.
d.   John passed all his required courses *implies* John graduated from college.
e.   John took the bus to school *implies* John did not take the train to school.
f.   John did not take the train to school *implies* John took the bus to school.

4.1:2   Consider the following story.

> There were several boys in the room. Some were wearing blue jeans, some were wearing suits and ties. They were lined up against a wall, their belongings on a table. A man was walking behind them, looking to see if any had hidden anything in his hat.

Suppose the story is true. Which of the following are implied by what we are told in the story?

a.   There were no girls in the room.
b.   There was a man in the room.
c.   The room had furniture in it.
d.   All the boys had hats on.
e.   All the boys had long pants on.
f.   There were at least three people in the room.

4.1:3   Explain the difference between the following two claims:

> P does not imply Q.
> P implies *not* Q.

4.1:4   Show that if *P* and *Q* are contraries, then *P* implies *not Q*.

4.1:5   Show that if *P* and *Q* are contraries, then *not P* does not imply *Q*.

Study Vocabulary: **imply**
                     implication
                     infer
                     transitive

4.2   IMPLICATION AND VALIDITY

In this section, we will explore the specific implications of conjunctions. We will also see how implications can be recast as **arguments**.

Here is, perhaps, the most obvious implication of a conjunction:

A conjunction implies each of its conjuncts.

In other words, if a conjunction is true, then each of its conjuncts must also be true. For example, if John went both to dinner and to the movies, then he must (at least) have gone to dinner, and he must (at least) have gone to the movies.

We can also express this implication as follows:

$$P \text{ and } Q$$
$$\text{SO, } P$$

Here, we set up the implication as an argument. The statement after *So* is supposed to follow from the statement in front of it. The statement after *So* is called the **conclusion** of the argument. It is the statement being argued for. The statement before *So* is the **premiss** of the argument: it is the statement we are arguing from. We will say:

If the implication holds, the argument is valid; if the implication does not hold, the argument is invalid.

Clearly, the argument above is a **valid argument**, since *P and Q* implies *P*.
      Let's look at another argument:

$$P$$
$$\text{SO, } P \text{ and } Q$$

Is this a valid argument? Does *P* imply *P and Q*? How do we figure this out? We start by going back to the definition of implication. If one statement implies another, then whenever the first is true, the second must also be true. So, to determine whether the implication holds in *this* case, we must ask: Must *P and Q* be true whenever *P* is true? If the answer is yes, the implication holds; if the answer is no, the implication does not hold.

How do we go about trying to answer this question? One way is to substitute statements for our variables, *P* and *Q*. Remember, the point of using variables is to speak generally; the implication is supposed to hold for any two statements whatsoever. Whenever we use variables, then, we are in effect expressing a generalization.

As with any other generalization, it is appropriate to try to find a *counterexample*. Can we find specific statements for which the generalization will fail? That is, can we find actual statements for *P* and *Q* such that *P* is true and *P and Q* is false? Take the statements we used earlier. Suppose that John went to dinner. Would it follow that he went both to dinner and the movies? Clearly not! Just because he went to dinner, it would not have to be the case that he went both to dinner and the movies. So, let's assign *P* and *Q* as follows:

P: John went to dinner.

Q: John went to the movies.

Then we have our *counterexample*. In this case, it is perfectly possible for *P* to be true and *P and Q* to be false. The implication doesn't hold.

But you might still be a little worried about the example we have chosen. Suppose you say that John is one of those fellows who always goes to the movies whenever he goes to dinner. In fact, if you know he is going to dinner, then you can always predict that he will be going to the movies afterwards. You might even have a standing joke with him; when he tells you that he is going out to eat, you ask him, "What are you going to see?" If that's the situation, then you would most probably think that it will follow that if John goes to dinner, then he will be going both to dinner and to the movies. So, you might be persuaded that the implication does hold.

But that the implication happens to work in this case does not mean that it works in *all* cases. And that is precisely what has to be shown if we maintain that an implication holds: that the implication works in all cases. An example is only *one* case. And the particular example chosen is quite special; it is not representative of *all* cases. Does everyone who goes to dinner go both to dinner and to the movies? Clearly not! Take your own case: would it follow that you go to dinner and to the movies whenever you go to dinner? We hardly think so.

Once you begin to recognize the peculiarity of this case, it is easy to come up with lots of examples where the implication fails. If it rains, does it have to both rain and snow? Obviously not. If John takes French, does it follow that he takes both French and Spanish? Obviously not. If John is eating breakfast, does it follow that he is both eating breakfast and singing a song? Obviously not. The point is that it is not *in general* true that whenever P is true, P *and* Q is true. In some cases it works, and in some cases it doesn't.

Substituting statements for P and Q helps bring to life a cold, abstract way of talking. With actual statements we can see what is going on, and we are therefore more comfortable with the problem. This is true for most people. Concrete examples are a tremendous aid in understanding the abstract claims we make in logic. But when we do use examples, we have to be careful not to rely on special or peculiar cases. Using the abstract P and Q prevents this from happening. As you become more familiar with our use of symbolic letters, you will find that you actually become more comfortable working out problems at the abstract level than at the concrete level.

Here is how we might argue abstractly in this case. In order for a conjunction to be true (by definition), both conjuncts must be true: P would have to be true *and* Q would have to be true. But if we are told only that P is true, and we are given no information about Q, we do not yet have enough information to determine whether the conjunction P *and* Q is true.

Note that when we have a valid argument, we do not have to worry about peculiar cases. If an argument is valid, then it holds true in every case; so, whatever case might come to mind, it will work. But if an argument is invalid, then it doesn't hold true in every case. That is, it might hold in some cases but not in others. This means that if an argument is invalid, then we should be able to come up with a counterexample. But if, on the other hand, the argument is valid, we should not be able to come up with a counterexample.

This tells us that our use of examples is limited. For if an argument is valid, examples will never show it to be valid. No matter how many individual cases we come up with, we will never be able to show that it works for *all* cases. The only way we can show that it holds for all cases is to reason abstractly from the properties of the logical connectives.

In summary, here are the two argument patterns we have studied, side by side:

(1)	(2)
P	P and Q
SO, P and Q	SO, P

(1) is invalid. In order for the conjunction to be true, *both* conjuncts must be true. However, we know that only one of them, P, is true. The other might be true or it might not be; we don't know. So we are not entitled to infer P *and* Q from the information we have so far—namely, that P is true.

(2), on the other hand, is valid. Why? Because, if the conjunction is true, then P has to be true and Q has to be true. This follows directly from our truth-table definition of conjunction. Look at it another way. Could P *and* Q be true while P is false? Impossible.

EXERCISES

4.2:1   Which of the following are valid arguments? That is, in which of the following does the premiss imply the conclusion? If the argument is valid, show that it is valid by arguing abstractly. If the argument is invalid, give a counterexample.

a.   *P and Q*
     SO, *Q*
b.   *Q*
     SO, *P and Q*
c.   *not P but Q*
     SO, *not P*
d.   *P and not Q*
     SO, *not P*

4.2:2   Is the following argument valid or invalid?

$$-(P \text{ \& } -Q)$$
$$P$$
$$\text{SO, } Q$$

Look back at our example of John, who went to dinner whenever he went to the movies. Show how that example is related to this argument.

4.2:3   The college catalog says that a student must take Math 200 if he did not take Math 100. Suppose that Harry did not take Math 100. Must he take Math 200? Suppose that Harry took Math 150 but not Math 100. Must he take Math 200?

4.2:4   The college catalog says that students must take Math 200 if they have taken Math 150 but not Math 100. Suppose that Harry did not take Math 100. Must he take Math 200? Suppose that Harry took Math 150 and Math 170 but not Math 100. Must he take Math 200? Suppose Harry took Math 150 and Math 100. Must he take Math 200?

4.2:5   Suppose you know that John went both to dinner and to the movies last night. Your friend asks you, "Where did John go last night?" You say, "John went to dinner." Is what you said false? How would you criticize the answer you gave in this case?

Study Vocabulary: argument
                       conclusion
                       premiss
                       valid argument

4.3   USING TRUTH TABLES

Now that we have developed this notion of implication, let us try some more complicated problems. Consider the following two arguments:

(1)	(2)
not P	*not both P and Q*
SO, *not both P and Q*	SO, *not P*

One of these is valid; one is invalid. Which one is which? Can you work it out?

Let's look at (1) first, and let's use examples. If John didn't go out to dinner, then obviously he couldn't have gone out to dinner and the movies. Again, if it didn't snow on Tuesday, then it couldn't have snowed both on Tuesday and Wednesday. The examples we have given make it very likely that the argument is valid. But they do not clinch the case. There is always the possibility that the argument does not work in all cases. The only way we can be sure that it *will* work in all cases is to show abstractly, using the truth-table definitions of conjunction and negation, that whatever examples we choose, the argument will be valid.

Let's argue abstractly. The conclusion of the argument is the negation of a conjunction; we are denying that both statements are true. And we are inferring this from the fact that one of these conjuncts—namely, *P*—is not true. But clearly, if one of the conjuncts isn't true, it couldn't be that both are true. So, whatever statements we substitute for *P* and *Q*, there is no way for *not P* to be true and *not both P and Q* to be false.

Now, let us look at (2). Of course, if we were right when we said at the beginning of the exercise that one and only one of the two arguments is valid, then since (1) is valid, (2) must be invalid. But we still have to argue for it to make sure we understand what is going on. Again, there are two avenues of approach. Either we can use examples, or we can argue abstractly.

Let us use examples first. From the fact that John didn't take both French and Spanish, would it follow that he didn't take French? Clearly not. From the fact that it didn't both rain and snow, would it follow that it didn't snow? Clearly not. We have two solid counterexamples. The implication therefore does not hold generally, and so the argument is invalid.

Now let us argue abstractly. We are told that *P* and *Q* are not both true, but we are not told specifically which one is not true. For all we know, *Q* might be the one that isn't true. It doesn't *have to be* that *P* isn't true in order for the conjunction of *P* and *Q* not to be true. So, it is possible for the premiss to be true and the conclusion false.

To a certain extent, arguing abstractly in words is difficult. The words get in our way. We can make things easier for ourselves if we leave the words out of the abstract explanation and deal almost entirely with symbols. We can use our truth-table definitions for conjunction and negation to help us.

Here is how we can use a truth table to determine whether argument (1) is valid or not:

P	Q	PREMISS −P	P & Q	CONCLUSION −(P & Q)
T	T	F	T	F
T	F	F	F	T
F	T	T	F	T
F	F	T	F	T

How did we set this table up? How did we get our column headings? On the left, we have columns for each of the letters occurring in the argument. We have a column for the premiss, −P, and we have a column for the conclusion, −(P & Q). The P & Q column is included as an intermediate step in the process of figuring out −(P & Q).

How did we fill in the truth table? For the P and Q columns, we listed all possible combinations of truth values for P and for Q. There are four such possibilities. Then we worked across the table, using the logical properties of negation and conjunction.

Let's work across the top line. −P is the negation of P; since P is T, −P must be F. Next, since P and Q are both T, P & Q will also be T (since a conjunction is true whenever both conjuncts are true). And, since P & Q is T, −(P & Q) will be F (since a statement and its negation always have opposite truth values).

Let's try the second line. P is T, so −P must be F. Next, since P is T and Q is F, P & Q is F. And, since P & Q is F, its negation, −(P & Q), is T.

You can work out the bottom two lines for yourself.

How do we use the truth table to determine whether the argument is valid? We need to find out whether it is possible for the premiss, −P, to be true while the conclusion, −(P & Q), is false. If it is possible, the argument is invalid; if it is impossible, the argument is valid. But we have all the possibilities right on our truth table. Each line on the table corresponds to a possibility. All we need do is check down each line of the table to see if there is one in which the premiss comes out true and the conclusion comes out false. Try it. Check down the lines. You should find no such line in the table. So, the argument is valid.

To determine whether (2) is valid we can use the same truth table we used with (1). All we have to do is relabel the columns for the premiss and conclusion:

		CONCLUSION		PREMISS
P	Q	$-P$	$P \& Q$	$-(P \& Q)$
T	T	F	T	F
T	F	F	F	T
F	T	T	F	T
F	F	T	F	T

Now, check to see whether there is a line in which the premiss comes out true and the conclusion comes out false. You will find that in the second line $-(P \& Q)$ comes out true and $-P$ comes out false. So, this argument is invalid. It is not the case that whenever $-(P \& Q)$ is true, $-P$ is also true.

We actually have three procedures for determining whether an argument is valid:

(1)   We give examples.
(2)   We argue abstractly using the properties of negation and conjunction.
(3)   We argue abstractly using truth tables.

Let us apply each of these procedures to the following arguments:

$$(3) \qquad\qquad (4)$$
$$-(P \& Q) \qquad\qquad -P \& -Q$$
$$\text{SO, } -P \& -Q \qquad\qquad \text{SO, } -(P \& Q)$$

One of these is valid; one is invalid. Our task is to find out which is which.

We'll consider argument (3) first. Let P be "The Red Sox won the pennant," and let Q be "The Red Sox won the World Series." The argument then becomes

The Red Sox didn't win both the pennant and the World Series;

so,

the Red Sox didn't win the pennant and didn't win the World Series.

Now, let's suppose that the premiss is true: suppose the Red Sox didn't win both the pennant and the World Series. Would it follow that the Red Sox didn't win either one—that they didn't win the pennant and they didn't win the World Series? No. Just because they didn't win both, it doesn't follow that they won neither. It is perfectly possible for the Red Sox to have won the pennant and lost the World Series (indeed, half the teams that play in the World Series do this); as such, they wouldn't have won both, but they wouldn't have won neither either. So, we have a counterexample. The argument is invalid.

Let's now argue abstractly, using the second procedure. Suppose that

P and *Q* are not both true. Then, one or the other or both are false. But these are three distinct possibilities; the conclusion—namely, that *P* and *Q* are both not true—is only one of them. So it would seem that it is possible for the premiss to be true and the conclusion false.

Now, let's construct a truth table:

P	*Q*	−*P*	−*Q*	CONCLUSION −*P* & −*Q*	*P* & *Q*	PREMISS −(*P* & *Q*)
T	T	F	F	F	T	F
T	F	F	T	F	F	T
F	T	T	F	F	F	T
F	F	T	T	T	F	T

Let's go over how this truth table has been constructed. First, the column headings. *P* and *Q* are the statement letters occurring in the argument. The −*P* and −*Q* columns are included so that we can work out −*P* & −*Q*, which is the conclusion of the argument. *P* & *Q* is included so we can work out the premiss, −(*P* & *Q*).

Next, we list all possible truth values for *P* and *Q*, and then calculate the rest of the table. Instead of working out the table line by line, however, we find that it is much faster to do it column by column. −*P* is the negation of *P*; whatever truth value is in the *P* column, we put the opposite in the −*P* column. Similarly for −*Q*. To figure out −*P* & −*Q*, we look back to the −*P* column and the −*Q* column: −*P* & −*Q* is T when and only when there is a T in both the −*P* and the −*Q* columns. Next, we put a T in the *P* & *Q* column when and only when there is a T in both the *P* column and the *Q* column. Finally, −(*P* & *Q*) is the negation of *P* & *Q*; whatever truth value is in the *P* & *Q* column, we put the opposite in the −(*P* & *Q*) column.

Finally, we check to see whether there is any line in which the premiss, −(*P* & *Q*), comes out T and the conclusion, −*P* & −*Q*, comes out F. If there is, the argument is invalid; if there is none, the argument is valid. Which is it? Clearly, the argument is invalid, because in the second and third lines (in other words, in two cases), the premiss comes out true and the conclusion comes out false.

You can work out argument (4) for yourself. You should find that it turns out to be valid.

EXERCISES

4.3:1   Which of the following are valid arguments? That is, in which of the following does the premiss imply the conclusion? If the argument is valid, show that it is valid by arguing abstractly. If the argument is invalid, argue abstractly and give a counterexample.

a. *not both P and not Q*
    SO, *not P*
b. *not P*
    SO, *not both not P and Q*
c. *P and not Q*
    SO, *not both P and Q*

4.3:2 Which of the following are valid arguments? Explain.

a. Harry and Sam don't both like classical music. So, neither Harry nor Sam likes classical music.
b. Harry and Sam don't both like classical music. So, Harry doesn't like classical music.
c. Harry and Sam both don't like classical music. So, Harry doesn't like classical music.

4.3:3 Suppose the college catalog says that students must take Math 200 if they have not taken both Math 150 and Math 170. Suppose Harry took neither Math 150 nor Math 170. Must he take Math 200? Suppose Harry took Math 150 but not Math 170. Must he take Math 200? Suppose Harry took Math 150. Must he take Math 200? Suppose Harry didn't take Math 150. Must he take Math 200?

4.3:4 Show that the following argument is valid by symbolizing it and constructing a truth table:

> Arguments (1) and (2) are not both valid. But argument (1) is valid. So, argument (2) is not valid.

REVIEW

1. *P* implies *Q* if whenever *P* is true, *Q* must be true. The other way of saying this is that *P* implies *Q* if *P* and $-Q$ cannot both be true. Every statement implies itself. Just because *P* implies *Q*, it does not mean that *Q* also implies *P*: *Q* will also imply *P* only when *P* and *Q* say the very same thing—that is, when they are logically equivalent.

2. An argument is valid if the premises imply the conclusion. So, every argument can be understood as an implication, and every implication as an argument.

3. There are three ways for determining whether an argument is valid. One way is to argue concretely, using examples. If you can come up with an example with true premises and a false conclusion, then you know the argument is invalid. But, to show an argument to be valid, you must argue abstractly, either in words, using the properties of the logical particles, or using truth tables.

4. To use a truth table for determining the validity of arguments, proceed as follows. There must be a column for each premiss, a column for the conclusion, and also columns for the atomic statements out of which the premisses and conclusion are constructed. Assign all possible truth values to the atomic statements (for two letters, there will be four distinct cases), and then figure out each of the columns, using the truth-table definitions of the connectives. When you have done this, look for a line in the table in which all the premisses come out true and the conclusion comes out false. If there is such a line, the argument is invalid. If there is no such line, the argument is valid.

5

DISJUNCTION

"I'll take your money or take your life," snarled the mugger wielding a knife. "You'll get nothing from me," said the muggee, who then turned around, attempting to flee. What then ensued was terrible strife. They struggled. They fought. But all was for naught. Muggee gave up his wallet and life; the wallet was empty, Mugger was rife. To the judge he was brought; he proceeded to plea: "All I did, Your Honor, oh please, don't you see, was speak the truth— that's no felony." The judge was appalled; out came his decree: "Either I speak the truth and you'll hang from a tree, or, Mr. Mugger, with all honesty, I'll say to you what you said to Muggee."

5.1   WHAT IS A DISJUNCTION?

When two statements are connected by *or*, the resulting complex statement is a **disjunction**. A disjunction, such as

John speaks French or John speaks Spanish,

contains two constituent statements, called **disjuncts**: "John speaks French" is the *left disjunct* and "John speaks Spanish" is the *right disjunct*.

As with *and*, we frequently find *or* connecting names or sentence fragments. For example:

He took either the bus or the train to school.

Such sentences can be taken to be contracted versions of sentences in which *or* connects statements. We could restate our example as

Either he took the bus to school or he took the train to school.

The left disjunct is "he took the bus to school" and the right disjunct is "he took the train to school." Other cases can be handled in the same way.

When you claim that a disjunction is true, you commit yourself to the truth of at least one disjunct. When you say

John took physics or John took chemistry,

you claim that one or the other of the two constituent statements is true. You are not claiming that John took physics. You are not claiming that John took chemistry. You claim something a good deal weaker than either of these statements taken individually. You claim that John took physics *or* chemistry.

Our object in this section is to determine the truth conditions of disjunction, and this means completing the following truth table:

P	Q	Either P or Q
T	T	
T	F	
F	T	
F	F	

Disjunction is a bit more complicated than conjunction, as we will come to understand in this section. However, some of the lines in the table are easier to fill in than others. We will fill in the table, working from the bottom line on up to the top. Let's use a concrete example. Consider the statement

Either Sally is at Macy's or Sally is at Gimbel's.

That is, we'll adopt the following assignments for P and Q:

P: Sally is at Macy's.
Q: Sally is at Gimbel's.

Bottom Line.   Both disjuncts are false. So, Sally is neither at Macy's nor at Gimbel's, but rather at, say, Bloomingdale's. Would the disjunction be true or false? The claim is that she is at one or the other of these two stores whereas, in fact, she is at neither. We think it's clear that the claim is false. So, our truth table is filled in like this:

P	Q	Either P or Q
T	T	
T	F	
F	T	
F	F	F

Third Line. The left disjunct is false and the right disjunct is true. So, Sally is not at Macy's but she is at Gimbel's. Would the statement be true? The claim is that she is at one or the other of the two places, and, indeed, she is at one of them—Gimbel's. So she *is* at one or the other of the two places mentioned. The statement is true. Our truth table now looks like this:

P	*Q*	*Either P or Q*
T	T	
T	F	
F	T	T
F	F	F

Second Line. The left disjunct is true and the right disjunct is false. Sally is at Macy's but not at Gimbel's. This case is essentially the same as the previous one. She is at one of the two places; so she is at one or the other of the two places. The claim is true. Our truth table to this point now looks like this:

P	*Q*	*Either P or Q*
T	T	
T	F	T
F	T	T
F	F	F

Top Line. Both disjuncts are true. This is the problematic case. Is the disjunction true or false? We will have to consider this possibility in some detail.

Let's go back to our example again:

Either Sally is at Macy's or Sally is at Gimbel's.

Suppose that she is at both places, Macy's and Gimbel's. Is the disjunction true or false? Someone who realizes that Macy's and Gimbel's are a block apart might argue as follows:

> She cannot be at both places at the same time (after all, no one can be at two places at the same time); so, the disjunction has got to be false.

This reasoning is, however, confused. Our questions was: What happens if Sally is at both places? The argument is that she cannot be at both places. But that doesn't tell us whether the disjunction is true or whether it is false if she *were* at both places.

So far, we have seen only an argument for the claim that the disjunction is false in this case. We will soon present an argument for its being true. But first, we'll consider different examples, where the issues are a bit clearer. Then we'll return to the puzzling case of Sally's being either at Macy's or at Gimbel's.

Let's suppose that the requirement for getting into Physics 415 is that the student has taken either Physics 300 or Math 300. Clearly, if you had taken Math 300 you would be allowed into Physics 415. Also, if you had taken Physics 300 you would be allowed into Physics 415. Now, suppose you had taken *both* Physics 300 *and* Math 300. Would this bar you from taking Physics 415? Surely not.

Here's another example. Suppose you place a bet with your friendly neighborhood bookie. Your bet is that either the Packers win their game against the Rams or the Bears win their game against the Patriots. Now remember, you are not simply betting that the Packers win, and you are not simply betting that the Bears win. You are also not betting that both of them win. You are betting that one or the other of them wins. (Clearly, you will not be getting odds as good as you would have gotten if you had bet on the teams individually.)

Under what conditions will you win the bet? Clearly, if the Bears win, you collect. Clearly, if the Packers win, you collect. What happens if both of them win? Would you rip up your ticket and suppose that you had lost? Not at all. You would be hightailing it down to your friendly neighborhood bookie to collect your winnings. The only way you could have lost that bet is if neither one of the teams had won.

These examples show that for the most part, we do not take a disjunction to be false when both disjuncts are true. On the contrary, if both disjuncts are true, we take the disjunction to be true. So what happened in the case of Sally? Earlier, it was claimed that the disjunction must be false because Sally couldn't be both at Macy's and at Gimbel's at the same time. However, consider the following science fiction story.

Let's suppose that Sally leaves her home in the Bronx one morning and hops on the downtown train to go shopping. Along the way, the train is bombarded by strange rays from outer space, which begin to have a strange effect on her. They make her grow bigger and bigger so that by the time the train gets downtown, she is as huge as Godzilla. She crashes up through the subway entrance and stands astride Thirty-fourth Street. Meanwhile, back in the Bronx, Sally's friend Harold comes to the door and asks where Sally is. Sally's mother answers, "She's either at Macy's or Gimbel's." And at that moment, there is Sally, like a colossus, with one foot in Macy's and one foot in Gimbel's. End of story. Question: Is what Sally's mother said to Harold true or false? We think it's true. Sally *is* at Macy's or Gimbel's; indeed, she is at both places.

What's the point of this little story? It is to show you that those who thought that the disjunction must be false in the top row are mistaken. What led them to think so was not the way they understand the word *or*. Rather, it was their background beliefs about how big Sally is and about how far apart Macy's and Gimbel's are. Of course Sally cannot be at two places at the same time; Sally is where she is. But, if she were as big as Godzilla, then she could be at both stores at the same time, although she would be in only one place. And if she were at both stores at the same time, then the disjunction would be true.

Our problem, then, is to fill in the top slot of our truth table for *or*. If we put a T in that slot, then we take our English *or* to be what is called the **inclusive** *or:*

Inclusive or: One or the other or both.

If we put an F in that slot, we take our English *or* to be what is called the **exclusive** *or:*

Exclusive or: One or the other but not both.

Do native speakers of English use *or* inclusively or exclusively? Other languages have conventions different from ours. Latin, in fact, has two words for *or: aut* is understood as exclusive *or*, and *vel* is understood as inclusive *or*. The difference is clearly exhibited in the truth table:

P	*Q*	*P vel Q*	*P aut Q*
T	T	T	F
T	F	T	T
F	T	T	T
F	F	F	F

The two differ only in the top case. When *P* and *Q* are both true, *P vel Q* is true but *P aut Q* is false. Now the question for us is: Does the English *or* correspond to the Latin *aut* or to the Latin *vel*? The only way we can distinguish the two is by the top case; we have to see what happens to a disjunction when both disjuncts are true.

You can see why the case of Sally's being either at Macy's or at Gimbel's would not tell us whether we had inclusive or exclusive *or*. Since Sally could not be at both places at the same time, we could not get both disjuncts true. That eliminates the only case that could decide the issue. Our science fiction story was designed to test your intuitions about what would happen if both disjuncts were true. Only then could we determine the logical properties of *or.* So, examples like

> Either Sally is at Macy's or Sally is at Gimbel's
>
> Either it's raining or it's not raining
>
> Either $x = 0$ or $x = 1$,

which are the sorts of examples that make one think the English *or* is exclusive, do nothing of the sort. To be sure, it cannot both rain and not rain (in the same place, at the same time, etc). But it is not the *or* that is doing the excluding; it's the logical fact that a statement and its negation cannot both be true. Similarly, in the third example: it can't be that $x = 0$ *and* $x = 1$, for then it would turn out that $0 = 1$, and this is mathematically impossible. Again, it is not the *or* that is doing the excluding; it is the mathematical facts we have just outlined.

Once we have eliminated the cases just discussed, there is very little reason left to support the view that the English *or* is exclusive. On the other hand, we've given a number of examples to show that we use *or* inclusively. So, we take *or* to be inclusive.

We will adopt the symbol v (for *vel*) to represent *or*. Our truth table, finally, looks like this:

P	*Q*	*P* v *Q*
T	T	T
T	F	T
F	T	T
F	F	F

In short,

> **A disjunction is false when and only when both disjuncts are false. Otherwise it is true.**

Another way of putting it is

> **A disjunction is true when and only when at least one disjunct is true. Otherwise it is false.**

Make sure you understand that these two definitions are equivalent.

EXERCISES

5.1:1   Identify the disjuncts in each of the following disjunctions.

a.   Either Mondale or Hart will be the Democratic nominee.

b.   John either isn't a Democrat or isn't a Republican.

c. Either Mary went to the party or she wasn't feeling well.
d. Harry took the Mercedes or he didn't drive.

5.1:2 Which of the following disjunctions are true? Which are false?
a. Either 0 equals 1 or it doesn't.
b. Either 0 does not equal 1 or 3 + 2 = 5.
c. Either 3 + 2 does not equal 5 or 0 does not equal 1.

Study Vocabulary: disjunction
disjunct
inclusive *or*
exclusive *or*

5.2 DISJUNCTION AND NEGATION

A disjunction, like any other statement, can be denied. We can negate the disjunction

The Republicans will win the election this year or next

by using our mechanical procedure:

It is not the case that the Republicans will win the election either this year or next.

We insert the word *either* for clarity, in just the same way we use the word *both* in the case of conjunction. Just as *both* goes with *and* to help group a conjunction, so *either* goes with *or* to help group the disjunction. What is being denied is the disjunction, the claim that either of these two events will occur.

A statement and its negation have opposite truth values. The negation of a disjunction will therefore be true when the disjunction is false, and it will be false when the disjunction is true. Since a disjunction is false when and only when both disjuncts are false, the negation of a disjunction will be true when and only when both disjuncts are false. So, to deny a disjunction is to claim that neither of the statements is true. We can see this clearly in a truth table:

P	*Q*	*P* v *Q*	−(*P* v *Q*)
T	T	T	F
T	F	T	F
F	T	T	F
F	F	F	T

As in the case of conjunction, we want now to consider whether we can negate a disjunction by placing a *not* inside the sentence. We will use a concrete example to help clarify our intuitions. Let's adopt the following abbreviations:

P: The Packers win.

Q: The Bears win.

So, *either P or Q* will abbreviate

Either the Packers win or the Bears win.

And let's compare:

(1)   Either the Packers *don't* win or the Bears win.

(2)   Either the Packers *don't* win or the Bears *don't* win.

(3)   It is *not* the case either that the Packers win or that the Bears win.

Now suppose you make another trip down to your friendly neighborhood bookie. Let's suppose that he knows at least as much logic as you do and also that he will accept crazy bets. You place ten dollars on each of the bets (1), (2), and (3). Under what conditions do you win? Under what conditions do you lose? A truth table will help us consider the four possibilities.

		(1)	(2)	(3)
P	*Q*	$-P \vee Q$	$-P \vee -Q$	$-(P \vee Q)$
T	T			
T	F			
F	T			
F	F			

First Case.   The first possibility is that P and Q are both true: the Packers and the Bears both win. What happens with our bets?

Our first bet, (1), was that either the Packers don't win or the Bears do. Since in this case the Bears do win, one of the disjuncts is true, so the disjunction is true. *We collect on (1).* Our second bet, (2), was that the Packers wouldn't win or the Bears wouldn't win. But, we are supposing in this case that both teams win. Both disjuncts in (2) are false, so the disjunction is false. *We lose on (2).* Our final bet, (3), is that neither team wins. But both teams win, so one or the other of them has won; hence, $P \vee Q$ is true and $-(P \vee Q)$ is false. *We lose bet (3).*

		(1)	(2)	(3)
P	*Q*	$-P \lor Q$	$-P \lor -Q$	$-(P \lor Q)$
T	T	T	F	F
T	F			
F	T			
F	F			

Second Case.   P is true and Q is false: the Packers win but the Bears don't. What happens in this case?

Bet (1) is that either the Packers don't win or the Bears do win. Since the Packers do win, the left disjunct is false; and since the Bears don't win, the right disjunct is false. Both disjuncts are false, so the disjunction is false. We lose on (1). Bet (2) is that one or the other of the two teams *doesn't* win. On our supposition, the Packers win but the Bears don't. So, one of the teams didn't win. In this case, then, the right disjunct comes out true. We *collect on (2)*. Bet (3) is that neither one of the two teams wins; it is not the case, (3) says, that either one of them wins. Since the Packers win, however, it must be true that either the Packers or the Bears win, so it must be false that it is not the case that either one of them wins. We *lose (3)*.

		(1)	(2)	(3)
P	*Q*	$-P \lor Q$	$-P \lor -Q$	$-(P \lor Q)$
T	T	T	F	F
T	F	F	T	F
F	T			
F	F			

Third Case.   We suppose P is false and Q is true: the Packers don't win but the Bears do.

Bet (1) was that either the Packers don't win or the Bears do: one or the other of these would come true. Both came out true in this case, so the disjunction is true. We *collect on (1)*. Bet (2) was that either the Packers didn't win or the Bears didn't win—in other words, that one or the other of them wouldn't win. And one of them—the Packers—didn't win. One disjunct is true, so the disjunction is true. We *collect on (2)*. The final bet, (3), was that it was not the case that either one would win—in effect, that neither team would win. But one of the teams did win—namely, the Bears. We *lose (3)*.

		(1)	(2)	(3)
P	*Q*	$-P \lor Q$	$-P \lor -Q$	$-(P \lor Q)$
T	T	T	F	F
T	F	F	T	F
F	T	T	T	F
F	F			

Fourth Case. We suppose *P* and *Q* are both false: the Packers don't win *and* the Bears don't win.

Bet (1) was that either the Packers don't win or the Bears do. Since the Packers don't win, the left disjunct is true, so the disjunction is true. *We collect on (1).* Bet (2) was that either the Packers don't win or the Bears don't win—that one or the other of the two teams wouldn't win. Since both didn't win, both disjuncts are true. *We collect on (2).* Bet (3) was that it was not the case that either team would win—in other words, that neither team would win. And, neither did win. *We collect on (3).*

		(1)	(2)	(3)
P	*Q*	*−P* v *Q*	*−P* v *−Q*	*−(P* v *Q)*
T	T	T	F	F
T	F	F	T	F
F	T	T	T	F
F	F	T	T	T

In short, to deny a disjunction is not the same as to deny each of the disjuncts. That is,

$$(4) \quad -(P \vee Q)$$

is not equivalent to

$$(5) \quad -P \vee -Q.$$

Although (4) implies (5), (5) does not imply (4). This is the same position we found ourselves in when we discussed conjunction in Chapter 3. To deny a conjunction is not the same thing as to deny each of the conjuncts. That is,

$$(6) \quad -(P \mathbin{\&} Q)$$

is not equivalent to

$$(7) \quad -P \mathbin{\&} -Q.$$

(7) implies (6), but (6) does not imply (7).

Is there a way of driving the negation sign inside the conjunction—or the disjunction? Or are we faced with having to use the stilted denials "It is not the case both that . . . and . . . ," and "It is not the case either that . . . or . . . "?

The answer is that we do not have to use these stilted denials. We can drive the negation signs in, but to do so we must change the logical connective from *or* to *and*, or from *and* to *or*. These are **De Morgan's Laws:**

$-(P \& Q)$ *is logically equivalent to* $-P \vee -Q$.
$-(P \vee Q)$ *is logically equivalent to* $-P \& -Q$.

We will use the truth table to show that (6) and (5) are equivalent.

			(6)			(5)
P	Q	$P \& Q$	$-(P \& Q)$	$-P$	$-Q$	$-P \vee -Q$
T	T	T	F	F	F	F
T	F	F	T	F	T	T
F	T	F	T	T	F	T
F	F	F	T	T	T	T

You can see from the table that (6) and (5) have exactly the same columns; they always have the same truth value.

De Morgan's Laws tell us that to deny a conjunction is to say that one or the other of the two conjuncts is not true. And to deny a disjunction is to say that both of the disjuncts are not true. In English, this means that

It is not the case both that the Packers and Bears win

is equivalent to saying

Either the Packers don't win or the Bears don't win.

And

It is not the case either that the Packers or the Bears win

is equivalent to saying

The Packers don't win and the Bears don't win.

EXERCISES

5.2:1   Put the following entirely in symbols.

a.   Either P or Q
b.   Neither P nor Q
c.   Either P or *not* Q

5.2:2   Symbolize each of the following.

a.   Either Plato or Socrates wrote the *Republic*.
b.   It is not the case either that Plato was a Sophist or that Socrates was a Sophist.

c.   Either it is not the case that Plato wrote the *Republic* or Socrates wrote the *Republic*.

d.   It is not the case that neither Plato nor Socrates wrote the *Republic*.

5.2:3   Let *P* abbreviate "John is handsome," and let *Q* abbreviate "Mary is beautiful." Write each of the following statements in English.

a. $P \vee Q$
b. $-P \vee Q$
c. $-(P \vee Q)$
d. $-(-P \vee -Q)$

5.2:4   Suppose that *P* and *Q* are true and *R* is false. Which of the following are true? Which are false?

a. $-P \vee Q$
b. $-Q \vee R$
c. $-(-R \vee Q)$
d. $-(-P \vee -Q)$
e. $-(P \vee R) \vee (R \vee -Q)$

5.2:5   Show that $-(-P \ \& \ -Q)$ is logically equivalent to $P \vee Q$.

5.2:6   What would be a simpler way of saying $-(-P \vee -Q)$?

Study Vocabulary: **De Morgan's Laws**

5.3   PARENTHESES

One of the most important aspects of understanding the structure of a complex statement is the *grouping* of the components. In logical symbolism, we use *parentheses* to group. We use parentheses in mathematics as well, although not in English. We will discuss the English devices shortly. In this section, we will explain how parentheses work.

Parentheses come in pairs; for every left parenthesis, '(', there must be a right parenthesis, ')'. There must always be an even number of parentheses in a formula, because each left parenthesis must be mated with a right parenthesis. Also, parentheses are sometimes nested, one set inside another, like this:

$$((\ )).$$

Which is the mate for the leftmost parenthesis? The rightmost parenthesis:

$$(\ (\ ) \ ) \ .$$
$$\uparrow \qquad \uparrow$$

The two outer parentheses connect up, and the two inner parentheses connect up.

Consider, as a more concrete example, the following mathematical formula:

$$((3 + 2) \times (4 + 3)).$$

How would you read this? Which would be the right mate for the leftmost parenthesis? There are three possibilities to consider:

(1)	(2)	(3)
((3 + 2) × (4 + 3))	((3 + 2) × (4 + 3))	((3 + 2) × (4 + 3)) .
↑ ↑	↑ ↑ ↑	↑ ↑

When you enclose a sequence of expressions in parentheses, you are taking them as a coherent whole. Note what happens for each choice. If you choose (1), then you are supposing that

$$(3 + 2$$

is a coherent subclause of the formula, and that

$$\times (4 + 3))$$

is also a coherent subclause of the formula. But this makes no sense. The first is a fragment. You can see that it is a fragment because there is one left parenthesis but no right parentheses. There is an odd number, and this is impossible. The second expression is also a fragment. For one thing, there is a multiplication sign, '×', and this requires two parts (you have to multiply two numbers), whereas there is only one. And again, there is an odd number of parentheses.

Now try (2). Remember how we analyze the situation. We imagine that everything *within* the two parentheses with the arrows underneath forms a coherent whole. When we follow this procedure, we are left with

$$(3 + 2) \times (4 + 3.$$

This is a fragment: the right parenthesis is missing. So this **parsing** is impossible.

We are left, then, with (3). This one works, because when we drop the outermost parentheses, we are left with

$$(3 + 2) \times (4 + 3),$$

and this makes perfectly good sense.

We are most familiar with parentheses in mathematical formulas. But we also use parentheses in logic. Their main function is to **disambiguate**. Without parentheses, very frequently the structure is not clear, and there might be more than one way of understanding the formula. Consider the following example:

P and Q or R.

This is ambiguous. We might read this as a conjunction, with *P* the left conjunct and *Q or R* the right conjunct. Using parentheses to show this, the reading is

P and (Q or R).

Alternatively, we might read this as a disjunction, with *P and Q* the left disjunct and *R* the right disjunct. Using parentheses, we get for this reading

(P and Q) or R.

You can see very clearly from this example how parentheses help us to group. In the first case, we are grouping *Q or R* as a coherent subclause of the whole formula; in the second case we are grouping *P and Q* as a coherent subclause.

There is a simple mechanical procedure for figuring out which parentheses are connected with which in a complex formula. Start at the far left side of the statement and proceed to the right until you find a right parenthesis. When you find one, connect it up with the nearest left parenthesis in front of it that is not already connected. Then continue proceeding to the right until you find another right parenthesis, and connect it up with the nearest unconnected left parenthesis that precedes it. Continue in this way until all parentheses are connected.

For example, suppose you had the following formula:

not (P and (Q or (R and S))).

This is an extremely complex, nested formula. Let us see what the structure is by using the procedure just described. Start at the left side of the formula and proceed to the right until you find a right parenthesis. You should now be pointing to where the arrow is pointing here:

not (P and (Q or (R and S))).
       ↑

You have to hook up this right parenthesis with the nearest unconnected left parenthesis in front of it:

not (P and (Q or (R and S))).
   ↑   ↑

Just to make clear what we have done, we will replace the left and right parentheses with brackets:

not (P and (Q or [R and S])).

Continue to the right until you find a right parenthesis. You should be here:

not (P and (Q or [R and S])).
       ↑

Now, connect it up with the nearest unattached parenthesis that precedes it. So, you have

not (P and (Q or [R and S])).
   ↑   ↑

Just to make clear what we have done, we will replace these parentheses with braces:

not (P and {Q or [R and S]}).

Continuing on, find the next right parenthesis:

not (P and {Q or [R and S]}) .
       ↑

And connect it up with the nearest unattached left parenthesis that precedes it:

not (P and {Q or [R and S]}) .
  ↑   ↑

There's no need to change these parentheses; we have finished.

We need parentheses to group. This means that parentheses are needed only when we have one complex formula occurring as part of another. Let's look at how we use parentheses in mathematics.

$$3 + 2$$

requires no parentheses around it. If we were to insert parentheses,

$$(3 + 2)$$

we would not enhance the clarity of the symbols. Similarly, there is no need to insert parentheses around the 3 or around the 2. That is, none of the following enhances the clarity of the original mathematical formula:

$$(3) + 2$$
$$3 + (2)$$
$$(3) + (2).$$

Actually, inserting so many parentheses eventually diminishes the readability of the formula. In each of these cases, there is no need to introduce parentheses because there is no ambiguity in the structure. The numeral 3 by itself has no structure. It is, if you like, an atom. There are no parts to this numeral that might be read in different ways. And since "3 + 2" is built up from atoms, again, there is no way this can be read in more than one way. Parentheses are needed only when a *complex* expression is embedded in a *more complex* expression.

For example, consider

$$(3 + 2) \times 4.$$

We need the parentheses around "3 + 2" because we want that particular string of symbols to be taken as a coherent whole. This formula tells us to add 3 to 2 and multiply that result by 4:

$$(3 + 2) \times 4 = 20.$$

If the parentheses are placed in a slightly different way, for example,

$$3 + (2 \times 4),$$

we are now taking "2 × 4" as a coherent whole. So, we are told to multiply 2 by 4 and add the result to 3:

$$3 + (2 \times 4) = 11.$$

You can see how different the results are in these two cases. You can also see that what we have is a *complex* expression embedded in a *more complex* expression. That is the only way in which ambiguity can crop up. Note again that there is no need to place parentheses around the whole expression. That is, there is no difference between

$$3 + (2 \times 4)$$

and

$$(3 + (2 \times 4)).$$

The reason is straightforward. Although we have a complex expression, it is not itself embedded in a larger expression.

We can sum up the correct use of parentheses as follows. Parentheses are required only when the following situation arises:

(1)   the expression in parenthesis is complex; and
(2)   the parenthesized expression is embedded in a larger expression.

Both (1) and (2) must be satisfied in order to use parentheses. If one or the other is not fulfilled, then there is no need to insert parentheses. In fact, putting in parentheses when none is needed makes the formula less readable. So there is a trade-off: inserting parentheses makes the formula unambiguous; inserting too many parentheses makes the formula unreadable.

EXERCISES

5.3:1   Connect up left and right parentheses in each of the following so that the structure of the complex formula is evident.

a. $-(P \vee -(-P \vee Q))$
b. $P \mathbin{\&} (Q \vee -(P \mathbin{\&} Q))$
c. $(-P \vee -(P \mathbin{\&} Q)) \vee -P$

5.3:2   Add parentheses to the following formulas so that they are unambiguous. If there is more than one way of adding parentheses, write each one.

a. $P \vee -Q \mathbin{\&} R$
b. $-(P \vee Q \mathbin{\&} R)$

Study Vocabulary: parse
                            disambiguate

5.4 EITHER AND BOTH

In logic, as in mathematics, we use parentheses to group symbols together into coherent units. We do not use parentheses for this purpose in English. In this section, we will examine ways in which we group in English.

Compare the following two English statements:

(1) It is not the case that either stocks will rise or bonds will rise.

(2) Either it is not the case that stocks will rise or bonds will rise.

These two statements say different things. Look closely at the two statements. You will notice that the important difference lies in the placing of the phrase *it is not the case that*. In the first statement, it occurs before *either*; in the second statement, it occurs after *either*.

In (1), we are negating the disjunction. We are saying

It is not the case that:

Stocks will rise or bonds will rise.

(1) is *not* a disjunction; it is the negation of a disjunction. If (1) were a disjunction, it would have a left disjunct and a right disjunct. Suppose that we try to parse (1) in this way. Then the left disjunct would be

It is not the case that either stocks will rise,

and the right disjunct would be

bonds will rise.

This parsing is incoherent. And the reason is that in the left disjunct, we find *either* without *or*. The *either* is left hanging. *Either* must go together with *or*. So, in parsing (1) we have to treat

either stocks will rise or bonds will rise

as a coherent unit. If we used parentheses in English, (1) would have been written as

It is not the case that (stocks will rise or bonds will rise),

and our meaning would be perfectly clear. So, *either* serves in this particular statement as a left parenthesis.

Now, let us look at (2). Since *either* must go along with *or*, we know that what occurs between *either* and *or* must be a disjunct. In (2), then, the disjunct would be

It is not the case that stocks will rise.

You can see, then, that in (2), we do have a disjunction. We have already identified the left disjunct; the right disjunct is

bonds will rise.

Here are some more examples of how *either* helps us group complex statements. Consider

P and Q or R.

This formula is ambiguous. But we can disambiguate this formula by judiciously using *either*. Compare

Either P and Q or R

with

P and either Q or R.

In the first case, we take the formula as a disjunction. *P and Q* is the left disjunct (that is, everything between *either* and *or* is the left disjunct), and *R* is the right disjunct. You couldn't parse the statement in any other way. If, for example, you tried to make it into a conjunction, your left conjunct would have been

Either P

which is not a coherent unit; the *either* is left hanging. The second statement, however, is a conjunction. *P* is the left conjunct, and *either Q or R* is our right conjunct. If you had tried to take this statement as a disjunction, you would have had to treat

P and either Q

as a coherent whole, and it is plain that it is not a coherent whole.

Either goes along with *or*. It is not actually part of the connective; it is more like a parenthesis that is used in connection with *or*. Similarly, *both* goes along with *and*. It is not part of the connective, but it is a special parenthesis that goes along with *and*. Note, by the way, that it makes no sense to say

Either . . . and . . . ,

nor does it make any sense to say

Both . . . or . . . .

It is as if *or* has its own special parenthesis—namely, *either*—and *and* has its own special parenthesis—namely, *both*. This differs from our use of parentheses in mathematics and logic, where '(' and ')' are universal and not dependent upon the particular connective used.

We can see how *both* helps us to disambiguate in the following example:

P or Q and R.

Again, this particular formula is ambiguous. We can disambiguate it with judicious placement of *both*. Compare

Both P or Q and R

with

P or both Q and R.

The first is a conjunction. What occurs between *both* and *and* is the left conjunct, namely, *P or Q*; the right conjunct is *R*. The second statement is a disjunction. The left disjunct is *P*; the right disjunct is *Q and R*. These particular choices are forced upon us; there is no other way of reading these statements. Try a different way; that is, try to read the first as a disjunction and the second as a conjunction. You will find that you cannot do so.

This use of *either* and *both* as purely structural features of the language is rather interesting. It is also somewhat surprising. We tend to think of all words as serving a similar purpose. But really, we can use words to do all sorts of things. It is fairly clear that in a language such as English, in which we are able to construct complex statements, we need some devices such as these to help us group subclauses and make transparent the structure of the complex. We think of punctuation marks—the period, '.', or the comma, ',',—as serving that purpose, and we are somewhat surprised to find words doing the same job. But there is no rule that says that a language cannot do this. It might be fun for you to try to devise your own techniques for establishing subclause structures in a complex statement.

EXERCISES

5.4:1   Give at least two possible interpretations for each of the following.
a.   You may have cake or ice cream and soda or milk.
b.   You must take philosophy and sociology and biology or chemistry.
c.   I want Tom and Sally or John to go to the store.
d.   Senior men and women are excused from the final.

5.4:2   Let *P* be "John is happy" and let *Q* be "John is sad." Symbolize each of the following.
a.   Either John is happy and sad or John is not happy.

b. John is happy or he is not both sad and happy.

c. Both John is happy or not and John is sad.

d. It is not the case both that John is happy or sad and that he is not sad.

5.4:3   For each of the following, write at least two corresponding English statements.

a. $P \& (Q \vee R)$

b. $(P \& Q) \vee R$

c. $(P \& -Q) \vee -R$

d. $-(P \& Q) \vee -(P \& R)$

e. $-[(P \vee Q) \& (R \vee S)]$

5.5   DISJUNCTION AND IMPLICATION

In this section, we will consider some of the implications that hold for disjunctions. Of course, we will not study them all, for there are an infinite number of different arguments involving disjunction. We need study only some in order to clarify our intuitions about disjunction.

Let's begin by comparing the following two arguments:

$$
\begin{array}{cc}
(1) & (2) \\
P & P \text{ or } Q \\
\text{SO, } P \text{ or } Q & \text{SO, } \quad P
\end{array}
$$

One of these arguments is valid and one invalid. Our problem is to decide which is which.

Let's start with (1), using a concrete example. Suppose you had taken French in high school. Then it would follow that you had taken either French or Spanish in high school. The latter claim,

You took either French or Spanish in high school,

is a much weaker claim than

You took French in high school.

To say that you took French in high school is much more definite than to say you took French or Spanish. How might this implication be important? Well, suppose that when you get to college, you find out that anyone who took either French or Spanish in high school is exempt from the foreign-language requirement. If you took French in high school, then you would immediately suppose that you are exempt from the foreign-language requirement; if you took French, then you took either French or Spanish.

Of course, such examples only make it *plausible* that the argument is valid; they do not prove the point. The only way we can prove that the argument is valid is to argue abstractly.

So, let's try to show that (1) is valid by using a more abstract line of reasoning—appealing to the logical properties of disjunction. We want to show that P implies P or Q. Is it possible for P to be true and P or Q to be false? Clearly not. Why? Because P or Q will be true whenever one of the disjuncts is true. So, if one of the disjuncts *is* true—namely, P—the disjunction will have to be true. Let us construct a truth table for the argument:

PREMISS		CONCLUSION
P	*Q*	*P* v *Q*
T	T	T
T	F	T
F	T	T
F	F	F

Under P and Q we list all possible combinations of truth values; under P v Q, we list the truth value of the disjunction, according to our rule for disjunction. Now, to test whether the argument is valid, we check to see whether, in any line, the premiss comes out true and the conclusion comes out false. Check it now. You should find that there is no such line. Hence, the argument is valid.

It is worthwhile pointing out that each of the following will also be valid, and for the same sorts of reasons that (1) is valid:

not P	*P*	*not P*
SO, *not P or Q*	SO, *P or not Q*	SO, *not P or not Q*

The reasoning is clear: as long as one disjunct is true, the disjunction must be true.

Now, let's look back at argument (2). We know, since (1) is the valid argument, that (2) must be the invalid argument. However, we want now to show that the argument is invalid.

The easiest way to see that (2) is invalid is to use the truth table we constructed for argument (1). To use that table for argument (2), however, we need to make a small adjustment in the way we label the columns: now P v Q is the premiss and P is the conclusion.

CONCLUSION		PREMISS
P	*Q*	*P* v *Q*
T	T	T
T	F	T
F	T	T
F	F	F

We have to check down each line in the table to see if there is a case in which the premiss is true and the conclusion is false. You should find that result in the third line on the table. So, the argument is invalid: it is possible for the premiss to be true and the conclusion false.

The reasoning here is straightforward. For $P \vee Q$ to be true, one or the other (or both) of the disjuncts has to be true. So $P \vee Q$ might be true even when P isn't, for Q might be true. It doesn't follow, therefore, that whenever $P \vee Q$ is true, P must also be true.

EXERCISES

5.5:1   Show that each of the following arguments is valid.

a.   *not P*
   SO, not P or Q

b.   *P*
   SO, P or not Q

c.   *not P*
   SO, not P or not Q

5.5:2   Which of the following arguments are valid? Explain your reasons.

a.   *P and not Q*
   SO, P or Q

b.   *P and not Q*
   SO, not P or not Q

c.   *Q*
   SO, Q or not Q

d.   *P and not Q*
   SO, not P or Q

5.5:3   Which of the following arguments are valid? Explain your reasons.

a.   Socrates was not a Sophist. So, either he wasn't a Sophist or he was a Persian warrior.

b.   Either Richard the Lionhearted was captured by the Saracens or he was killed in battle. So, he was captured by the Saracens.

c.   Abelard was the teacher of Plato. So, he either taught Plato or he didn't.

5.5:4   The college catalog says that students must take French 200 if they either have taken French 100 or have not taken French 150. Suppose that Harry has taken French 100. Must he take French 200? Suppose that Harry took French 100 and French 150. Must he take French 200? Suppose that

Harry took French 112 and French 115, and these are the only French courses he took. Must he take French 200?

5.5:5   Suppose you know that John went both to dinner and to the movies last night. Your friend asks you, "Where did John go last night?" You say, "John went either to dinner or the movies." Is what you said false? How would you criticize the answer you gave in this case?

5.6 MORE COMPLICATED CASES

Let us try some arguments that are a bit more complicated and require that we think a bit harder about disjunction. Compare the following two arguments:

(1)	(2)
not either P or Q	*not P or not Q*
SO, *not P or not Q*	SO, *not either P or Q*

Again, of these two arguments, one is valid and the other is invalid. Why don't you take a minute before reading on to try out for yourself which you think is the valid one and which you think is the invalid one. (Don't just guess! Try to back up your choice with reasons!)

Okay, now we'll figure them out together, starting with (1). We will begin with a concrete example. Let's adopt the following assignments for *P* and *Q*:

P: Einstein won a Nobel prize.
Q: Salk won a Nobel prize.

Then, our premiss in (1) says

It is not the case either that Einstein won a Nobel prize or that Salk won a Nobel prize.

In our premiss, we are denying that either one of them won the prize. Another way of saying this is: *neither* one of the two won the prize. Einstein didn't win *and* Salk didn't win. Now, what does our conclusion in (1) say? Substituting our statements for *P* and *Q*, we get

Either Einstein didn't win a Nobel prize or Salk didn't win a Nobel prize.

But if *neither* of the two won the prize, then the much weaker statement, that *either* Einstein didn't win *or* Salk didn't win, must surely follow.

If neither one of them is true, then *P* isn't true and *Q* isn't true. But, then, if *not P* is true, then *either not P or not Q* must be true (since if one disjunct is true, the disjunction must be true). We can set this piece of reasoning out as follows:

It is not the case either that Einstein won the prize or that Salk won the prize.	START
Neither Einstein nor Salk won the prize.	REPHRASE
Einstein didn't win the prize and Salk didn't win the prize.	REPHRASE
Einstein didn't win the prize.	$-P$ *and* $-Q$; SO, $-P$
Either Einstein didn't win the prize or Salk didn't win the prize.	$-P$; SO, $-P$ *or* $-Q$

This sequence of statements reflects the way in which we figure out whether one statement follows from another. On the left we have our statements, and on the right we have the justification for each statement. The first statement in the sequence actually requires no justification. It is our *premiss*, our starting point for the argument. The problem is to get from that starting point to the end point, the *conclusion* of the argument. This is the essence of argument. You try to rephrase a statement or draw some consequence, using the most obvious and elementary valid argument patterns, in order to get from some starting point to the end point. In logic, this is called **natural deduction**. It is logically the ideal way of setting forth an argument. We study natural deduction in more detail in Chapter 10 of this text.

Let's now look at argument (2). Our premiss is *not P or not Q*. So, either *P* isn't true or *Q* isn't true. The conclusion, however, is that *neither* of the two statements is true. And this conclusion surely doesn't follow from the premiss. Here is a counterexample. From the fact that you either didn't take French or didn't take Spanish in high school, it does not follow that you took neither of these two subjects. You might have taken one but not the other. So, if you took French, say, but you didn't take Spanish, then the following would be true:

Either you didn't take French or you didn't take Spanish.

But the statement

It is not the case that you either took French or Spanish

would be false. So, argument (2) is invalid.

Here is the truth table:

P	*Q*	*P* v *Q*	$-P$	$-Q$	$-P$ v $-Q$	$-(P$ v $Q)$
T	T	T	F	F	F	F
T	F	T	F	T	T	F
F	T	T	T	F	T	F
F	F	F	T	T	T	T

How did we plan this truth table? On the left side of the table, we list all the statement letters that occur in the premiss or in the conclusion. Then, we work out each column in stepwise fashion until we have built up our premiss and our conclusion. For example, the conclusion is $-(P \vee Q)$. Since this is the negation of $P \vee Q$, we first have to figure out the truth values for the disjunction, and then we can work out its negation. Similarly with $-P \vee -Q$. This is a disjunction, with $-P$ as the left disjunct and $-Q$ as the right disjunct. In order to work out this disjunction, we first have to work out each of the disjuncts, so we make a column for each part we have to work out.

How did we work out the first line in the table? Since P and Q are both true, the disjunction $P \vee Q$ is true; so we put a T in that column. $-P$ is the negation of P; so, since P is T, its negation is F. Similarly, $-Q$ is the negation of Q; since Q is T, $-Q$ is F. To work out $-P \vee -Q$, we look back to the $-P$ column and the $-Q$ column, for these are the two disjuncts. The disjunction will be true if we find a T in either of these two columns. There is an F in both columns. Both disjuncts are false, so the disjunction is false. We therefore put an F in the $-P \vee -Q$ column. Finally, $-(P \vee Q)$ is the negation of $P \vee Q$. And since the disjunction is T, its negation is F. You can similarly work out all the other lines in the truth table.

Once we have worked up our truth table, we can easily determine whether our two arguments are valid. Remember, for an argument to be valid, there can be no line (that is, no possibility) in the table in which the premiss comes out true and the conclusion comes out false. Alternatively, if there *is* a line in the table in which the premiss comes out true and the conclusion comes out false, then *it is possible* to have a true premiss and false conclusion, so the argument is *invalid*.

In argument (1), $-(P \vee Q)$ is the premiss and $-P \vee -Q$ is the conclusion. Check the lines in the table and you will find no line in which the premiss is true and the conclusion is false. So, (1) is valid. Next, we test argument (2). Here, $-P \vee -Q$ is the premiss and $-(P \vee Q)$ is the conclusion. You will note that in the second and third lines, the premiss comes out true and the conclusion comes out false. So, it is possible to get a true premiss and false conclusion. Argument (2) is invalid.

EXERCISES

5.6:1   Which of the following arguments are valid? Which are invalid? Explain your answers.

a.   *not either P or Q*
     SO, *P*

b.   *not either P or Q*
     SO, *not both P and Q*

c.   *either not P or not Q*
     SO, *not either P or Q*

5.6:2   Which of the following arguments are valid? Which are invalid? Explain your answers.

a.   Neither the president of the United States nor the vice-president of the United States is a Democrat. So, the president of the United States is not a Democrat.

b.   It is not the case that both New York and Maryland are north of West Virginia. So, neither New York nor Maryland is north of West Virginia.

c.   It is not the case that either New York City or Buffalo is the capital of New York State. So, either New York City is not the capital of New York State or Albany is the capital of New York State.

5.6:3   Show that the following argument is valid.

Either argument (1) is not valid or argument (2) is not valid. But we have already shown that argument (1) is valid. So, argument (2) is not valid.

Study Vocabulary: **natural deduction**

REVIEW

1.   When two statements are joined by *or*, we have a disjunction. The two constituent statements are disjuncts. There are two possible senses of *or*: the *inclusive or*—one or the other or both—and the *exclusive or*—one or the other but not both. We will use the inclusive *or* and symbolize it by 'v'. A disjunction is true when at least one of the disjuncts is true. Otherwise it is false. Here is the truth table for disjunction:

P	Q	$P \vee Q$
T	T	T
T	F	T
F	T	T
F	F	F

2.   In order to negate a disjunction, we must place *It is not the case that either* in front. We cannot negate the disjunction by negating each disjunct. *Either* serves as a left parenthesis for *or*, just as *both* serves for *and*. We express *not either P or Q* by $-(P \vee Q)$. We express *either not P or not Q* by $-P \vee -Q$.

3.   De Morgan's Laws relate disjunction and conjunction in the following way: $-(P \& Q)$ is logically equivalent to $-P \vee -Q$, and $-(P \vee Q)$ is logically equivalent to $-P \& -Q$.

4.   Parentheses help us to group coherent subclauses in some complex formulas. Parentheses are required when the expression in parentheses is complex and the parenthesized expression is embedded in a larger, more complex expression.

6

TRUTH TABLES

The College Requirement in Foreign Language is as follows:

Either (A) for a student with NO MORE THAN ONE YEAR OF HIGH SCHOOL CREDIT IN A FOREIGN LANGUAGE: *two five-credit language courses at the 100-level or the equivalent sequence in the School of General Studies; or (B) for a student with* MORE THAN ONE YEAR OF HIGH SCHOOL CREDIT IN A FOREIGN LANGUAGE, *either (1) after consultation with the appropriate language department, either (a) two five-credit language courses at the 100-level or the equivalent sequence in the School of General Studies; or (b) the five-credit second semester of the 100-level sequence; or (c) a 200-level course in the foreign language; or (d) a 300-level course in the foreign language; or (2) demonstration of proficiency in the foreign language sufficient to pass a final examination for a 300-level language course as determined by the appropriate department; or (3) two five-credit language courses at the 100-level in a new language or the equivalent sequence in the School of General Studies.*

Adapted from the *Lehman College Bulletin.*

Do you satisfy this requirement? If not, how could you satisfy it?

6.1 GRAMMATICAL TREES

Every complex formula we have dealt with is built up step by step from simpler formulas, by means of the logical connectives we have defined so far: negation, conjunction, and disjunction. At each step, the complex is built up from simpler formulas in only one of the following ways: it is the *negation* of a simpler formula, or it is the *conjunction* of two simpler formulas, or it is the *disjunction* of two simpler formulas. Using these facts, we can re-create the grammatical history of any formula: we can show how the complex formula was built up from the *atomic letters.*

Consider, for example, the complex formula

not both P and either Q or R.

In symbols, this is expressed as

(1) $-[P \And (Q \lor R)]$.

Let us see how this complex is built up. The first thing to recognize is that this is a *complex formula.* This means that it is either the negation of a simpler formula, or the conjunction or disjunction of two simpler formulas. Since all three connectives occur in the formula, we have to decide which is the **main connective.** Every complex formula must have a main connective.

Could it be a disjunction? If so, we would have to read everything to the left of the disjunction sign—namely, $-[P \And (Q$—as the left disjunct, and everything to the right—namely, $R)]$—as the right disjunct. But these are fragments. The parentheses,

$$-[P \And (\underset{\uparrow}{} Q \lor R \underset{\uparrow}{})],$$

require us to take $Q \lor R$ as a whole unit.

Could the formula be a conjunction? If so, we would have to read everything to the left of the conjunction sign—namely, $-[P$—as the left conjunct, and everything to the right—namely, $(Q \lor R)]$—as the right conjunct. Again, we end up with fragments. The brackets,

$$-[\underset{\uparrow}{} P \And (Q \lor R) \underset{\uparrow}{}],$$

require us to take $P \And (Q \lor R)$ as a whole unit.

Could we take the formula as a negation? Yes. It would be the negation of

(2) $P \And (Q \lor R)$.

So, the main connective in the original formula, (1), is the negation sign right in front.

Now, (2) is also complex, and so it must also have been built from simpler formulas by means of conjunction, disjunction, or negation. Since there is no negation sign in this formula, it must be either the conjunction or the disjunction of two simpler elements. Which is it? The parentheses are the tip-off. It is a *conjunction*; that is, the conjunction sign is the main connective here. The left conjunct is *P*; the right conjunct is *Q* v *R*. The left conjunct is not complex; it is simply a statement letter. The right conjunct is complex, and so we must determine the main connective. *Q* v *R* was formed by putting together *Q* and *R* with the disjunction symbol.

The formula that we have just worked out can be represented by the following diagram:

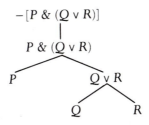

Think of the formula as having been built from the bottom up. We started with *Q* and *R*, and we disjoined them to form *Q* v *R*. Next, we took this disjunction and conjoined it with *P* to form *P* & (*Q* v *R*). Finally, we negated this to get our complex. This picture gives us a **grammatical tree**. It shows us how the complex was constructed from the parts.

Here is another example: Consider the complex formula

either not P or not both Q and R.

In symbols, this would be expressed as

$$-P \lor -(Q \;\&\; R).$$

Since this is a complex formula, it must have been built up from simpler formulas, by means of negation, conjunction, or disjunction. Is it the *negation* of a simpler formula, as in our previous example? The occurrence of the negation sign in front makes this plausible. But since there is no open parenthesis after the negation sign, we must read the negation sign as operating only on *P*. So, this cannot be the negation of a simpler formula. Could it be the *conjunction* of two simpler formulas? If so, everything to the left of the conjunction sign—namely, −*P* v −(*Q*— would have to be the left conjunct, and everything to the right—namely, *R*)—would have to be the right conjunct. But this makes no sense. In order to do this, we would have to break up something in parentheses. But *Q* & *R* must be taken as a unit because of the parentheses around it. So, the formula could not be a conjunction. Could it be a *disjunction?* Yes. *P* is the left disjunct and − (*Q* & *R*) is the right disjunct. We have found our main connective. So, our formula was formed by disjoining two simpler formulas. The left disjunct is itself complex: − *P* was formed by negating *P*. The right disjunct is the negation of *Q* & *R*, and this conjunction is also complex. It was formed by conjoining *Q* with *R*.

The grammatical tree for this formula would look like this:

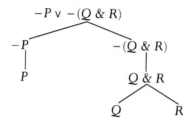

That is, we started with *P* and negated it, to get − *P*. Then, we took *Q* and *R* and conjoined them to form *Q* & *R*. Next, we negated this conjunction to form − (*Q* & *R*). Finally, once we constructed − *P* and − (*Q* & *R*), we disjoined them to form our complex.

We construct these trees to re-create the grammatical history of the particular formula we are interested in. Working from the top down, we slowly unfold at each level in the tree the subformulas out of which the complex was constructed. If the formula is the negation of some formula, then it has only one subformula. But if the formula is a conjunction or disjunction, then it has two subformulas, and that is how we obtain our branchings.

We can always ensure that our formula is built up in only one way. If we should find more than one possibility, then the formula is ambiguous and we need to insert parentheses into it in order to eliminate the ambiguity. We can always add parentheses to a formula to achieve this end.

EXERCISES

6.1:1   Identify the main connective in each of the following formulas.

a.   *P* v (*Q* & *R*)

b.   (*P* v *Q*) & *R*

c.   − *P* & − (*Q* v *R*)

d.   − (*P* v *Q*) & *R*

e.   − (*P* v (*Q* & *R*))

6.1:2   Construct a grammatical tree for the following formulas.

a. $(P \& Q) \vee (-P \& -Q)$
b. $-(P \vee -(Q \vee -R))$

6.1:3   Identify the main connective in each of the following statements.

a.   John did not take both French and Spanish in high school.
b.   Either John took French in high school or he took no language at all.
c.   John took either French or Spanish in high school.
d.   John took either French or Spanish in high school but not both.
e.   John didn't take either French or Spanish in high school.

Study Vocabulary: **main connective**
grammatical tree

6.2   ASSIGNING TRUTH VALUES

We can use these grammatical trees to determine the truth value of any complex formula, no matter what truth values are assigned to the atomic letters occurring in it.

Consider again the last tree we worked out in the previous section:

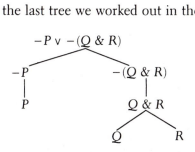

Suppose that P, Q, and R are all true. Let's put this information in our tree diagram:

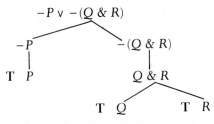

Next, let's figure out the truth value of the complex. We work from the bottom up. Working up the right branch of the tree, since Q is T and R is T, the conjunction Q & R is T.

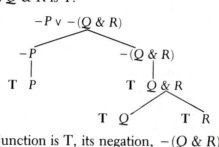

And since the conjunction is T, its negation, $-(Q$ & $R)$, will be F.

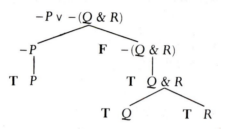

Now, we cannot work up this right branch any more until we have worked up the left branch. Since P is T, its negation, $-P$, is F.

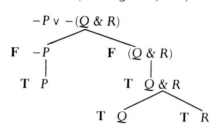

Finally, since $-P$ is F and $-(Q$ & $R)$ is F, the disjunction $-P$ v $-(Q$ & $R)$ will be F (because a disjunction is false when both disjuncts are false).

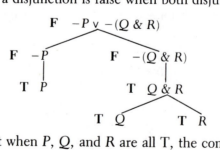

We now know that when P, Q, and R are all T, the complex formula will be F.

We can do the same for some other assignment of truth values to P, Q, and R. For example, suppose P and Q are both T but R is F.

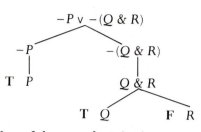

What is the truth value of the complex? Again, we work up the tree. Since Q is T and R is F, the conjunction Q & R will be F.

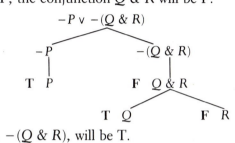

So its negation, $-(Q$ & $R)$, will be T.

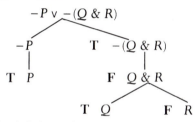

Next, we work up the left branch. Since P is T, $-P$ will be F.

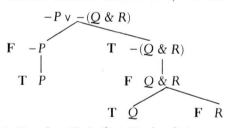

Finally, since $-P$ is F and $-(Q$ & $R)$ is T, the disjunction $-P \vee -(Q$ & $R)$ will be T.

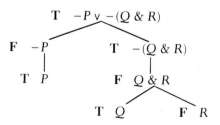

We now know that when P and Q are T and R is F, the complex formula will be T. In like manner, we can figure out the truth value of the complex for any possible assignment of truth values to P, Q, and R.

EXERCISES

6.2:1   Suppose P and Q are both F while R is T. Construct a grammatical tree for each of the following formulas, and determine its truth value.

a. $P \lor (Q \,\&\, R)$
b. $(P \lor Q) \,\&\, R$
c. $-P \,\&\, -(Q \lor R)$
d. $-(P \lor Q) \,\&\, R$
e. $-(P \lor (Q \,\&\, R))$

6.3   TRUTH TABLES

There is a drawback, however, to using these trees. We must rewrite the tree each time we assign different truth values to the atomic statements. As a result, we have no easily usable record of what we did previously. This is why truth tables are preferable. In this section, we will explain the connection between grammatical trees and truth tables.

Consider the following formula:

$$-(-P \lor Q)$$

We want to determine the truth value of this complex formula for any possible assignment of truth values to its constituent atoms, P and Q. Our first job, then, is to create a grammatical tree for this formula, so that we can determine how the complex was constructed out of the atoms. Here is the tree:

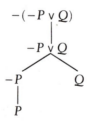

To construct this formula, we start with P and negate it to form $-P$. We then disjoin $-P$ with Q to form $-P \lor Q$. Finally, we negate the disjunction to form our complex.

We form a truth table by taking the grammatical tree we have just constructed and redrawing it horizontally. We start at the left with our atoms, P and Q, and then we work across, re-creating the nodes on the tree. (First we work up the left branch as far as we can go, and then we work up the right branch as far as we can go.) Thus far, our truth table should look like this:

P	*Q*	$-P$	$-P \vee Q$	$-(-P \vee Q)$

Now, let us work out the truth value of the complex given a particular assignment of truth values to the atoms. Let us suppose P and Q are both T. If we were to work up the tree, we would reason as follows. Since P is T, its negation, $-P$, is F. And since Q is T, the disjunction $-P \vee Q$ will be T. Finally, since the disjunction is T, its negation, $-(-P \vee Q)$, is F. The finished tree would look like this:

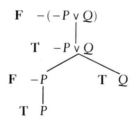

In the truth table, we work across the table and come out with the same result. Our supposition is that P and Q are both T. So we write this in the P and Q columns of our table:

P	*Q*	$-P$	$-P \vee Q$	$-(-P \vee Q)$
T	T			

Next, we work across the table. We need to work out the next column, $-P$. This is the negation of P. Since P is T, $-P$ must be F. We enter this in the table:

P	*Q*	$-P$	$-P \vee Q$	$-(-P \vee Q)$
T	T	F		

Next, we figure out $-P \vee Q$. To do so, we look back at the $-P$ column and the Q column, since these are the two disjuncts. $-P$ is F and Q is T. Since one disjunct is T, the disjunction is T and we enter this in the table:

P	*Q*	$-P$	$-P \vee Q$	$-(-P \vee Q)$
T	T	F	T	

Our final column, $-(-P \vee Q)$, is the negation of $-P \vee Q$; so we have to look back to that column. Since this disjunction is T, its negation must be F. We enter it this way:

P	Q	-P	-P v Q	-(-P v Q)
T	T	F	T	F

We have now re-created our original chain of reasoning on the grammatical tree; instead of working out our problem vertically, we did so horizontally. Note, however, that we now have an easily usable *record* of our calculations. We can try a new assignment of truth values without having either to erase our old calculations or rewrite the tree.

For example, let us continue constructing our truth table by considering the possibility that P is T and Q is F:

P	Q	-P	-P v Q	-(-P v Q)
T	T	F	T	F
T	F			

We look back at the P column and we find a T. Since a statement and its negation have opposite truth values, we put an F in the $-P$ column:

P	Q	-P	-P v Q	-(-P v Q)
T	T	F	T	F
T	F	F		

Next, we need to work out the disjunction $-P \vee Q$, so we look back to the $-P$ column and the Q column. We find an F in the $-P$ column and an F in the Q column. Since both disjuncts are F, the disjunction is F.

P	Q	-P	-P v Q	-(-P v Q)
T	T	F	T	F
T	F	F	F	

Our final column is the negation of $-P \vee Q$. Since we find an F in the $-P \vee Q$ column, and since a statement and its negation always have opposite truth values, we put a T in the $-(-P \vee Q)$ column:

P	Q	-P	-P v Q	-(-P v Q)
T	T	F	T	F
T	F	F	F	T

Constructing a truth table means calculating what the truth value of the complex will be for each possible assignment to the atomic statements *P* and *Q*. There are four such possibilities. We have already considered two of them: the two that remain are *P* F and *Q* T, and finally *P* F and *Q* F. The fully worked out table looks like this:

P	*Q*	*−P*	*−P* v *Q*	*−(−P* v *Q)*
T	T	F	T	F
T	F	F	F	T
F	T	T	T	F
F	F	T	T	F

Our truth table shows us that our formula will be true only in the second case, when *P* is T and *Q* is F. In all other cases, our formula turns out to be false.

Let us try another example, *−(−P* & *−Q)*. We need first to construct the grammatical tree for the formula. Here it is:

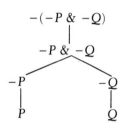

We started with *P* and negated it to form *−P*. We then took *Q* and negated it to form *−Q*. Then, we conjoined the two to form *−P* & *−Q*, and finally, we negated the conjunction to get *−(−P* & *−Q)*.

Constructing the truth table for this complex formula entails first setting out the atomic statements on the left, in this case *P* and *Q*, and then moving across with a column heading corresponding to each node on the tree. Remember that we are, in effect, flattening out the preceding tree— turning it on its side, so to speak—so that we can work horizontally instead of vertically. Here is what the column headings would look like:

P	*Q*	*−P*	*−Q*	*−P* & *−Q*	*−(−P* & *−Q)*

Once we have done this, our next task is to consider all possible combinations of truth values assigned to the atomic statements *P* and *Q*. Remember that there are four such possibilities:

P	*Q*	*−P*	*−Q*	*−P* & *−Q*	*−(−P* & *−Q)*
T	T				
T	F				
F	T				
F	F				

P and Q might both be true (top case), or P and Q might differ in truth value (two middle cases), or P and Q might both be false (bottom case). We need, next, to calculate the rest of the table.

Instead of going line by line, however, it is actually faster to go column by column. Let's start with the $-P$ column. $-P$ and P must always have opposite truth values, so we have

P	Q	$-P$	$-Q$	$-P \,\&\, -Q$	$-(-P \,\&\, -Q)$
T	T	F			
T	F	F			
F	T	T			
F	F	T			

Next, the $-Q$ column. Q and $-Q$ must always have opposite truth values:

P	Q	$-P$	$-Q$	$-P \,\&\, -Q$	$-(-P \,\&\, -Q)$
T	T	F	F		
T	F	F	T		
F	T	T	F		
F	F	T	T		

Our next column is a conjunction, with $-P$ the left conjunct and $-Q$ the right conjunct. The conjunction is T when and only when both conjuncts are T:

P	Q	$-P$	$-Q$	$-P \,\&\, -Q$	$-(-P \,\&\, -Q)$
T	T	F	F	F	
T	F	F	T	F	
F	T	T	F	F	
F	F	T	T	T	

Our final column is the negation of $-P \,\&\, -Q$:

P	Q	$-P$	$-Q$	$-P \,\&\, -Q$	$-(-P \,\&\, -Q)$
T	T	F	F	F	T
T	F	F	T	F	T
F	T	T	F	F	T
F	F	T	T	T	F

So, our formula comes out F only in the bottom case—namely, when P and Q are both false. Otherwise the formula is true.

EXERCISES

6.3:1   Work out a truth table for each of the following formulas, after using a grammatical tree to determine the column headings.

a. $(P \& Q) \vee (-P \& -Q)$
b. $(P \vee Q) \& -(P \& Q)$
c. $(-P \vee Q) \& P$

6.4   THE GENERAL METHOD OF TRUTH TABLES

In order to work out truth tables in general, we need to know, first, how to set up the table; second, how many different possible truth-value assignments there are for the statement letters; and third, how to determine what those truth-value assignments are.

The first part of our problem is solved by working out the grammatical tree for the formula. Once the tree has been built, we know what our atomic-statement letters are, and we have our column headings, a column for each node on the tree. We saw how this is done in the last section.

How many different truth-value assignments are there for the statement letters in a formula? Here is one way to work it out. If we had only one statement letter, P, there would be two possibilities: either P is T or P is F. That is, there would be two ways of filling in the slot:

$$P$$

T
F

If we now added a second letter, Q, how many possible ways could there be of filling in the two slots? For each assignment to the first slot, there are *two* ways of filling in the second slot: whatever assignment we give to P, Q will be either T or F. So, since there are two ways of filling in the first slot, and for each of these there are two ways of filling in the second slot, there will be $2 \times 2 = 4$ possible ways of filling in the two slots. We can picture our result so far like this:

Now suppose we added a third letter, *R*. How many different ways would there be of filling in the three slots? Since there are four ways of filling the first two slots, and for each of these there are two ways of filling the third slot, there will therefore be 4 × 2 = 8 ways of filling in all three. Our picture now looks like this:

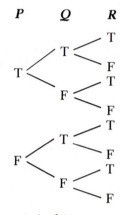

And so on.

Once we know how many ways there are of assigning truth values to the statement letters, how can we make sure that we have them all? That is, how can we make sure that we have not repeated any or left any out? The idea is to fill out the picture we have above.

Start at the rightmost column and write T, F, T, F all the way down:

P	*Q*	*R*
		T
		F
		T
		F
		T
		F
		T
		F

Then, move left one column and double the groupings of Ts and Fs. That is, since in the previous column we wrote one T and one F, here we write two Ts and two Fs:

P	Q	R
	T	T
	T	F
	F	T
	F	F
	T	T
	T	F
	F	T
	F	F

Then, move left one column and again double the groupings of Ts and Fs. That is, since in the Q column we wrote two Ts and two Fs, we write in the P column four Ts and four Fs:

P	Q	R
T	T	T
T	T	F
T	F	T
T	F	F
F	T	T
F	T	F
F	F	T
F	F	F

Here is the general rule:

If there are n statement letters, then there are 2^n different truth-value assignments.

For 1 letter there are 2^1 =   2 assignments.
For 2 letters there are 2^2 =   4 assignments.
For 3 letters there are 2^3 =   8 assignments.
For 4 letters there are 2^4 = 16 assignments.
For 5 letters there are 2^5 = 32 assignments.
and so on.

Let us now work out a complete problem. Let us work out a complete truth table for the following formula:

$P \lor (Q \ \& \ R)$.

First, we figure out the grammatical tree:

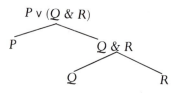

That is, we take Q and R and conjoin them to form $Q \& R$. Next, we disjoin this with P to form our formula.

Second, we set up our truth table, with a column heading corresponding to each node on the tree:

P	*Q*	*R*	*Q & R*	*P v (Q & R)*

Third, we figure out how many different truth-value assignments there are to the atomic letters occurring in the formula. Since there are three letters, there are $2^3 = 8$ different assignments. These are as follows:

P	*Q*	*R*	*Q & R*	*P v (Q & R)*
T	T	T		
T	T	F		
T	F	T		
T	F	F		
F	T	T		
F	T	F		
F	F	T		
F	F	F		

Last, we figure out the truth table. You can easily verify that it will look like this:

P	*Q*	*R*	*Q & R*	*P v (Q & R)*
T	T	T	T	T
T	T	F	F	T
T	F	T	F	T
T	F	F	F	T
F	T	T	T	T
F	T	F	F	F
F	F	T	F	F
F	F	F	F	F

EXERCISES

6.4:1 Work out a truth table for each of the following formulas.

a. $P \lor (Q \ \& \ R)$
b. $(P \lor Q) \ \& \ R$
c. $-P \ \& \ -(Q \lor R)$
d. $-(P \lor Q) \ \& \ R$
e. $-(P \lor (Q \ \& \ R))$
f. $(P \ \& \ -Q) \lor (-P \lor Q)$

6.4:2 If a formula has four letters, how many different truth-value assignments will there be? Show all the possibilities.

REVIEW

1.   Every complex formula is built up from its atoms in one and only one way. We can identify the main connective and re-create the grammatical history of the formula by constructing a grammatical tree.

2.   With a grammatical tree, we can figure out the truth value of the complex by plugging in truth values for the atoms at the bottom of the tree and working our way up the nodes. A truth table is a way of representing the same information, except that we work vertically on the tree, but we work horizontally on the truth tables.

3.   We can use the grammatical tree to determine the column headings for our truth table. Each node on the tree corresponds to a column heading in the table.

4.   If we have n statement letters, we will have 2^n different truth-value assignments.

7

THE CONDITIONAL

"If, if, if. That's all you ever say," said the girlfriend. "If you get promoted and if you get the loan from the bank, then you'll be financially secure and we will get married. But I'm tired of waiting. You won the lottery and you're financially secure. So you've got to fulfill your promise and marry me." "But," said the boyfriend, "I didn't get promoted and I didn't get the loan from the bank. So, I'm afraid you'll have to wait."

Who is right—the boyfriend or the girlfriend?

7.1 WHAT IS A CONDITIONAL?

When two statements are joined by *if,then*, the resulting complex statement is called a **conditional**. Each of the following is a conditional:

If his fever gets worse, then we'll have to call the doctor.

If the drought continues, then corn prices will soar.

The two constituent statements in a conditional have special names. The statement occupying the *if* clause is called the **antecedent**. The statement occupying the *then* clause is called the **consequent**. In the first of the preceding conditionals, for example, "his fever gets worse" is the antecedent, and "we'll have to call the doctor" is the consequent.

What do we commit ourselves to when we assert a conditional? Suppose, for example, we were to claim

If the United States deploys MX missiles, then it will be more secure.

Do we claim that the United States will deploy MX missiles? Clearly not.

We claim that something will happen—that the United States will be more secure—*if* the United States deploys MX missiles. This is quite different from claiming that the United States will deploy MX missiles. Do we claim that the United States will be more secure? Clearly not. We are saying that the United States will be more secure *if* it deploys MX missiles. And this too is different from claiming that the United States will be more secure.

When we assert a conditional, we claim that one statement is true *if* another statement is true, that *if* something happens, *then* something else happens. *If P then Q* does not say that *P* is true, nor does it say that *Q* is true. It says that *Q* is true if—or, *on the condition that*—*P* is true.

The ordering of the constituent statements in a conditional is therefore crucially important. Compare

> If you've had a quart of milk today, then you've had enough calcium today

with

> If you've had enough calcium today, then you've had a quart of milk today.

The first statement is true. A quart of milk contains the recommended minimum requirement of calcium. But the second statement is false. A person might have gotten a sufficient amount of calcium by eating cheese, for example, and not have had any milk at all. Note that the only change between the two statements is the *ordering* of the constituents. The two constituents of a conditional play different logical roles: the antecedent expresses the condition under which the consequent is said to be true.

There are slight variations of *if,then* that we often use:

(1) *If P then Q.*
(2) *If P, Q.*
(3) *Q, if P.*

These are simple grammatical variations of one another. We drop the *then* in (1) and replace it with a comma to get (2). We put the consequent before the *if*, separating it by a comma, to get (3). Each of the following says the same thing:

(1) If the fever gets worse, then we'll have to call the doctor.
(2) If the fever gets worse, we'll have to call the doctor.
(3) We'll have to call the doctor if the fever gets worse.

Sometimes we use other words to express the conditional. Each of these says the same thing:

If P then Q.

Q provided that P.

Q on the condition that P.

Just to be clear about our ability to recognize conditionals, let's look at some more examples:

The economy will slow down provided that interest rates go up.

The Yankees will win the pennant on the condition that they get Billy back.

If the Yankees get Billy back, they'll win the pennant.

Germany would have won the war if it had invaded England.

If you get off at Astor Place, you'll be near the theater.

You'll go to heaven if you live a good life.

In each case, it is being claimed that one thing will happen *if* another thing happens.

EXERCISES

7.1:1   For each of the following conditionals, identify which constituent is the antecedent and which is the consequent.

a.   Japan will export more cars to the United States if there is no trade agreement negotiated soon.

b.   Albania will participate in the Olympic games provided that China participates in the games.

c.   If the rent is not paid by the fifteenth of the month, the tenants will have abrogated their lease.

d.   Provided that they install a new stove and refrigerator, landlords are entitled to a 3 percent increase in rent.

e.   Your car's air-conditioning unit will be replaced on the condition that it fails to operate during the first ninety days of ownership.

7.1:2   Which of the following conditionals say the same as "If John took French in high school, then he is exempt from the language requirement"?

a.   John is exempt from the language requirement if he took French in high school.

b.   John took French in high school if he is exempt from the language requirement.

c.   If John is exempt from the language requirement, then he took French in high school.

d. John is exempt from the language requirement provided that he took French in high school.

e. On the condition that he took French in high school, John is exempt from the language requirement.

Study Vocabulary: **conditional**
antecedent
consequent

7.2   NECESSARY AND SUFFICIENT CONDITIONS

Suppose the doctor tells you

If you stay in bed for a week, you'll get better.

The doctor has told you that staying in bed for a week is sufficient to get you better. Has she told you that it is also necessary—that you won't get better if you don't stay in bed? No, not at all. She has only told you one way to assure your getting better; she has not told you it is the only way you can get better. Indeed, she might very well have gone on to say

If you take penicillin, you'll get better.

The two claims are consistent with each other. You'll get better if you stay in bed for a week; you'll also get better if you take penicillin. You have a choice.

The *if,then* idiom is closely connected with the notions of **necessary condition** and **sufficient condition**. In this section, we will examine these notions to help clarify the logic of conditionals. First, let us define the two notions.

P is a sufficient condition for Q if P's being true is enough to assure Q's being true.

P is a necessary condition for Q if P wouldn't be true without Q's being true.

Here are some examples:

Being eighteen or over is a necessary condition for voting in the United States. You can't vote unless you're eighteen or over. Although necessary, being eighteen or over is not sufficient. There are other requirements you must satisfy to vote. You must also, for example, be a United States citizen.

Being a father is a sufficient condition for being a parent. Anyone who is a father is a parent. But it is not necessary. You don't have to be a father in order to be a parent. You might be a mother.

Having a child is both necessary *and* sufficient for being a parent. Anyone who has a child is a parent, and you can't be a parent without having a child.

These two say the same thing:

If P then Q.

P is a sufficient condition for Q.

You can just as easily say

If you're a freshman then you're a student

as

Being a freshman is sufficient for being a student.

We run back and forth between the two idioms comfortably. It is, of course, true that being a freshman is sufficient for being a student. So, if it is true that Harry is a freshman, you can immediately infer that he is a student. Suppose it is false that Harry is a freshman. Can you infer that he is a student? No. He might not be a student at all. Can you infer that he is not a student? No. He might be a senior. He might or might not be a student. You need more information to make either inference.

We can also use the *if,then* idiom to express the notion of a necessary condition. We can just as easily say

Being a student is necessary for being a freshman

as

If you're a freshman, then you're a student.

Both say that you wouldn't be a freshman without being a student. Suppose it's false that Harry is a student. Then you can immediately infer that he is not a freshman. Suppose, on the other hand, it's true that Harry is a student. Can you infer that he is a freshman? Can you infer that he is not a freshman? No, not at all. You are told only that being a student is necessary for being a freshman; you are not told whether it is also sufficient. You need more information before you can make either inference.

So, each of the following says the same thing:

If P then Q.

P is a sufficient condition for Q.

Q is a necessary condition for P.

(Watch the ordering of *P* and *Q*.)

Here's an example to test you. We are all familiar with the notion of a prerequisite. It is quite common for algebra to be a prerequisite for physics; you need the algebra to do the physics problems. Which of the following captures the idea that algebra is a prerequisite for physics?

(1) If anybody takes algebra, then he takes physics.

(2) If anybody takes physics, then he takes algebra.

The answer is (2). (1) says that anyone who has taken algebra takes physics. That is, taking algebra is a sufficient condition for taking physics. But that's not what it means for algebra to be a prerequisite for physics. A student might very well take algebra and then not go on to physics.

(2) does capture the notion of a prerequisite. It says that if anyone is in the physics course, then he either took, or is now taking, algebra. Taking algebra is a necessary condition for taking physics. (Of course, although taking algebra is necessary for taking physics, we do not yet know if it is also sufficient. There might be other requirements that must also be satisfied in order to take physics. Our statement does not say.)

Taking algebra, we have said, is a *necessary* condition for taking physics. This might seem a bit odd to you. The way we ordinarily speak, if algebra is a prerequisite for physics, we would perhaps say that taking algebra is *sufficient* for taking physics. But we have to be careful here. There is a subtle difference we must be alert to. In the ordinary use of the word *sufficient*, what is meant is that taking algebra is *all* that is required for taking physics. Once you have taken algebra, you *may* take physics. The logical use of the word *sufficient* is slightly different. To say that P is sufficient for Q is not to say

If P is true, Q *may* be true.

Rather it is to say

If P is true, Q *is* true.

No ifs, ands, or buts.

There is another surprising characteristic of the conditional. If algebra is a prerequisite for physics, then, as we have seen, if anyone takes physics, then he takes algebra. This might seem odd, because one might very well take physics *after* one takes algebra. So it is important to recognize that *if,then* carries no time element. There is no reason to think that *If P then Q* requires P to come before Q.

It is also important to distinguish the conditional *if,then* from the notion of *cause*. Taking physics is sufficient for taking algebra, but it doesn't *cause* or *make* a student take algebra. There is, however, a relation between the two notions:

X is the cause of Y

implies

X is a sufficient condition for Y.

The two notions differ, however, because the implication does not work the other way:

X is a sufficient condition for Y

does *not* imply

X is the cause of Y.

Finally, it is important to distinguish the following two:

Q if P.
Q only if P.

Compare:

You will pass logic *if* you pass the final.
You will pass logic *only if* you pass the final.

The first tells us that passing the final is a sufficient condition for passing logic. It doesn't say that one has to pass the final to pass logic; it says only that passing the final will assure one's passing logic. There might be other ways to pass. The second statement, however, says that passing the final is a *necessary* condition for passing logic. One must pass the final in order to pass logic. There might be other conditions as well. So, these two say the same thing:

Q if P
If P then Q,

and these two say the same thing:

Q only if P
If Q then P.

In summary, each of the following says the same thing (be careful about the ordering of P and Q):

If P then Q.
Q if P.
P only if Q.
P is sufficient for Q.
Q is necessary for P.

EXERCISES

7.2:1 Which of the following statements are equivalent to "If John took French in high school, then John is exempt from the language requirement"?

a. John's having taken French in high school is a sufficient condition for his being exempt from the language requirement.

b. John's having taken French in high school is a necessary condition for his being exempt from the language requirement.

c. John took French in high school only if he is exempt from the language requirement.

d. John's being exempt from the language requirement is a necessary condition for his having taken French in high school.

7.2:2 Suppose that John is exempt from the language requirement if he took one year of either French or Spanish in high school, or if he had two years of German in high school, or if he had one year of Latin and one year of Greek in high school. Which of the following are true?

a. A sufficient condition for John's being exempt from the language requirement is that he had one year of German in high school.

b. A sufficient condition for John's being exempt from the language requirement is that he had one year of Greek in high school.

c. A sufficient condition for John's being exempt from the language requirement is that he had two years of Latin and one year of Greek in high school.

d. A necessary condition for John's being exempt from the language requirement is that he had two years of language in high school.

Study Vocabulary: **necessary condition**
sufficient condition

7.3 ARGUMENTS USING CONDITIONALS

Suppose you bet ten dollars on the following claim:

> If Billy Martin lasts out the season as Yankee manager, then the Yankees will win the pennant.

Now, suppose Billy Martin does last out the season as the Yankee manager, but the Yankees do not win the pennant. Obviously, you lose the bet.
A conditional is false when the antecedent is true and the consequent

false. So, if a conditional *If P then Q* is true, and the antecedent *P* is also true, then the consequent *Q must* be true. That is,

$$\begin{array}{c} \textit{If P then Q} \\ P \\ \text{SO, } Q \end{array}$$

is a valid argument pattern. Indeed, it is probably the most fundamental valid argument pattern. Medieval logicians gave it a name: **modus ponens**. It is also called **affirming the antecedent**.

Using the language of necessary and sufficient conditions makes the argument's validity even clearer. *If P then Q*, remember, is the same as *P is sufficient for Q*. Now, if *P is* sufficient for *Q*, and *P* is true, then *Q must* be true.

Here is another example of a modus ponens argument:

> If John is eighteen years old, he can vote in a United States election.
> John is eighteen years old.
> SO, John can vote in a United States election.

Again, the argument is valid. If the premisses were all true, the conclusion would have to be true. To be sure, being eighteen years old is not sufficient for voting in a United States election. The first premiss is, as a matter of fact, false. But that doesn't mean the argument is invalid. Although the first premiss is plainly false, if it *were* true, and if it were true as well that John is eighteen years old, then it would have to be the case that he can vote in a United States election.

A **sound argument** is one that is valid *and* has all true premisses. The above argument is valid, but it is not sound: it has a false premiss. So, we must distinguish carefully between attacking the validity of an argument and attacking the truth of its premisses. In everyday life, both are important. For we are interested in determining not only whether one statement is a consequence of others, but also whether these others are true and the conclusion therefore true as well. All instances of modus ponens are valid, but only some are sound. And only the sound instances establish the truth of the conclusion.

There is another argument that looks very much like modus ponens and is frequently mistaken for modus ponens. It is, however, different in important ways and is, in fact, *invalid*. This argument, known as the fallacy of **affirming the consequent**, looks like this:

$$\begin{array}{c} \textit{If P then Q} \\ Q \\ \text{SO, } P. \end{array}$$

Note that in this argument, the second premiss is the *consequent* of the conditional—thus its name. The conclusion is the *antecedent* of the conditional. (In modus ponens the second premiss is the *antecedent* of the conditional; the conclusion is the *consequent* of the conditional.)

The argument we are now looking at is called a **fallacy**. This means that the argument is a bad one; the conclusion does not follow from the premisses. This argument has also been given a name, because it is frequently used, even though it is fallacious. (Actually, there are many valid argument patterns and many invalid argument patterns—*infinitely* many in each case. Not all have names. This pattern is named because it comes up so frequently in our reasoning.)

We want now to establish that the fallacy of affirming the consequent is, as we have claimed, an invalid argument. To do this, we must show that the two statements taken together, *If P then Q* and *Q*, do *not* jointly imply the truth of *P*. Suppose the following were both true:

> If I have a Pontiac, then I have a car.
> I have a car.

Would it follow that I have a Pontiac? No. Suppose I have a Mercury. If so, then both premisses would be true, but the conclusion would be false. Our conditional tells us, in effect, that all Pontiacs are cars. It does not, however, tell us that Pontiacs are *the only* cars.

Many people fall prey to this argument because they fail to distinguish a sufficient condition from a necessary condition. We must be very careful to distinguish the two. *If P then Q* tells us that *P* is *sufficient* for *Q*. It does not say whether *P* is or is not *necessary* for *Q*. Consider the conditional

> If John is born on American soil, he is an American citizen.

This is true. Now, if it is also true that John is born on American soil, then we may infer that he is an American citizen (modus ponens). But if, on the other hand, it were true that he is an American citizen, we would not be entitled to infer that he was born on American soil; he might, for example, have been naturalized (fallacy of affirming the consequent).

So far, then, we have identified the following:

Modus Ponens	Affirming the Consequent
If P then Q	*If P then Q*
P	*Q*
SO, *Q*	SO, *P*
Valid	Invalid

Let's now consider the following problem. Suppose *If P then Q* is true but *Q* is false. What can we infer about *P*? We can infer that *P* is also false. For if *P* is sufficient for *Q*, and *Q* is not true, *P* couldn't be true. If it were, *Q* would have to be true.

This is another fundamental valid inference pattern, called **modus tollens** (or **denying the consequent**):

$$If\ P\ then\ Q$$
$$-Q$$
$$\text{SO},\ -P.$$

In modus tollens, the first premiss is a conditional, the second premiss is the denial of the consequent, and the conclusion is the denial of the antecedent. From the two statements

If I have a Pontiac, then I have a car.
I don't have a car.

you can clearly infer that I don't have a Pontiac. Pontiacs are cars, so if I don't have a car, I couldn't possibly have a Pontiac.

Again, we must be careful to distinguish modus tollens from the fallacy of **denying the antecedent**:

$$If\ P\ then\ Q$$
$$-P$$
$$\text{SO},\ -Q.$$

First, notice its form. The first premiss is a conditional. But the second premiss is the negation of the antecedent—hence the name—and the conclusion is the negation of the consequent.

This pattern is invalid. Suppose the following two statements were both true:

If I have a Pontiac, then I have a car.
I don't have a Pontiac.

Could you infer that I don't have a car? No. Pontiacs are cars, as the first premiss says. But they are not the only cars, and the first premiss does not say that they are the only cars. So, just because I don't have a Pontiac, it does not follow that I don't have a car. I might have a Mercury.

If P then Q says that *P is sufficient for Q*. It does not say whether *P* is necessary for *Q*. So, from the fact that *P* is false, we cannot infer that *Q* is false. On the other hand, from the fact that *Q* is false, we know that *P* must be false.

<table>
<tr><td align="center">Modus Tollens</td><td align="center">Denying the Antecedent</td></tr>
<tr><td align="center">*If P then Q*</td><td align="center">*If P then Q*</td></tr>
<tr><td align="center">$-Q$</td><td align="center">$-P$</td></tr>
<tr><td align="center">SO, $-P$</td><td align="center">SO, $-Q$</td></tr>
<tr><td align="center">Valid</td><td align="center">Invalid</td></tr>
</table>

EXERCISES

7.3:1 Identify the argument pattern by name and say whether it is valid or invalid.

a. If Socrates is a man, then Socrates is mortal. Socrates is not mortal. So, Socrates is not a man.

b. If Socrates is a man, then Socrates is mortal. Socrates is not a man. So, Socrates is not mortal.

c. If Socrates is a man, then Socrates is mortal. Socrates is a man. So, Socrates is mortal.

d. If Socrates is a man, then Socrates is mortal. Socrates is mortal. So, Socrates is a man.

7.3:2 Symbolize each of the following arguments, using *P* and *Q* for the atomic statements, and say which is valid.

a. If Sue likes rock and roll, then she likes Michael Jackson. Sue likes rock and roll. So, she likes Michael Jackson.

b. If Sue likes rock and roll, then she hates classical music. Sue hates classical music. So, she likes rock and roll.

7.3:3 Suppose it is true that taking French in high school is a sufficient condition for John's being exempt from the language requirement in college. Which of the following are true? Which are false? Which are indeterminate?

a. John took French in high school only if he is exempt from the language requirement in college.

b. John's having taken French in high school is a necessary condition for his being exempt from the language requirement in college.

c. John's being exempt from the language requirement in college is a necessary condition for his having taken French in high school.

d. John's being exempt from the language requirement in college is a sufficient condition for his having taken French in high school.

7.3:4   Consider the following argument:

If the mechanics had fixed my car, then they would have called me.
They didn't call me. So, they didn't fix it.

Now consider the following criticism of the argument:

That argument's no good. Sometimes the mechanics don't call when
they've finished fixing a car.

Discuss this criticism of the argument. What has been shown to be "no
good" about the argument?

Study Vocabulary: modus ponens (affirming the antecedent)
sound argument
affirming the consequent
fallacy
modus tollens (denying the consequent)
denying the antecedent

7.4   THE MATERIAL CONDITIONAL

There is considerable controversy about whether *If,then* can be captured
in a truth table. The restrictions (1) that we have but two truth values, true
and false, and (2) that the truth value of an *if,then* statement be determined
solely by the truth value of its constituents, lead to differences between the
logical *if,then* and ordinary usage. Indeed, logicians call theirs the **material
conditional**, acknowledging its difference from the ordinary conditional. In
this section, we will explain the truth table for the material conditional and
note some of the ways in which it diverges from ordinary usage.

Here is the truth-table definition of the material conditional:

P	*Q*	If *P* then *Q*
T	T	T
T	F	F
F	T	T
F	F	T

*A conditional is false when and only when the antecedent is
true and the consequent is false. In all other cases, it is true.*

Let's now explain how we got this table. This table is geared to the
four argument patterns we discussed in the previous section. We want the

valid argument patterns to be valid in the truth table; we want the invalid argument patterns to be invalid in the truth table. Finally, we want our two fundamental valid patterns, modus ponens and modus tollens, to be **useful**. That is, not only should they turn out to be valid, but it should be possible to have sound arguments involving modus ponens or modus tollens so that we can use them to establish the truth of a conclusion.

With these criteria in mind, we will explain how the table was filled in.

The second line is clear-cut. When the antecedent is true and the consequent is false, the conditional is false. For example, suppose someone says

If the star gets ill, the concert will be canceled.

Well, suppose the star does get ill, but the concert is not canceled. Then the conditional is false.

P	Q	If P then Q
T	T	
T	F	F
F	T	
F	F	

Notice, moreover, that had we put a T in the conditional column, modus ponens would turn out to be invalid. For then, *If P then Q* and *P* could both be T and *Q* would be F.

Our intuitions, however, are nowhere near as clear for the other three lines. Consider the first line. What is the truth value of a conditional when antecedent and consequent are both true? Suppose I say

If Mary goes out with John, Sally will sulk for a week.

Well, suppose Mary does go out with John, and Sally goes off to her room and sulks for a week. I would be justified in saying, "I told you so."

So we certainly wouldn't want to say that a conditional is false when antecedent and consequent are both true. On the other hand, there are reservations about saying that the conditional is true in this case. Since, in dealing with the material conditional, all we are looking at are the truth values of the antecedent and consequent, we are overlooking any connection between the two. This means that

If 2 + 2 = 4, then Ronald Reagan is a Republican

and

If the sky is blue, then Canada is north of Idaho

would each turn out true, since each has a true antecedent and a true consequent. These are odd because there is no apparent connection between antecedent and consequent. But remember, our notion of *if,then* is purely logical; we eliminate any temporal connection—indeed, any causal connection—between the antecedent and the consequent. The only relevant connection between the two is truth value. Understood this way, the truth of the above two conditionals is harmless.

Most important, however, we want a T in the top line so that modus ponens turns out to be a useful argument pattern. If we had an F in that line, then, since we have already put an F in the second line, *If P then Q* would be F whenever *P* is T. As a result, we could never get *P* and *If P then Q* both T. So, we could never have a sound modus ponens argument. And so, we take the conditional to be T when antecedent and consequent are both T:

P	*Q*	*If P then Q*
T	T	T
T	F	F
F	T	
F	F	

Let us look at the third row. What is the truth value of a conditional when the antecedent is F and the consequent is T? In order to show that affirming the consequent is invalid in our truth table, we must assign T in the third row. Only then is it possible to have the two premises, *If P then Q* and *Q*, be true and yet have the conclusion, *P*, be false. If we were to put an F in that third slot, affirming the consequent would turn out to be valid. We don't want that. So, we take the conditional to be T when antecedent is F and consequent T:

P	*Q*	*If P then Q*
T	T	T
T	F	F
F	T	T
F	F	

Finally, we consider the bottom line. What is the truth value of the conditional when antecedent and consequent are both F? This is a particularly troublesome case, as we'll see in a moment. We take the conditional to be true in this case, and the main reason is to render modus tollens useful. If the conditional were F when antecedent and consequent were both F, we would never be able to use a modus tollens argument to derive a conclusion. For we would never be able to get both *If P then Q* T and $-Q$ T, so we would never be able to conclude the truth of $-P$.

So, our truth table is now complete:

P	Q	If P then Q
T	T	T
T	F	F
F	T	T
F	F	T

The conditional is T in the top case to ensure the usefulness of modus ponens. The conditional is F in the second case because of clear intuitions. The conditional is T in the third case so that affirming the consequent will be invalid. And the conditional is T in the bottom case so that modus tollens will be useful.

Still, there are differences between the ordinary *If,then* and the material conditional we have just defined. Consider the following two conditionals:

> If Germany had invaded England in 1940, then Germany would have won World War II.

> If Hitler had used deodorant, then Germany would have won World War II.

These are called **counterfactual conditionals**, because the antecedent expresses something that is contrary to the facts. Each has a false antecedent and false consequent; so, according to the truth table, each is true. But no historian would accept this as adequate reason for thinking each true.

The first conditional is debatable, but at least plausibly true. It has been argued that the strategic error Germany made was in failing to close the western front before turning east and attacking the Soviet Union. So, if Germany had invaded England in 1940 (and, it is assumed, conquered England), then it would have had a secure western border and could have devoted all its energies to the eastern front. As events turned out, however, Germany ultimately had to fight a two-front war and eventually got squeezed between the two sides.

Not all historians agree with this argument, but none would be inclined to support the second conditional. After all, what connection could there be between Hitler's using deodorant (or not) and the outcome of World War II? So, even though we have a false antecedent and a false consequent in each case, historians might very well assign different truth values to these two conditionals. And, in any event, no historian would be inclined to think that both conditionals are true because both have false antecedents and false consequents.

Although the material conditional does not capture all the uses of our ordinary *if,then*, it does capture the use of the conditional by mathematicians. A number of you will have already started to learn a programming language, most likely BASIC, and will have become familiar with commands that involve *If,then*. For example, a line on one of your computer programs might look like this:

35   IF X>0 THEN N=X+2.

When you run your program and the computer comes to this instruction it is going to check to see if "X>0" is true. If it is, then it will set N=X+2. But, if "X>0" is false (that is, if X is not greater than 0), then the machine will ignore the rest of the *If,then* command (that is, it will not carry out the command in the *then* clause), but simply proceed on to the next instruction in the program.

    This way of understanding an *If,then* command follows precisely the material conditional defined in this section. Essentially, the computer takes each instruction to be a command that says: make this true. So, when the computer comes to an *If,then* statement, it must make it true. How does it make the conditional true? Well, if the antecedent is true (in our example, if "X>0" is true), then in order to make the conditional true, the computer must make the consequent true. But, if, on the other hand, the antecedent is false, then the conditional is already true and the computer does not have to do anything to make it true. It therefore ignores the command in the consequent and simply moves on to the next instruction in the program.

    There ought, perhaps, to be no surprise at this. Mathematicians do not have to deal with causal connections between numbers, geometric shapes, and the like. In our speaking about the world, however, causal connections are frequently at issue. And that's where the material conditional departs from the ordinary conditional. Further work needs to be done in analyzing the notion of cause. Only then will we have a complete understanding of our ordinary use of *if,then*.

    We will introduce a special symbol for the conditional. We will abbreviate *If P then Q* as $P \rightarrow Q$:

P	*Q*	$P \rightarrow Q$
T	T	T
T	F	F
F	T	T
F	F	T

A conditional will be false when and only when the antecedent is true and the consequent is false. Otherwise it will be true.

EXERCISES

7.4:1   Work out a truth table for each of the following formulas. What do the truth tables reveal about them?

a. $P \rightarrow Q$

b. $-P \lor Q$
c. $-(P \And -Q)$

7.4:2   Suppose P is T, Q is F, and R is unknown (in other words, it could be either T or F). Determine which of the following are T and which are F.

a. $R \to (P \lor R)$
b. $(Q \And P) \to R$
c. $(P \lor Q) \to (P \And Q)$
d. $(P \And R) \to (P \lor R)$

Study Vocabulary: material conditional
                      useful argument
                      counterfactual conditional

7.5   NEGATION AND THE CONDITIONAL

In this section, we will examine how to negate a material conditional.

First, however, we must understand how *if* and *then* serve to group in English. Consider

If P then if Q then R.

What is the structure here? Which *if* goes with which *then*? The trick is to think of *if* as a left parenthesis.

Suppose we tried to connect the first *if* with the last *then*:

If P then if Q then R.
↑   ↑

This would require us to take what comes between *if* and *then*, namely, *P then if Q*, as the antecedent of the conditional. But

P then if Q

is no more a coherent unit than is

P)(Q.

The *then* cannot come before the *if* it belongs with.

So, let us connect up the first *if* with the first *then*:

If P then if Q then R.
↑   ↑

P would be the antecedent of the conditional (because it goes between *if* and *then*), and *if Q then R* would be the consequent, (since it is the smallest coherent unit following *then*). We would symbolize this conditional as

$$P \rightarrow (Q \rightarrow R).$$

And this makes good sense.

Here is another example:

If if P then Q then R.

How is this to be parsed? Let's try

If if P then Q then R.
↑   ↑

On this reading, the antecedent would have to be what comes between *If* and *then*—namely, *if P*. But this is not a coherent subclause. *If P* is a sentence fragment: the *if* is left dangling without a *then* to connect up with. We cannot separate *ifs* and *thens* any more than we can separate parentheses; they come in pairs. So, the proposed structuring of the statement is incorrect. Let us therefore try to hook up the first *if* with the second *then*:

If if P then Q then R.
↑   ↑

This does make sense. The antecedent of the conditional will be *if P then Q*, a coherent whole subclause, and the consequent of the conditional will be *R*, which is also a coherent whole subclause. In symbols:

$$(P \rightarrow Q) \rightarrow R.$$

Now we are ready to turn to negation. The simplest way of negating a conditional is to place *It is not the case that* in front of it. The negation of *If P then Q* is *It is not the case that if P then Q*. In symbols:

$$-(P \rightarrow Q).$$

The parentheses are needed because we are negating the conditional as a whole unit.

It is, however, important to distinguish the following three formulas:

(1) $-P \rightarrow Q$ *If not P then Q*
(2) $-P \rightarrow -Q$ *If not P then not Q*
(3) $-(P \rightarrow Q)$ *Not if P then Q*

(1) is a conditional. $-P$ is the antecedent and Q is the consequent.

Remember, since there are no parentheses, the negation sign operates just on P.

(2) is also a conditional. $-P$ is the antecedent and $-Q$ is the consequent. The English rendering of (2) is clear: what occurs between *If* and *then* (namely, *not P*) is the antecedent; what occurs after *then* (namely, *not Q*) is the consequent.

(3), however, is *not* a conditional. It is the negation of the conditional $P \to Q$. We can see from the English rendering that the *not* occurs in front of the *if*. This *if* operates like a left parenthesis in English; so the *not* will be understood to apply to the whole *if,then* statement.

It is important to recognize that (2) and (3) are not logically equivalent. We can see this in the truth table for these two formulas:

P	Q	$-P$	$-Q$	$P \to Q$	$-(P \to Q)$	$-P \to -Q$	$Q \to P$
T	T	F	F	T	F	T	T
T	F	F	T	F	T	T	T
F	T	T	F	T	F	F	F
F	F	T	T	T	F	T	T

$-(P \to Q)$ has different truth conditions from $-P \to -Q$. The two columns do not agree in all cases.

$-P \to -Q$ is logically equivalent to $Q \to P$. Indeed, $-P \to -Q$ is called the **contrapositive** of $Q \to P$. The general rule for forming the contrapositive of a conditional is this: switch antecedent and consequent and negate both. (Some further terminology: $Q \to P$ is called the **converse** of $P \to Q$. To form the converse of a conditional, simply switch antecedent and consequent).

A conditional and its converse are not in general equivalent, as we have seen earlier. For example, compare

If John is a freshman, then John is a student.

If John is a student, then John is a freshman.

The first is true; the second is not. On the other hand, a conditional and its contrapositive are equivalent. Compare

If it's twelve o'clock, then this is logic class.

If this is not logic class, then it's not twelve o'clock.

These say exactly the same thing.

One final point. We have said that a conditional is false when and only when the antecedent is true and the consequent is false. So, to deny a conditional is equivalent to claiming that its antecedent is true and its consequent is false.

$-(P \to Q)$ is logically equivalent to $P \,\&\, -Q$.

P	*Q*	*P* → *Q*	−(*P* → *Q*)	−*Q*	*P* & −*Q*
T	T	T	F	F	F
T	F	F	T	T	T
F	T	T	F	F	F
F	F	T	F	T	F

EXERCISES

7.5:1   Insert parentheses appropriately in the following.

a.   *If if if P then Q then P then P.*

b.   *If either P or if not Q then P then not P.*

7.5:2   Does −(*P* → *Q*) *imply P* → −*Q*?

7.5:3   Which of the following are equivalent to *P* → −*Q*?

a.   −*P* → *Q*

b.   −*Q* → *P*

c.   *Q* → −*P*

7.5:4   Is *P* → *Q* equivalent to −*P* ∨ *Q*?

7.5:5   Let *P* abbreviate "It rains," let *Q* abbreviate "The concert is canceled," and let *R* abbreviate "We get a refund." Express each of the following in good English.

a.   (*P* → *Q*) → *R*

b.   −(*P* → *Q*) → *R*

c.   −((*P* → *Q*) → *R*)

7.5:6   Which of the following are equivalent to the conditional "If John comes to the party, then Mary will sulk"?

a.   If Mary sulks, then John came to the party.

b.   If Mary doesn't sulk, then John didn't come to the party.

c.   If John doesn't come to the party, then Mary won't sulk.

d.   John will come to the party only if Mary sulks.

e.   John will come to the party if Mary sulks.

f.   Mary will sulk if John comes to the party.

g.   Mary won't sulk only if John doesn't come to the party.

Study Vocabulary: contrapositive
converse

7.6   IMPLICATION AGAIN

There is a close connection between the notion of *implication* we defined in Chapter 4 and the conditional we have introduced in this chapter. Of course,

(1)   *P implies Q*

does not *mean* the same thing as

(2)   *If P then Q.*

(2) is true when *P* and *Q* are both true. But that's not enough to make (1) true. It is not the case that any two statements that are, as a matter of fact, true imply each other. One implies the other only if the second *has to be* true when the first is. Nevertheless, there is a connection between (1) and (2).

Let us introduce some terminology.

A statement is a tautology (or a logical truth) if it comes out true for every line in the truth table.

A statement is consistent if it comes out true for at least one line in the truth table.

A statement is inconsistent if it comes out false for every line in the truth table.

It follows from these definitions that every tautology is consistent, since, if it's true in every line, then it must be true in at least one line. But the converse does not hold: it is not the case that every consistent formula is a tautology. $P \rightarrow Q$ is consistent but not a tautology since it is true in some lines, but not in all.

Here are some examples of tautologies:

$$P \vee -P$$
$$-(P \ \& \ -P)$$

The first says that for any statement *P*, either it or its negation must be true. For example:

Either it's raining or it's not.

This statement is true, whatever the weather conditions. The second example says that a statement and its negation are not both true. For example:

It's not both raining and not raining.

This, too, is a tautology. It is not simply true; it is true on logical grounds alone.

A conditional will be a tautology if there is no line in the table in which the antecedent comes out true and the consequent comes out false. Here are some examples:

(1) $P \rightarrow P$
(2) $P \rightarrow (P \vee Q)$
(3) $(P \& Q) \rightarrow P$

Let us see that each of these *is* a tautology. Here's the strategy. We try to find out whether we can get the antecedent true and the consequent false. If not, then the formula is a tautology. Consider (1). There is no way the antecedent P can be true and the consequent P false, since antecedent and consequent are the same, and so must have the same truth value. Consider (2). Whenever P is true, the left disjunct of $P \vee Q$ will be true, so the disjunction will be true. So, there is no way of getting the antecedent, P, true and the consequent, $P \vee Q$, false. Finally, consider (3). Whenever the conjunction $P \& Q$ is true, both conjuncts are true, so, in particular, P is true; so there is no way to get the antecedent true and the consequent false.

P	Q	$P \rightarrow P$	$P \rightarrow (P \vee Q)$	$(P \& Q) \rightarrow P$
T	T	T	T	T
T	F	T	T	T
F	T	T	T	T
F	F	T	T	T

Since (1) is a tautology, we know that every statement implies itself. Since (2) is a tautology, we know that a disjunction is implied by each of its disjuncts. And, since (3) is a tautology, we know that a conjunction implies each of its conjuncts.

This is how implication is connected with the conditional:

P implies Q if, and only if, $P \rightarrow Q$ is a tautology.

P implies Q if there can be no circumstance in which the conditional $P \rightarrow Q$ is false. We can extend this to the case where a group of statements implies another. Given a group of statements $P1, P2, P3, \ldots Pn$, we will say

$P1, P2, P3, \ldots Pn$ implies Q if, and only if,
$(P1 \& P2 \& P3 \& \ldots Pn) \rightarrow Q$ is a tautology.

We can now use our notion of implication also to help make our notion of the validity of arguments more precise. We say

An argument is valid if it is impossible to get the premisses all true and the conclusion false.

This is now seen to be equivalent to

> **An argument is valid if the conjunction of the premises implies the conclusion.**

This is actually the procedure we have been following in determining whether or not an argument is valid. We have simply omitted working out the conditional. Instead, we set up a truth table with each of the premises and the conclusion as a column heading, and then checked to see whether there is a line in which the premises come out true and the conclusion comes out false. If there is such a line, the argument is invalid. If there is no such line, then it is *impossible* to get all the premises true and the conclusion false, so the argument is valid.

EXERCISES

7.6:1   Work out a truth table for each of the following formulas. Which are tautologies?
a. $((P \rightarrow Q) \rightarrow P) \rightarrow P$
b. $-P \rightarrow (P \rightarrow Q)$
c. $Q \rightarrow (P \rightarrow Q)$
d. $(-P \rightarrow P) \rightarrow -P$

Study Vocabulary: **tautology (logical truth)**
consistent statement
inconsistent statement

REVIEW

1.   A conditional is a statement formed from other statements by means of *If,then* or one of its equivalent idioms. The *if* clause is called the antecedent; the *then* clause is called the consequent.

2.   If *P then Q* says that *P* is a sufficient condition for *Q*—in other words, that *P*'s being true is enough to assure *Q*'s being true. It also says that *Q* is a necessary condition for *P*—that *P* wouldn't be true without *Q*'s being true. Each of the following says the same thing:

> If P then Q.
> If P, Q.
> Q, if P.
> P only if Q.

If not Q then not P.
P is a sufficient condition for Q.
It is sufficient for Q that P.
Q is a necessary condition for P.
It is necessary for P that Q.

3.   There are two fundamental valid argument patterns that involve the conditional:

Modus Ponens	Modus Tollens
If P then Q	*If P then Q*
P	*not Q*
SO, *Q*	SO, *not P*

In each case, an invalid pattern is frequently mistaken for the valid one:

Affirming the Consequent	Denying the Antecedent
If P then Q	*If P then Q*
Q	*not P*
SO, *P*	SO, *not Q*

4.   We define the material conditional, abbreviated '→,' according to the following truth table:

P	*Q*	*P → Q*
T	T	T
T	F	F
F	T	T
F	F	T

Thus, a conditional is false when and only when the antecedent is true and the consequent false. Otherwise it is true.

5.   *If* and *then* serve as parentheses to help group a conditional. *Not if* is different from *if not.* $-Q \to -P$ is the contrapositive of $P \to Q$, and is logically equivalent to it. $Q \to P$ is the converse of $P \to Q$, and is not logically equivalent to it.

6.   A tautology is a formula that comes out true for every line in the truth table. We say that P implies Q if, and only if, the conditional $P \to Q$ is a tautology.

8

ARGUMENTS

8.1 WHY ARGUE?

In the remainder of the text we will focus more deeply on arguments. Our discussion of arguments will occur in two main parts. In this and the next chapter we will focus on how to recognize arguments and how to determine their structure. In the last two chapters, we will focus on how to evaluate arguments—that is, on how to determine whether an argument is good or bad.

When we speak about arguments in everyday life, we often think of shouting matches, where people get hot under the collar and yell at each other, call each other names, and possibly end up physically struggling with each other. People argue about politics, about baseball, about who's to blame for an automobile collision, about what television show the family will watch tonight, about whether a youngster may stay out late or whether he or she may sleep at a friend's house. Such disputes are often emotional, noisy, possibly even dangerous engagements. Many of us like to avoid arguments because of the unpleasantness we associate with them. We prefer to have things on an even keel. True, some people love to get into arguments with others. But we tend to think of these people as exhibiting a kind of bravado, even if they limit themselves only to words.

This picture of argument and of arguing is completely different from the one we wish to paint. In logic, arguments are *rational* affairs. For the most part, in logic, we are interested in *figuring things out*, in working out the *implications* of a group of statements, and in determining what *evidence* there might be to support a claim.

Some readers might associate the notion of *figuring out* with complex puzzles, mathematical problems, or some other abstract subject matter. But figuring out problems is the heart of our dealing with the everyday world. We are rational agents; we cannot help it. It is a fact about us. Insofar as we do more than flip a coin or throw dice to determine what to do, we are making *reasoned choices*. In this sense, then, arguing is the most natural thing in the world, and we use argument in virtually every dimension of our lives, from the most trivial choices, such as figuring out what clothes to wear, to the most important, such as what occupation to follow or whether we should undergo a particular surgical procedure. There is no end to it. And each of these figurings out can be reconstructed as an argument. We have reasons for most everything we do.

Choosing what to do also involves us in argument. Suppose, for example, that you have to meet your friend at the movies this afternoon; you are running late and you want to get there on time. Should you drive? And if so, what route should you take? Will you be able to park? Should you take the train? Which will get you there faster? And so on. These are the sorts of questions you have to mull over in your mind before you decide which course of action to follow. When you make your choice, you will have figured out a problem.

We can represent this figuring out as an argument you have constructed in your mind, the conclusion of which is, say, that you should take the train. For you have looked over the alternatives, weighed their various advantages and disadvantages, and then selected what you take to be the best choice.

Sometimes our reasoning works in the other direction. Instead of trying to figure out what *will* happen or what we are justified in believing to be true, we try to figure out *why* something happened. That is, we seek an *explanation* for something. The car won't start, so we try to figure out what went wrong. We finally notice, say, that the battery is dead, and we explain the situation as follows: the car won't start because the battery is dead. This is a piece of reasoning, similar in structure to an argument, although here we are interested not in justifying the conclusion (since we already know it to be true), but in explaining why it is true. If the explanation is good, the conclusion follows from the reason. We can thus treat explanations as arguments as well, because both are pieces of reasoning whose structure is subject to the same logical principles.

And, of course, argument is intimately involved when we decide what to believe. We do not believe everything some individual tells us, and we do not believe everybody. When someone tells us something, we sometimes disregard it; when others tell us something, we believe it immediately. These, too, are choices we make. These are also, most likely, rational choices. We usually have reasons why we believe one person and not another, or why we believe one statement a person makes but not another statement that very same person makes. When we listen to the radio and hear the weather report, we tend to believe what the forecaster says. We assume the legitimacy of the station and the authority of its forecaster. Either the forecaster is himself an authority on the weather or he relies on others who are authorities. If, however, it should turn out that the predictions are not very reliable, we begin to doubt what he says and either find a better forecaster or simply temper his statements in the light of experience. We are all familiar with this. Similarly, if we're ill, we go to a doctor, believing that doctors are more likely to know what to do to cure us than, say, architects. We take the doctor's advice on illness. But we don't necessarily listen to her advice on how to build a building. For that, we go to an architect. Thus, we choose whom to listen to, and for the most part these choices are also reasoned choices.

This is not to say that when someone—say, the doctor—makes a claim such as "You have an inflamed kidney" that she is therefore giving us an argument. Not at all. She is simply making a claim. We, however, in our own minds, construct an argument about whether we should believe her. But *she* is not arguing for the claim. The argument *we* construct goes something like this:

> Jones said that *P*.
> Jones is a reliable authority on the subject.
> SO, It is likely true that *P*.

(Of course, we would normally suppose that since Jones is a reliable authority on the subject, she could, if we asked her, give us a good reason for her claim.)

We accept most information not on the basis of argument, but on the basis of the authority of the individual making the claim. Consider, for example, your experiences in school. For the most part, you were not given reasons for believing the things you were told. You believed them because you believed that your teachers were authorities in their fields, so what they were telling you was quite likely true. Our beliefs about current affairs are also for the most part based on authority. We rely on reporters and newscasters for our information; we rely on their honesty, integrity, and reliability in getting the correct information. When younger, we relied on the authority of our parents to determine what is right or wrong to do in a given situation. In few of these cases were we given arguments to support the claims that were made. Our choice to believe their statements, however, was based on arguments that we constructed in our own minds.

Nevertheless, we ultimately need to figure many things out for ourselves. For one thing, it is in our interests to know why a particular claim is true. For unless we are able to see the reasons why the claim is true, we will be unable to comprehend fully its implications, and so we will be unable to generalize to other, similar situations. If we rely on the authority of others to determine what to believe, we run into problems. Authorities aren't always available; we cannot carry them around with us. Moreover, each of us is ultimately responsible for what he or she believes. Whether an action is right or wrong, for example, is not something that we will readily allow someone else to decide for us. But more important, if the authority is wrong, *we* are the ones who pay the piper.

EXERCISES

8.1:1   Give three examples of things that you reasoned or figured out today.

8.1:2   Give three examples of things that you *could have* reasoned or figured out but didn't.

8.1:3   Give three examples of arguments from the newspaper.

8.1:4   Give an example of a situation in which you accept someone's saying something as evidence for its truth. Why do you accept this person's word as authoritative? Do you accept this person's word on everything? Give an example of a situation in which you do *not* accept someone's saying something as evidence for its truth. Why *don't* you accept this person's word as authoritative?

8.2   WHAT IS AN ARGUMENT?

We can define an argument as follows:

> **An argument is a collection of statements, one of which, the conclusion, is the statement being argued for, and the rest of which, the premisses, are the reasons put forward to justify the conclusion.**

An argument is a collection of statements. This is the first point to note about our definition. An argument is never a single statement. A single statement by itself is a *claim*. If someone were to say to you

> The earth is bigger than the moon,

he would simply be making a claim. As such, it is either true or false, and we may either believe it or not. But no *reason* has been given to believe this claim; no evidence has been put forward that would lead us to think that the claim is true. If such a reason had been given, as in

> The gravitational attraction of the moon is less than that of earth. *So,* the earth is bigger than the moon,

then we would have an argument. The *conclusion* is that the earth is bigger than the moon; the *premiss* is that the gravitational attraction of the moon is less than that of earth.

There is, of course, nothing wrong with making claims. We do it all the time. Making claims has its proper place in the overall scheme of communication. We don't always expect people to give reasons for everything they claim to be true. If you ask someone which airlines fly to Great Britain, you expect a simple answer, not an argument. Or, when you listen for the weather report in the morning, you want to hear the prediction, not the reasons the forecaster has for making the prediction. And so on. Making statements has its proper place. But arguments also have their proper place. We often face the question of whether to believe a given statement to be true, so we often want to examine its justification—the reasons put forward to support its claim to truth.

The *premisses* of an argument are meant to justify the conclusion, to give support for the truth of the conclusion. This simply reflects the primary purpose of argument: to put forward good *reasons* for believing the conclusion. To support the truth of the conclusion is to provide good reasons for believing it.

The *conclusion* of an argument is the point at issue; it is the claim that is being justified. Every argument *must* have a conclusion, and an argument can have *only one* conclusion. But an argument must also include the reasons put forward to justify the conclusion. An argument may contain any number of premisses.

An argument, therefore, divides into two parts. There is the statement one is arguing for—the conclusion—and there can be only one such statement in an argument. And there are the statements put forward to justify the conclusion—the premisses—and there can be any number of them in an argument. Abstractly, then, an argument will look like this:

$$
\begin{aligned}
&P1 \\
&P2 \\
&P3 \\
&\quad\vdots \\
&\underline{Pn} \\
&SO,\ C.
\end{aligned}
$$

Note that there can be good and bad arguments. For, although the premisses of an argument are *meant* to justify the conclusion, they do not always do so. When the premisses do justify the conclusion, the argument is good; when the premisses do not justify the conclusion, the argument is bad. What distinguishes arguments from other forms of discourse is that in an argument some statements are put forward for the purpose of supporting another. What distinguishes good arguments from bad is that the premisses of a good argument actually do justify the conclusion. Logic provides us with the means to determine when a person is putting forward a good argument and when he is putting forward a bad argument. We shall examine these means in Chapters 10 and 11.

Although, we have already seen a number of arguments in the first seven chapters of this textbook, these arguments have been presented in a highly stylized form. It is rare, however, that the arguments we encounter in everyday life appear in such a neat form. Our first problem, then, is quite practical. We want to be able to determine when, in ordinary discourse, we are being presented with an argument. This is often not a simple matter. And, unlike the work we have been doing to this point, it is often a matter of interpretation. We must try to reconstruct the author's thinking, to put the most reasonable interpretation on what has been said.

We will now look at a number of examples of "collections of statements" to determine whether or not they contain arguments. We will discuss a number of clues to look for in order to decide whether a passage contains an argument.

Consider the following passage:

> Adolf Hitler was one of the meanest men who ever lived. There have been other mean men besides him—for example, Attila the Hun, Barbarossa, Genghis Khan. But Adolf Hitler was the meanest of them all.

Is this an argument? If it is an argument, then what is its conclusion? What is the author arguing for? What is the point at issue? Clearly the author's main point is that Adolf Hitler was one of the meanest men who ever lived. Actually, the author goes on to say something even stronger: Hitler was not merely *one* of the meanest men, but he was *the* meanest of all. But, although this is the point of the paragraph, the author does not seem to be offering any reasons to support his claim. To be sure, he lists other mean men in history. But this list provides no reason to believe that Adolf Hitler belongs in the list. So, we have no argument here. The author has given you no reason to believe that Adolf Hitler was one of the meanest men to have ever lived. The author simply asserts it.

Let us try another example:

> Adolf Hitler was one of the meanest men who ever lived. He started a world war and killed many millions of people for no good reason.

Is there an argument here? Is there a conclusion? First, let's see what the author's main point is. Again it is

> Adolf Hitler was one of the meanest men who ever lived.

But what is the rest of the passage doing? The author goes on to say (1) that Adolf Hitler started a world war, and (2) that Adolf Hitler killed many millions of people for no good reason. Is there any relation between these claims and the main point of the passage? Yes. These claims seem to be presented as *evidence* to support the claim that Adolf Hitler was one of the meanest men who ever lived. We would undoubtedly be making the author's intentions perfectly clear if we inserted a *because* into the paragraph:

> Adolf Hitler was one of the meanest men who ever lived *because* he started a world war and killed many millions of people for no good reason.

The *because* makes the relation between the parts of the paragraph explicit. The argument of the passage goes as follows:

Adolf Hitler started a world war.
Adolf Hitler killed many millions of people for no good reason.
SO, Adolf Hitler was one of the meanest men who ever lived.

Two reasons are put forward to support the conclusion.
Let us look at a third example:

> Adolf Hitler was one of the meanest men who ever lived. I say this because I hate him and I want everyone else to hate him too.

Is this an argument? If so, what is its conclusion? It certainly seems reasonable to take the first sentence as the main point of the paragraph. But can we reconstruct the passage as an argument for this claim? The second sentence seems rather to be an explanation of why the writer *says* that Adolf Hitler was one of the meanest men who ever lived. The emphasis is on why the author *says* it. So, even though

Adolf Hitler was one of the meanest men who ever lived

is the main point of the paragraph, the author does not argue for it; he provides no reasons for believing it to be true. He simply asserts it. What the author does provide are reasons for his *saying* that Adolf Hitler was one of the meanest men who ever lived.

So, if the passage contains any argument at all, its conclusion is

I *say* that Adolf Hitler was one of the meanest men who ever lived.

But, then what are the reasons or premises put forward to support this conclusion? We can take our cue from the word *because*. *Because* answers the question *Why?* So, what follows the *because* must be the reasons supporting the conclusion. These are (1) that the author hates him and (2) that the author wants others to hate him too. The argument in the paragraph, then, looks like this:

> I hate Adolf Hitler.
> _I want others to hate Adolf Hitler._
> SO, I say that Adolf Hitler was one of the meanest men
> who ever lived.

This sequence reconstructs the author's reasoning. The author hates Adolf Hitler and he wants others to do so also. What he suggests is that the proper course of action is to tell others exactly how he feels, and this will, he supposes, affect their attitude towards Adolf Hitler. Note, however, that the author gives us reasons that are meant to justify his _doing_ what he is doing. He does not give us reasons for believing that Adolf Hitler was one of the meanest men who ever lived.

Finally, consider the following passage:

> Jones said: "Adolf Hitler was one of the meanest men who ever lived. He started a world war and killed many millions of people for no good reason."

Do we have an argument here? If so, what is its conclusion? Be careful; the example is somewhat tricky. Apparently, what the author is doing here is _directly quoting_ Jones. The author is not committing herself to Jones's words. She is reporting them. So, the author is not herself arguing anything at all. She is merely quoting Jones. Jones, however, is clearly arguing for Adolf Hitler's being one of the meanest men who ever lived.

Let us summarize some of what we have learned in this section. Our primary concern is with pieces of reasoning, examples of which can be found in virtually every dimension of our discourse. Such pieces of reasoning we have called _arguments_. We have given this word a quite precise definition, which might differ in part from the meaning some of us ordinarily give to it. An **argument** is a collection of statements containing a **conclusion**, and **reasons** (which we call **premises**) that are put forward to justify the conclusion. If the argument is good, the premises do support the conclusion; if the argument is bad, the premises do not support the conclusion. We examined some sample passages to determine whether or not they are arguments. What we looked for in each case was a conclusion—a main point at issue—and then we looked to see whether the rest of the passage can be viewed as presenting reasons or evidence to support this conclusion. If so, the passage is an argument; if not, it is not an argument.

EXERCISES

8.2:1 Some of the following are arguments and some are not. Identify which are arguments, and explain your reasons for saying so.

a. The team had a lot of good plays for Hutchinson, so they were able to overwhelm the opposition.

b. John meant to punch Harry, but he hit Sam because he was closer.

c. Humans have hunted animals ever since the dawn of time.

d. Put up or shut up.

e. Sticks and stones may break my bones, but names will never harm me.

f. Inflation came to be a terrible problem in America because President Johnson refused to choose between guns and butter.

g. Humans cannot fly because God didn't mean them to.

8.2:2   Indicate for each of the following passages whether it is an argument. If it is, identify its premisses and conclusion.

a. Richard Nixon was the first president to come from California. Other presidents have come from the western part of the country, but no one else has come from California.

b. Richard Nixon said that Herbert Hoover was one of the greatest presidents America ever had. Hoover, Nixon said, kept the peace and was not in any way responsible, as so many people have claimed, for the Great Depression. Finally, Nixon said, Hoover was a great humanitarian and a moral leader to all Americans.

c. Richard Nixon believed in the free market and was against government intervention. He also believed that taxes should be lowered and that America should increase its spending for defense.

d. Richard Nixon believed in the free market and was against government intervention. I know this because I heard him say so many times.

e. Since Richard Nixon is a Republican, and all Republicans are out to help the poor, Richard Nixon is out to help the poor.

f. Richard Nixon said that lowering taxes for the rich will help all Americans. But, he's rich, and lowering taxes is in his own interests. So, what he said is probably false.

Study Vocabulary: argument
conclusion
premiss
reason

8.3   ARGUMENT INDICATORS

Sometimes it is difficult to decide whether a passage contains an argument and, if so, to determine which statement is the conclusion and which are the premisses. You no doubt discovered this when you worked out the exercises in the last section. To a large extent, we have to rely on common sense: we must try to figure out what the writer is attempting to do in the passage. And this means that we have to try to put ourselves into the writer's shoes. Our job can be made easier by attending to the words the writer uses to indicate that he is drawing a conclusion and the words the writer uses to indicate that he is giving a reason. In this section, we will examine some of these **argument indicators** and attempt to specify the information they give us.

In English, we use many little indicators or signposts to determine whether a statement is serving as a premiss or as a conclusion. Each of the following **conclusion indicators**, for example, tells us that a conclusion is coming:

thus	*as a result*
therefore	*which entails that*
hence	*we may infer that*
it follows that	*so*
consequently	*for this reason*

There are other expressions that do the same job; you might, perhaps, try to add some to the list.

Whenever you see one of these words or phrases, you may be reasonably sure that a conclusion is coming. Consider

Smith is a physicist. So, he is very bright.

As you look through this sequence of statements, you see the word *so*. *So* is a conclusion indicator: it tells us that the statement after *so* must be a conclusion. *So*,

He is very bright

is the conclusion of the argument. And since this *is* an argument, you know, by a process of elimination, that the other statement,

Smith is a physicist,

must be the premiss. You would therefore take this passage to look like this:

Smith is a physicist.
***
SO, he is very bright.

Without the word *so* in the passage above, you would have none of this information. For example, suppose you were presented with this:

Smith is a physicist. He is very bright.

You might well take this as a list of descriptive statements about Smith, neither of which is being put forward as evidence or justification for the other. And even if you decided (from the context) that an argument is being presented, it would not be clear which statement is the premiss and which is the conclusion. You might, for instance, suppose that the writer is arguing for the claim that Smith is a physicist, on the grounds that Smith is very bright. With the word *so* in the passage, however, there can be no doubt that the writer is presenting us with an argument, and there can be no doubt about which statement is the conclusion of the argument.

Just as there are words that indicate that a conclusion is coming, so there are words that indicate that a *reason*, or *premiss*, is coming. We may call these **premiss indicators**. Here is a list of some of these words:

> *because*
>
> *since*
>
> *for*

These words are a bit more complicated than the conclusion indicators we have just discussed. Take the word *because*. This word actually indicates *both* a premiss and a conclusion. The general form is:

CONCLUSION *because* PREMISS.

That is, what follows *because* is the reason or premiss; what precedes *because* is the conclusion, the statement being argued for. (Note that *because* is often used to indicate that what follows is not just a reason, but a cause. We will ignore this distinction here because we are interested only in the structure that *because* imposes.)

In the example of the physicist Smith we could have given the information about the direction of the argument by using the word *because*:

> Smith is very bright because he is a physicist.

The conclusion here is "Smith is very bright." The premiss is "He is a physicist."

What follows *because* answers the question *Why?* that is prompted by the statement that precedes it. Smith is very bright. Why? Because he is a physicist. If we had rearranged the order of the statements to read

> Smith is a physicist because he is very bright,

then "Smith is a physicist" would be the *conclusion* and "He is very bright" would be the *premiss*. Smith is a physicist. Why? Because he is very bright.

Take another example:

> She failed because she was bored.

What is being argued for, the *conclusion*, is "She failed." Why? *Because* "She was bored." This is the premiss. What follows *because* is the reason why.

Each of the other argument indicators in the preceding list has the same form:

CONCLUSION *because* PREMISS.
CONCLUSION *since* PREMISS.
CONCLUSION *for* PREMISS.

So, each of the following presents the same argument:

She failed *because* she didn't do her homework.
She failed *since* she didn't do her homework.
She failed *for* she didn't do her homework.

We can also perform a small grammatical change on each of these forms. We could equally have said:

Because PREMISS, CONCLUSION.
Since PREMISS, CONCLUSION.
For PREMISS, CONCLUSION.

For example, each of the following pairs says the same thing:

She failed *because* she didn't do her homework.
Because she didn't do her homework, she failed.

She failed *since* she didn't do her homework.
Since she didn't do her homework, she failed.

In looking for these argument indicators, however, one must be careful. It is not a mechanical matter. For example, *since* can also be used as a time indicator. The statement

I haven't seen him since he was three years old

does not present an argument. *Since* does not serve here to indicate that a premiss is coming. We could not understand this to be an argument whose conclusion is

I haven't seen him.

What follows *since*—namely, "he was three years old"—does not answer *why* I haven't seen him. Rather, the author is saying that she hasn't seen him for a certain length of time.

Be careful about *for* also. You cannot mechanically assume that whenever you see *for* you have an argument. *For* also serves as a preposition. In, for example,

This is for you,

no argument is presented. *For* does not indicate here that a premiss is coming. Again, in *for example* no argument is presented; you cannot take "example" as a premiss.

Also, be careful not to confuse *for*, which indicates that a reason is coming, with *therefore*, which indicates that a conclusion is coming.

Be careful about *so* as well. Earlier, we said that *so* indicates that a conclusion is coming. But, again, there are exceptions to this rule. In

Why do you use so many words?

so does not indicate that an inference is occurring. You have to be very careful and use your common sense throughout.

One final point we wish to make here concerns *If,then*. Compare the following two sentences:

(1)   Smith is a physicist; therefore, he is very bright.

(2)   If Smith is a physicist then he is very bright.

There is a close connection between these two, which we explained back in Chapter 7: (1) is valid if, and only if, (2) is a tautology. Nevertheless, (1) and (2) are importantly different. (1) is an argument; (2) is not.

(1) contains two claims, the first of which is the premiss ("Smith is a physicist"), and the second of which is the conclusion ("Smith is very bright"). The writer is committing himself to the truth of both of these claims. He is saying that *it is true* that Smith is a physicist and also that *it is true* that Smith is very bright. Moreover, in indicating that Smith's being a physicist is a reason for believing that Smith is very bright, he is also committing himself to the truth of (2).

(2), however, is only a single statement: it is a conditional. The writer is *not* committing himself to the truth of the claim that Smith is a physicist. He is saying only that *if* Smith is a physicist, then he is bright. A conditional, you will recall, does not commit one to the truth of either the antecedent or the consequent. So, do not suppose that *then* indicates that a conclusion is coming. Most likely, *then* indicates that a *consequent* is coming.

EXERCISES

8.3:1   Give three phrases that have not been mentioned in this text that serve to indicate that a conclusion is coming. Give three phrases that have not been mentioned in this text that serve to indicate that a reason is coming.

8.3:2   Some of the following are arguments; some are not. Identify which are which, and explain your answer.

a.   Since time immemorial, humans have hunted animals.

b.   For Pete's sake, stop what you are doing.

c.   Since too much time elapsed between plays, the team was penalized five yards.

d.   You'll be late if you don't start right now.

e. In conclusion, I want to thank all the people who made this event possible.

f. John is poor, but he is honest.

g. Although Arthur and Lancelot were friends, Arthur had to punish Lancelot.

h. There are, finally, many personal reasons why I cannot continue on my contract.

8.3:3 For each of the following simple arguments, circle the argument indicator, and indicate which is the premiss and which is the conclusion.

a. The concert was canceled because of bad weather.

b. Since all men are created equal, men and women are the same height.

c. The United States has the most athletes at the Olympic games, so it will win the most medals.

d. Because attendance was so low, the owners decided to fire the whole team.

e. John inferred that someone was in the house because the window had been jimmied open.

8.3:4 For each of the following arguments, identify the argument indicator and the conclusion.

a. Because genes are the smallest biological entities that carry information, they are the morphemes of our genetic language.

b. You have to know how to take orders in order to know how to give orders. Therefore, you must serve as a private before you become a general.

c. Isaac loved Jacob, for he was good and kind.

d. An individual who is kept artificially alive is no longer a person. For this reason, removing an individual's life-support system is not an act of murder.

e. Since an individual who is kept artificially alive is no longer a person, some individuals are not persons.

f. There's no fool like an old fool; so all fools are young.

g. Because the gang used the mail to advertise stolen property, they could be prosecuted by the federal government for mail fraud.

8.3:5 The following is an argument, even though there are no argument indicators explicitly showing the direction of the reasoning. Insert an appropriate argument indicator so that the argument is clearly delineated, and then explain why the passage *must* be understood this way rather than another.

> When in doubt, tell the truth. It will confound your enemies and astound your friends. attributed to Mark Twain

8.3:6   The following is an argument, but it is not clear which statement is the premiss and which is the conclusion. It could actually be read in either way. Set up the two arguments and explain how they differ (*Note:* Don't explain the difference simply by noting which is the premiss and which is the conclusion.)

> The politicians believe the public is more fearful of tax increases than it is of budget deficits. It's highly unlikely they'll balance the budget this year.

Study Vocabulary: **argument indicator**
conclusion indicator
premiss indicator

8.4   MORE COMPLICATED EXAMPLES

We will now examine some more complicated examples of arguments in order to become more familiar with the way in which argument indicators work. Consider the following passage:

> Since political philosophy is a branch of philosophy, even the most provisional explanation of what political philosophy is cannot dispense with an explanation, however provisional, of what philosophy is.

> Leo Strauss, *"What Is Political Philosophy?" and Other Studies*
> (Glencoe, Ill.: Free Press, 1959), pp. 10–11.

As we scan the passage, we find the argument indicator *since* appearing at the very beginning of the sentence. We know that there are two formats for *since*. These are

C *since* P

since P, C

And, since *since* occurs at the very beginning of the sentence, it must be the second of the two forms. Hence, what occurs between *since* and the comma will be our premiss, and what follows the comma will be our conclusion.

Since
political philosophy is a branch of philosophy,
even the most provisional explanation of what political philosophy is cannot dispense with an explanation, however provisional, of what philosophy is.

In our stylized format, then, we have

> <u>Political philosophy is a branch of philosophy.</u>
> SO, Even the most provisional explanation of what
> political philosophy is cannot dispense with an
> explanation, however provisional, of what philosophy is.

That is, what our author is arguing for (in simpler terms) is that you have to explain what philosophy is in order to explain what political philosophy is. And what is his reason? Because political philosophy is a branch of philosophy.

It is important to recognize that you cannot mechanically apply the principles that you have been implementing here. You must always use your common sense as well. For example, suppose that our illustration had gone like this:

> Since political philosophy, *shallow as it may be*, is a branch of philosophy, even the most provisional explanation of what political philosophy is cannot dispense with an explanation, however provisional, of what philosophy is.

Suppose we followed our recipe literally and took everything between *since* and the comma as our premiss. Our premiss would be

> political philosophy

and our conclusion would be

> shallow as it may be, is a branch of philosophy, even the most provisional explanation of what political philosophy is cannot dispense with an explanation, however provisional, of what philosophy is.

This makes no sense. We have split our premiss in the middle by literally going only to the first comma. The "premiss" we end up with is not a statement at all, and our conclusion is a run-on sentence fragment. The point to note is that the phrase *shallow as it may be* has been put *in apposition* and pertains to *political philosophy*. It belongs as part of the statement and does not serve to separate a premiss from a conclusion. The correct way of reading this example is to take the statement

> Political philosophy, shallow as it may be, is a branch of philosophy

as the premiss, and the remainder as the conclusion.

Here is another example. It exhibits a different pattern.

> If you believe the biblical admonition that killing is wrong, then you should oppose the death penalty.

This passage does not contain an argument. It is a conditional. As such, it is true or false. But it is not an argument, because no reason has been put forward to support the conditional. In an argument, the writer commits herself to the truth of the premisses as well as the conclusion. But in a conditional, the writer commits herself only to the claim that the truth of the antecedent is enough to assure the truth of the consequent; she does not commit herself either to the truth of the antecedent or to the truth of the consequent.

Let us now try a more complicated example in which more than one reason is put forward to support a conclusion. The way to figure out the structure of the argument—just as we did in the simple case—is first to locate the argument indicators and then to identify the conclusion of the argument. Then we can piece together how the remaining statements of the paragraph function. Consider:

> Animals do not respect the rights of others; so animals are not entitled to moral rights, since only those who respect the rights of others are themselves entitled to moral rights.

As we scan the argument, we note that there are two argument indicators— *so* and *since*. We know that what follows *so* is a conclusion. The conclusion is

> Animals are not entitled to moral rights.

This is what is being argued for. *Since* indicates that a premiss is coming. So,

> Only those who respect the rights of others are themselves entitled to moral rights

must be a premiss. So far, then we have

> Only those who respect the rights of others are
> themselves entitled to moral rights.
> _____
> SO, Animals are not entitled to moral rights.

But, what about the first statement in the argument: "Animals do not respect the rights of others?" How does this function? It certainly could not be the conclusion, because we have already located the conclusion of the argument, and an argument can have but one conclusion. So, it is either an irrelevant comment or it is another premiss. It is certainly not an irrelevant comment. It must be another premiss. And we know from the way our argument indicators work that so, while always followed by a conclusion, is frequently preceded by a premiss. In sum, then, we have determined the following format for the argument:

> Animals do not respect the rights of others.
> Only those who respect the rights of others are
> themselves entitled to moral rights.
> _____
> SO, Animals are not entitled to moral rights.

Our author is arguing that animals are not entitled to moral rights. What are his reasons to support this claim? That "animals do not respect the rights of others" and "only those who respect the rights of others are themselves entitled to moral rights."

Here is another complicated example:

> Only those who pass the course will be able to go on in philosophy. The rest will have to make do with an inferior education. And, since some of you will not pass, some of you will not be able to go on in philosophy.

As we scan the passage, we find only one argument indicator, *since*. There are two formats for *since*:

since P, C.

C since P.

The first format is the one used here; so, so far, we have

Some of you will not pass [the course].
_____
SO, Some of you will not be able to go on in philosophy.

But there are two sentences remaining in the passage. What is their function? Consider the first sentence:

> Only those who pass the course will be able to go on in philosophy.

How does this claim fit into the argument? Is it being argued for? No. It does not appear to follow from anything else in the passage. Is it being used to support the conclusion? Yes. So, the argument in the passage now looks like this:

Only those who pass the course will be able to
go on in philosophy.
Some of you will not pass [the course].
_____
SO, Some of you will not be able to go on in philosophy.

Now, we need only identify what is going on with the remaining sentence:

> The rest will have to make do with an inferior education.

How does this claim fit into the argument? Is it being argued for? Clearly not. The author is simply claiming that those who are unable to go on in philosophy will have an inferior education. Does the claim serve as a premiss for the conclusion that some will not be able to go on in philosophy? No. It does not seem to figure into the conclusion at all. So, we can, as far as the argument goes, ignore it; it is an irrelevant comment.

Note how different our analysis would be if the passage looked like this:

> Only those who pass the course will be able to go on in philosophy. The rest will have to make do with an inferior education. And, since some of you will not pass, some of you will have to make do with an inferior education.

Here the former irrelevant comment is intimately connected with the ultimate conclusion of the argument—namely, that some will have to make do with an inferior education.

Our analysis of this passage requires that we recognize two arguments in it. On top of the argument we have already recognized is the following:

> Some of you will not be able to go on in philosophy.
> Those who are not able to go on in philosophy will
> have to make do with an inferior education.
> _____
> SO, Some of you will have to make do with an
> inferior education.

The first premiss is the conclusion of the first argument. The second premiss is the former irrelevant comment.

EXERCISES

8.4:1   For each of the following arguments, circle the argument indicator(s) and underline the conclusion.

a.   Someone must have been telling lies about Joseph K., for without having done anything wrong he was arrested one fine morning.

Franz Kafka, The Trial, trans. Willa and Edwin Muir
(New York: Schocken Books, 1946), p. 1.

b.   An international agreement proscribes the use of gas, and so germ warfare must be developed.

c.   Since only those who respect the rights of others are entitled to moral rights, and criminals do not respect the rights of others, criminals are not entitled to moral rights.

d.   Only those who respect the rights of others are themselves entitled to moral rights; so, since animals do not respect the rights of others, animals are not entitled to moral rights.

e.   There are many different routes into a trap, but only one way out; so be careful how you plot your course.

f.   Since you can check in but not check out, and you want to be able to check out, you had better never check in.

g.   Our course is just. For God is with us, and God's course is always just.

h. I'm old; so I'm not a fool since there's no fool like an old fool.

i. Since no one is someone, I met someone walking down the street since I met no one walking down the street.

j. Since Tom had two pieces of pie with lunch, and he is not allowed more than three pieces a day, he will be able to have one more piece at supper.

k. The best advertisement for a product is the product itself. So any advertisement that gets people to buy the product is better than one that only tells you about how wonderful it would be if you bought it.

l. For God and country I would gladly lay down my life. But I will not bear arms for your cause since you are neither God nor my country.

m. The United States cannot publicly acknowledge the Soviet struggle in Afghanistan. For, to do so would only underline its unwillingness to do anything about it.

n. Cancer can be cured if treated early. It is therefore important for people to recognize the signs of cancer.

o. It's been said that computers will eventually be able to do all the work of translating from one language to another. But that will never happen, because computers will never be able to capture the poetic and the idiomatic in language.

p. Rumor had it that Jordan spent $500,000 on his campaign. No one who knows him believed that, however, since he spends that much each year on beer alone.

REVIEW

1. An argument is a collection of statements, one of which, the conclusion, is the statement being argued for, and the rest of which, the premisses, are the reasons put forward to justify the conclusion. An argument can have any number of premisses, but only one conclusion.

2. There are a number of words we use to tell us the direction or flow of reasoning in a passage. These are called *argument indicators.*
Premiss indicators tell us a premiss is coming. Examples are:

since

because

for

Conclusion indicators tell us a conclusion is coming. Examples are:

so	*for this reason*
thus	*it follows that*
therefore	*as a result*
hence	*which entails that*
consequently	*we may infer that*

9

ARGUMENT STRUCTURES

9.1 TYPES OF STRUCTURES

Arguments rarely occur so neatly spelled out that the reader can easily determine which statements are the premises and which is the conclusion. In the last chapter, we saw a number of examples in which we had to use various cues to determine what the structure of the argument is, and also to see which statements, if any, are irrelevant to the argument contained in the passage. In this chapter, we are going to examine more complicated passages, ones in which more than one argument is found. Though we shall limit ourselves to single paragraphs, the techniques we develop for dealing with them are applicable to any complicated sequence of arguments. They will apply to the flow of reasoning over several paragraphs, a long essay, or even an entire book.

Every argument must have a conclusion, and an argument cannot have more than one conclusion. This means that if we find more than one conclusion in a passage, we may immediately infer that it contains more than one argument. On the other hand, an argument can have any number of premises. So, just because we find a number of reasons put forward to support a given conclusion, it does not follow that there is more than one argument in the paragraph, although it is possible—for independent lines of reasoning might be put forward to support a conclusion.

For the most part, there is no great difficulty in determining what is going on in such complicated cases, as long as everything is spelled out in the argument. What is of interest to us in the present chapter are cases in which the flow of the argument is not spelled out. We are especially interested in cases in which a given statement does double duty (1) as the premiss of one argument and the conclusion of another, (2) as a premiss of two distinct arguments for two distinct conclusions, or (3) as the conclusion of two distinct arguments.

These three possibilities give rise to three frequently encountered, distinct structures:

(1) *sequential reasoning:* the author argues for a given claim, which then becomes a reason to support a later claim.

(2) *divergent reasoning:* the author puts forward the same reason to support two distinct conclusions.

(3) *convergent reasoning:* the author puts forward two independent lines of reasoning to support the same claim.

Our object in this chapter is to examine these various types of structures so that you will be able to recognize and deal effectively with them.

Before we begin, however, we should mention that in this chapter we will have to rely more extensively than we have before on principles that pertain to *interpreting* what we read. For the problems we face will frequently turn on how best to understand the passage. The point to note is that in a complex passage, it is not always immediately evident what the author is trying to do. The difficulty might arise from the way he words the passage, from the fact that the author himself is confused or unsure of what he is saying, or from the fact that the material itself is complex. The answers that we come up with might therefore not be as clear-cut as the answers we are usually able to come up with in logic. They will depend upon how we *interpret* the passage and on what assumptions we make about the author's intentions and beliefs. Different readers might well arrive at different interpretations.

It doesn't follow, of course, that one may read just anything into a passage; there are constraints on *acceptable* interpretation. In this chapter, we are especially interested in having you come to understand the sorts of reasons we use to arrive at an acceptable interpretation of a passage. That way you can appreciate and rationally assess disagreements in interpretation.

In reading a difficult passage, we must often employ the **principle of charity**. That is, we must assume that the person writing the passage is a rational human being, like ourselves. Unless we have reasons to think that she is trying to mislead us, we assume that she is presenting her beliefs as cogently as she can. This means that when a question arises about how to interpret a passage, we suppose, other things being equal, that our author is putting forward the best of the possible readings—insofar as we suppose her capable of being aware of its being best. We must, so to speak, put ourselves into the author's shoes to see how she sees the situation. We should not, however, attribute too much to her, and so we sometimes have to guess what she is aware of and what she is not aware of.

Consider the problems that arise in trying to understand a two- or three-year-old child who is just starting to talk and make himself understood. Think of how we try to figure out what the child is saying. We try to appreciate what is important from his vantage point, and we try to see the world from his conceptualization of it, in terms of his wants and likes. This is the principle of charity at work. When we do not immediately understand what he is saying, perhaps because his pronunciation is unclear or the words do not string together meaningfully, we accept the burden of trying to find out. We do not ignore the child and suppose that he is talking gibberish. That would be cruel, for a child of two or three is a pretty clever individual, often surprising in the depth of his understanding of the world around him. Rather, we assume that the child is a rational human being trying to make sense out of the world around him, that he is trying to communicate something to us that he considers important, and that he knows what he is trying to communicate. Our problem is to enter into his way of thinking, to reach into his soul, and to see past the difficulties he is having with the language. Sometimes, of course, we cannot tell which of two (or three or several) possibilities is the right one. Sometimes the communication is just a failure, but we do not start out supposing it's a failure. Now if, when you are reading a difficult passage, you can re-create the frame of mind with which you attempt to understand a child, then you will be well on the way to becoming an astute reader.

You should not infer that because of the principle of charity, we, as writers and speakers, are relieved of the responsibility of making our words as clear as possible. Far from it. If what we say is worth saying, then we want to include sufficient information, presented in a clear, reasonable order of exposition for a reasonable reader to understand what we are saying and fairly evaluate it. That is why it is often instructive for us, when we write, to recognize the difficulties we have as readers in making sense out of the text before us.

Although the principle of charity is, perhaps, the most important constraint on interpretation, there are several other principles of interpretation that we tend to rely on. We will mention some others to help you gain a sense of what is involved in interpreting a complex passage.

One such principle is that we assume the person speaking to us, other things being equal, is telling us what she takes to be the truth. Of course, people don't always tell the truth. There are clear situations in which we are pretty sure that someone is not telling the truth, and there are situations where we are aware that the speaker might very well succumb to lying. But, for the most part, we tend to assume—unless we have good reason to think otherwise—that a person is telling us the truth. If we didn't, we would be unable to distinguish those cases where a person is lying from those cases where a person is mistaken—a very important distinction. We certainly don't want to mistake mistakes for bad character traits.

Another principle is to suppose the author is being candid in what he says. That is, we suppose the author to be telling us everything he thinks is relevant to the situation. A person who omits crucial points is deceiving us in some way. (This is, of course, the distinction between "the truth" and "the *whole* truth.") There are many stories that are based on violations of this **principle of candor**. Consider this one:

> A man's car breaks down, and he walks down the road to find help. He meets a farmer and tells him what happened. The farmer says, "The same thing happened to my car." "What did you do?" asks the man. The farmer said, "I blew on the carburetor." So, the man goes back to his car and blows on the carburetor. But the car still won't start. So, he goes back to the farmer and tells him what happened. The farmer says, "It didn't work for me either." "Why didn't you tell me?" the man asks. The farmer replies: "You asked me what I did. You didn't ask me whether it worked."

This is a perfect example of not being candid. The farmer's answer entitled the man to infer that the procedure would work. And though the farmer said nothing false, he was being deceitful. He was allowing the man to make the inference, knowing full well that he would be led to a false conclusion.

Here is another example of how we make inferences on the basis of these principles of interpretation. Suppose your instructor comes into the classroom with the graded exams and announces: "Some of you have passed the exam." No doubt, you would immediately infer that some in the class have not passed the exam. Why? You might think that the inference is justified by the fact that 'some' means 'at least one, but not all'. Certainly, if that were so, the inference would be justified. But we think there is a better explanation. In logic, as you know, we take 'some' to mean 'at least one, possibly all.' So the inference that some did not pass the exam cannot be justified by appealing to the meaning of 'some'. Rather, we think the inference is justified because we reasonably make a further assumption, based on the principle of candor, that the instructor is giving the most information that he can. There's no reason to think that the instructor would lie to you, or that he would intentionally deceive you. Now, the instructor marked the exams, and he knows everybody's grades. So, we reason on the basis of the principle of candor that if everyone passed, the instructor would say that everyone passed. The fact that he said only that some passed means that he could not truthfully say that everyone passed.

Of course, the instructor might have been a wise guy. Suppose that everyone had actually passed. Then he did not say something false when he said that some passed; he said something misleading.

There are many other principles of this sort. The important thing to note is that we employ these principles of interpretation all the time, and we make inferences on the basis of them.

It is worth remarking, of course, that these principles of interpretation all depend upon a "friendly" environment, in which we may reasonably assume a mutual effort to arrive at mutual understanding. In an adversary situation, however—for example, in a law court or political arena, or the somewhat artificial world of debate—we don't make these assumptions. In such environments, to give the benefit of the doubt will quite likely lead to your being misled. You must, therefore, stick to the literal meaning of the words used.

In this chapter, then, we shall be alert to the differences of interpretation that sometimes arise out of the natural problems of communicating with one another, and we shall sometimes rely on some of the nonlogical principles that also guide our communication with one another.

EXERCISES

9.1:1   Professor Smith asks Professor Jones about a student who has taken many courses with Jones. All Professor Jones says is, "He has very fine penmanship." What inference should Professor Smith make? Why?

9.1:2   Imagine reading each of the following sentences in the newspaper. What do they literally say? What do they mean?
a.   Mary had been benched for bad grades. But after passing biology, she was allowed to rejoin the tea."
b.   For the second time in two days, a New Jersey firefighter suffered a fatal heart attack while fighting a fire.
c.   Mary tried very hard to play tennis without success.
d.   Last week we announced the election of Roger Smith to the Board. This is a mistake that we wish to correct.

9.1:3   A sign says, "No smoking allowed." John, who is smoking, is arrested by a policeman. John protests. "My actions are perfectly in accordance with that sign," he says. Why is John literally right? Why is John being a wise guy?

9.1:4   John asked Mary for a hot cup of coffee. When he picked it up, he burned his hand. When he complained, Mary said, "I gave you just what you asked for." Did she?

Study Vocabulary: **principle of charity**
                                  principle of candor

9.2   SEQUENTIAL STRUCTURES

Whether a statement is a premiss or a conclusion or neither depends on its role in the argument. The very same statement might be a premiss of one argument and the conclusion of another.

Consider, for example, the following argument:

John broke up with Mary because he was angry with her, and he was angry with her because she ate his piece of pizza.

There are two arguments in this passage. We can see this immediately from the two occurrences of *because* in it:

(1)   John broke up with Mary *because* he was angry with her.

(2)   He was angry with her *because* she ate his piece of pizza.

Consider argument (1). The statement

He was angry with her

must be the premiss since it occurs immediately after the *because*, and the statement

John broke up with Mary

must be the conclusion, since it comes before the *because*. In our stylized format, we express the argument as

$$(1) \quad \frac{\text{John was angry with Mary.}}{\text{SO, John broke up with Mary.}}$$

In argument (2), the statement

John was angry with her

is the conclusion, since it comes before the *because*, and the statement

Mary ate John's piece of pizza

is the premiss, since it comes after the *because*. So, in our stylized format we have

$$(2) \quad \frac{\text{Mary ate John's piece of pizza.}}{\text{SO, John was angry with her.}}$$

Note that the statement

John was angry with Mary

is the conclusion of (2) and the premiss of (1).

Although there are two arguments in this passage and, therefore, two conclusions, the two arguments are not unrelated. It is clear that the main point of the passage is to explain why John broke up with Mary. John broke up with Mary. Why? *Because* he was angry with her. And why was John angry with Mary? *Because* she ate his piece of pizza. We might express this very same argument in abbreviated form as

> Mary ate John's piece of pizza, so he got angry with her, so he broke up with her.

This is an example of a **sequential structure**. Had we seen the argument in this form and followed our suggestions for determining premisses and conclusion by using the argument indicators, we would have located the two occurrences of *so*. Can one argument have two conclusions? Clearly not. So, how can there be two occurrences of *so*? The answer is, of course, that there are *two* arguments in this passage. "John was angry with Mary" serves as the conclusion of the first and the premiss of the second.

It will be useful to introduce a slightly different format to capture the structure of this paragraph. We shall use arrows to indicate that an inference has been made. The arrow points to the conclusion, so the premiss will come above the arrow, and the conclusion will come below the arrow:

PREMISS

↓

CONCLUSION

Now we can represent the passage as follows:

(1)   Mary ate John's piece of pizza.
↓
(2)   John got angry with Mary.
↓
(3)   John broke up with Mary.

The argument, then, goes

(1) SO (2) SO (3).

Or, put another way,

> from (1) we infer (2), and
> from (2) we infer (3).

Such a sequence is a very common type of structure. Much of our reasoning moves one step at a time, from statement to statement, either rephrasing the statement or making some logical inference, until we reach our desired conclusion. We have seen such arguments throughout this book.

Here is another example of a sequential structure:

John didn't take his umbrella since he didn't believe it would rain today. So he got soaking wet.

As we scan this argument, we find two argument indicators: *since* and *so*. Let's follow our principles for operating with these indicators. To begin with, the *so* indicates that a conclusion is coming. So, we take the statement "John got soaking wet" to be a conclusion. But, when we look at the first sentence, we find a *since*:

John didn't take his umbrella

> *since*

he didn't believe it would rain today.

Following our rule for *since* "he didn't believe it would rain today" must be the premiss and "John didn't take his umbrella" must be the conclusion. What we have obtained so far is

John didn't believe it would rain today.   ?
      ↓   ↓
John didn't take his umbrella.   John got soaking wet.

The question mark represents the fact that although we have determined that

John got soaking wet

is a conclusion, we don't yet know from what it is inferred. It could not be inferred from the first sentence of the passage, because this sentence is an argument (not a statement), and only statements can be premisses or conclusions. So, what premiss could our conclusion that John got soaking wet have been inferred from?

It was inferred either from the fact that he didn't believe it would rain today or from the fact that he didn't take his umbrella with him. Although both are coherent, it is evident that the latter is the one that captures the author's intentions more cogently. Why would she have bothered to make the point that John didn't take his umbrella with him, if she didn't think that it was relevant to his having gotten soaking wet? It would certainly be odd for the author to think of John's not having taken his umbrella and his having gotten soaking wet as *independent* and *unrelated* conclusions. After all, John's not having taken his umbrella clarifies why he got wet. The second interpretation, then, exhibits a much tighter connection than the first. In accordance with the principle of charity, we put the strongest interpretation on the passage. So, we conclude that the statement "John didn't take his umbrella" is serving as both a premiss and a conclusion, and that we have a sequential structure here.

So, we have two arguments in this passage:

(3) $\dfrac{\text{John didn't believe that it would rain today.}}{\text{SO, John didn't take his umbrella today.}}$

(4) $\dfrac{\text{John didn't take his umbrella today.}}{\text{SO, John got soaking wet.}}$

In our new arrow notation,

(1) John didn't believe that it would rain today.
       ↓
(2) John didn't take his umbrella today.
       ↓
(3) John got soaking wet.

To summarize, one of the structures we will run into very frequently is what we call a sequential structure. It looks like this:

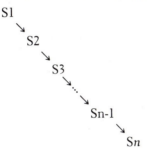

That is, this sequential structure is a sequence of arguments:

$$\frac{S1}{SO,\ S2}$$

$$\frac{S2}{SO,\ S3}$$

$$\frac{S3}{SO,\ S4}$$

$$\vdots$$

$$\frac{Sn\ -\ 1}{SO,\ Sn}$$

EXERCISES

9.2:1   Each of the following is a sequential structure. Set the argument out using our arrow notation.

a.   John insulted Harry, so Harry hit John, so John sued him.

b. Since the air controllers' union had supported Ronald Reagan's candidacy for president, the union believed Reagan, once in power, would support its wage demands; so the air controllers struck, believing they would go unpunished, when the wage demands were not met.

c. The federal government will have to take responsibility for water distribution in the area, for the rivers and streams flow across state boundaries, so no state has legal jurisdiction over the water.

d. Humans can learn from animals: the smartest animals are smarter than the dumbest humans, so some animals are smarter than some humans.

e. The assassination attempt on Reagan helped his presidency: it created a sense of invincibility about the man, therefore making him more powerful.

f. He didn't have a horseshoe nail; so, he couldn't shoe the horse; so, he couldn't ride the horse; so, he couldn't deliver the message; so, the general didn't move the troops; so, the battle was lost; so, the war was lost.

g. Since the new tax proposal prohibits deducting mortgage payments, it will hurt the middle class. So, no tax bill will pass this year.

Study Vocabulary: sequential structure

9.3   DIVERGENT STRUCTURES

Our guiding principle is that an argument can have but one conclusion. If we read a passage and find two conclusions, then we know that we really have two distinct arguments occurring in that passage. We have already examined one way in which this might occur: the passage contains a sequential structure. There is another way in which this might occur: one and the same statement serves as a premiss for two distinct arguments. This is called a **divergent structure**.

Here is an example of a divergent structure:

> John failed mathematics this semester. That means that he won't be allowed to declare a major. It also means that he won't get the new car his parents promised him.

As we scan this passage, we find two occurrences of the indicator *that means that*. We did not include this in our list of argument indicators in Section 8.3, but surely it too serves to help guide us in understanding the direction of the reasoning. *That means that* introduces a conclusion. And the fact that we have two occurrences of this indicator means that we have two conclusions in our passage. (As we mentioned earlier, the presence of two conclusions means that we have two arguments masquerading as one.) One conclusion is

John won't be allowed to declare a major.

The other conclusion is

John won't get the new car his parents promised him.

But what are the premisses that support these conclusions?

The argument indicator *that means that* has the following form:

PREMISS. *That means that* CONCLUSION.

This is explicitly the form of the first two sentences of the passage. So, "John failed mathematics this semester" is a premiss, and one of the arguments in the passage is

John failed mathematics this semester.
SO, John won't be allowed to declare a major.

Or, in our arrow notation

John failed mathematics this semester.
$$\downarrow$$
John won't be allowed to declare a major.

But, we still have our other conclusion:

John won't get the new car his parents promised him.

What is the premiss for this conclusion? Is this a sequential structure? If we followed the literal form in which *that means that* occurs in the third sentence, it might seem reasonable to suppose that the preceding sentence expresses the supporting premiss. This would make it look sequential:

John failed mathematics this semester.

That means that

John won't be allowed to declare a major.

That means that

John won't get the new car his parents promised him.

But this does not seem right. For one thing, on this reading, it appears that the condition for his getting the new car is that he be allowed to declare a major. But the passage doesn't say that his parents promised him a car if he were allowed to declare a major, and it does not seem likely that this would be the condition determining whether he would be getting the car or not. For another thing, the original wording in the passage is "It *also* means that," indicating that his not getting the car, like his not being allowed to declare a major, follows from his having failed mathematics. So, it does not seem plausible to read this passage as a sequential structure. We do not have one statement serving as the conclusion of one argument and the premiss of another. Rather, we have one statement (expressed in the first sentence) that is serving as a premiss for two distinct conclusions. We have already seen the first argument; the second is

John failed mathematics this semester.
_____
SO, John won't get the new car his parents promised him.

Using our arrow notation, we can exhibit the structure of the paragraph as follows:

(1)   John failed mathematics this semester.

(2)   John won't be allowed to declare a major.

(3)   John won't get the new car his parents promised him.

Our two arguments here are

(1)   SO (2) and
(1)   SO (3).

Here is another example of a divergent structure:

The Soviets are still not on good diplomatic terms with the Chinese. The Soviet resolution failed because of the Chinese veto in the Security Council.

We have only one argument indicator in this passage, *because*. This tells us that

The Chinese vetoed the Soviet resolution in the Security Council

is the premiss for the conclusion

The Soviet resolution failed in the Security Council.

So, we have identified one argument in this passage:

The Chinese vetoed the Soviet resolution in the
Security Council.
_____
SO, The Soviet resolution failed in the Security Council.

But this only takes care of the second sentence in the passage. What is the point of the first sentence? On reflection, it should be apparent that the second sentence is intended to back up the claim made in the first sentence. So,

> The Soviets are still not on good diplomatic terms with the Chinese

must also be a conclusion. From what claim is it being inferred? There are two possibilities. Either the evidence for the conclusion is the failure of the Soviet resolution, or the evidence is the vetoing of the Soviet resolution by the Chinese. The second makes the most direct connection, for the failure of the Soviet resolution does not by itself clarify the status of diplomatic relations between the Soviets and the Chinese. Only the premiss that identifies the Chinese as the ones responsible for its failure does that. So, by the principle of charity, we infer that the claim that the Chinese vetoed the resolution is serving as the premiss to support two distinct claims. We have an example of divergent reasoning here. In our arrow notation, it looks like this:

The Chinese vetoed the Soviet resolution in the Security Council.

| The Soviet resolution failed in the Security Council. | The Soviets are still not on good diplomatic terms with the Chinese. |

Here is a more difficult example to work out. The difficulty is in determining whether the reasoning here is sequential or divergent.

> John is going to be late for work because there was an accident on the West Side Highway, so he's taking the East River Drive downtown.

Here, again, we have two conclusions in the argument. One conclusion follows *so*:

> He's taking the East River Drive downtown.

The other conclusion is expressed by the part of the sentence preceding *because*:

> John is going to be late for work.

We have two conclusions. So, we have two questions. First, *why* is John going to be late for work? Second, *why* is he taking the East River Drive downtown? Since we have an argument in which both of these claims are being supported, the passage must contain answers to both of these questions.

The answer to the second question is clear: he's taking the East River Drive downtown because there is an accident on the West Side Highway. One argument, then, is

> There is an accident on the West Side Highway.
> _____
> SO, John is taking the East River Drive downtown.

The answer to the first question is the one that requires us to think. Is he going to be late because there is an accident on the West Side Highway, or is he going to be late because he's taking the East River Drive downtown? Put another way, is this a divergent structure or a sequential structure? If it's divergent, then we must suppose that the two conclusions, that "John is taking the East River Drive downtown" and that "John will be late for work," are arrived at independently from the fact that there is an accident on the West Side Highway. If it's sequential, on the other hand, then there is a connection between the two conclusions: one is also the reason for the other. It is pretty clear in this case that there is a connection between his taking the East River Drive and his being late for work. For the tightest way of understanding this passage is as follows: John is going to be late for work. *Why? Because* he took the East River Drive downtown. *Why? Because* there was an accident on the West Side Highway. So, the structure of the argument is sequential:

(1)   There is an accident on the West Side Highway.
$$\downarrow$$
(2)   John is taking the East River Drive downtown.
$$\downarrow$$
(3)   John will be late for work today.

Let us sum up the results of this section. We know that an argument can have only one conclusion (even though it can have any number of premises). So, when we find a passage with more than one conclusion, we know that embedded in that passage is more than one argument. And, in that case, we will have one of the following situations:

(1)   explicitly distinct arguments for these conclusions,
(2)   a sequential structure, or
(3)   a divergent structure.

When distinct arguments are provided explicitly, we have no problem understanding the paragraph. The only difficulty we have is in distinguishing (2) and (3). We choose (3) when the conclusions are unrelated to each other—that is, when one is not serving as a reason for the other. Otherwise, we choose (2).

EXERCISES

9.3:1   Each of the following passages contains an argument exhibiting a divergent structure. Diagram the argument using our arrow notation.

a.   Richard smokes cigarettes. That means that he is endangering his health. It also means that he is endangering the health of others.

b.   Richard stood on his head because he wanted to impress Marsha. That's also why he volunteered to head the Prom Committee.

c.   The reason John was late was that he had forgotten to put on his raincoat today. That explains why he's called an absentminded professor.

d.   Because he never drank liquor, Harry was awarded a prize by the Women's Christian Temperance Union. He also never had any fun.

9.3:2   Each of the following passages contains an argument exhibiting either a divergent structure or a sequential structure. Diagram the argument using our arrow notation, and explain why you take it one way rather than the other.

a.   Families rarely keep their heirlooms. For a child short of cash will readily sell an heirloom, since his need for money will overwhelm any attachment he has to it.

b.   Taxes will have to go up since Congress will never be able to reduce the enormous budget deficit by cutting programs. Consequently, Congress will lose any standing it has as guardian of the nation's purse.

9.3:3   Consider again the second sample argument presented in this section:

> The Soviets are still not on good diplomatic terms with the Chinese. The Soviet resolution failed because of the Chinese veto in the Security Council.

In the text, we urged that this be understood as a divergent structure. Try now to interpret it as a sequential structure, and explain how you would have to shift your understanding of the passage in order to do so. Which interpretation do you prefer, the sequential or the divergent? Why?

Study Vocabulary: divergent structure

9.4   CONVERGENT AND CONJOINED STRUCTURES

So far, we have been working only with cases in which there is more than one conclusion in a passage. In those cases, as we have seen, there is more than one argument put forward. Now we will examine what happens when there is more than one premiss in the paragraph. When this occurs, we have to decide whether we have one argument or two. When we have *two or more distinct lines of reasoning* leading to a conclusion, then we have a **convergent structure** and two or more arguments. When we have a *single complex line of reasoning* leading to a conclusion, we have a **conjoined structure** and only one argument.

Here is a good example of a convergent structure:

> John took the West Side Highway downtown today. For one thing, Harry passed him at Seventy-ninth Street, and, for another, John himself told me that he took it.

Here you have two distinct reasons supporting the claim that John took the West Side Highway. One reason is that Harry passed him. A completely independent reason is that John himself told us how he got downtown today. Either of these would provide a reason for believing the conclusion that he took the West Side Highway downtown today. So the passage contains two arguments:

(1)
$$\frac{\text{Harry passed John going downtown at Seventy-ninth Street on the West Side Highway today.}}{\text{SO, John took the West Side Highway today.}}$$

(2)
$$\frac{\text{John told me he took the West Side Highway downtown today.}}{\text{SO, John took the West Side Highway today.}}$$

Pictorially, the flow of reasoning in the paragraph looks like this:

(1) Harry passed John going downtown on the West Side Highway today.　　　　(2) John said that he took the West Side Highway today.

(3) John took the West Side Highway today.

That is, the passage reads

(1) SO (3), and
(2) SO (3).

　The overall effect of these two independent lines of reasoning is that we have a relatively strong case for believing that John took the West Side Highway downtown today, for the more independent evidence we have for a given claim, the more strongly it is supported. But what do we mean when we say that the reasons are *independent* of each other? For one thing, we mean that the reasons could stand individually, by themselves, in supporting the conclusion. Even if Harry never passed John on the West Side Highway, we would still have good reason to believe that John took that road on the basis of what John told us. Alternatively, the fact that Harry passed him would stand as evidence without our having to find out from John himself where he had been that day. The reasons don't interact with each other in order to obtain their cogency.

　To understand this concept of independent reasons, it might be helpful to look at a case in which we do not have independent evidence, where instead of independent lines of reasoning, we have a single conjoined line. Consider the following argument:

John likes theater. Harvey likes theater. Steven likes theater. So, all boys like theater.

In this argument, evidence is being piled up to support a generalization. Each statement provides some evidence by itself, but if we were to take them individually, we would have a host of very weak arguments. That is, it seems very odd to suppose that the author is reasoning

John likes theater.
_____

SO, All boys like theater.

Of course, this is an extremely weak argument. Could someone reasonably infer that *all* boys like theater from a single case? And piling up weak arguments only yields a pile of weak arguments. That is, if we take the passage to exhibit a convergent structure like this

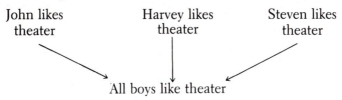

we would only be attributing to the author several bad arguments for the conclusion. On the other hand, if we suppose the premises to be joined together, constituting a complex line of reasoning designed to establish the conclusion, we have a better argument. It is certainly more reasonable to suppose that the author is making the inference that *all* boys like theater only after having come across many cases of boys who like theater. So, when we take all the reasons together, we have a more powerful argument for the claim that *all* boys like theater. We will represent the paragraph in the following way, using the + sign to indicate that the premises are joined together in a complex line of reasoning:

John likes theater. +

Harvey likes theater. +

Steven likes theater.
↓
All boys like theater.

Here is a slightly different case:

John likes theater. Harvey likes theater. Steven likes theater. So, most boys like theater.

Does this passage exhibit a convergent structure, with independent reasons put forward to support the conclusion? Or does it exhibit a conjoined structure? To be sure, if one of the premises is false, the conclusion might still be true. Just because one boy doesn't like theater, that doesn't falsify the claim that *most* boys do, and if all the rest do like theater, that would certainly make the conclusion at least plausible. Nevertheless, the passage does seem to be an example of a single, complex line of reasoning, for if we split up the reasons and treat them as independent arguments, we would again have imputed to the author a host of bad arguments. That is,

John likes theater.
SO, Most boys like theater

is, on the face of it, an extremely weak argument. How could anyone jump to the conclusion that *most* boys like theater from a single case of a boy who likes theater? That would be outrageous. To suppose that the author is putting forward a battery of outrageous arguments would be to put the worst interpretation on the passage. No. In accordance with the principle of charity, we should put the best interpretation on the passage, giving the author the benefit of the doubt. The strongest way of understanding what she is saying is to take the evidence as constituting a single complex line of reasoning for the conclusion. In our arrow notation, then, we structure the argument as follows:

John likes theater. +

Harvey likes theater. +

Steven likes theater.

$\downarrow$

Most boys like theater.

Here is another example:

John likes theater, and if he likes theater he likes dance, so he must like dance.

We have two reasons in this passage:

John likes theater.

If John likes theater, then he likes dance.

Are these independent reasons for the conclusion, or do they constitute a complex line of reasoning? If we were to take them as independent lines of reasoning, then we would have to suppose that the passage contains the following two arguments:

John likes theater.
SO, John likes dance.

and

> If John likes theater, then he likes dance
> _____
> SO, John likes dance.

These arguments are much too weak. If we look at the first argument, we wonder how the author could infer that John likes dance from the fact that he likes theater. We need some *connection* between his liking dance and his liking theater. And, of course, it is the conditional that makes the desired connection. If we look at the second argument, we wonder how the author could infer that John likes dance from the fact that *if* he likes theater, then he likes dance—unless she also believed that John likes theater. Combining the two premisses generates a much stronger argument for the conclusion. The passage has to be conceived of as exhibiting a single complex line of reasoning for the conclusion. In arrow notation,

John likes theater. +

If John likes theater then he likes dance.

$$\downarrow$$

John likes dance.

Whether we have a single complex line of reasoning—that is, a conjoined structure—or two (or more) independent reasons in a passage—that is, a convergent structure—depends upon the relation between the reasons given to support the conclusion. If the reasons, when joined together, generate a stronger case for the conclusion than they would have treated separately, then we impute a conjoined structure to the passage. If, on the other hand, the reasons, when joined together, give you no stronger a case than if they were treated and evaluated separately, then, because a position is stronger when there is independent confirmation of the conclusion, we impute a convergent structure to the passage. Our guiding principle is, of course, the principle of charity.

Just to be clear about the distinction, however, let us look at one more example:

> It is going to rain today because it is very muggy and it hasn't rained in a week.

The *because* tells us that the conclusion of this passage is

> It is going to rain today.

And what follows the *because* are the premisses put forward to support the conclusion:

> It is very muggy.
> It hasn't rained in a week.

Our problem is to determine whether we have a convergent structure

    (1) It is very muggy   (2) It hasn't rained in a week

                         ↘   ↙

            (3) It is going to rain today

or a conjoined structure.

    (1) It is very muggy +
    (2) It hasn't rained in a week
                   ↓
    (3) It is going to rain today.

Which do you think it is? Can the premisses be separated out, or should they be put together?

    Suppose we treated the premisses separately. Consider the argument

$$\frac{\text{It's very muggy.}}{\text{SO, It's going to rain today.}}$$

Would this argument be any stronger if we were to add a second premiss, as follows?

$$\frac{\text{It hasn't rained in a week.}}{\text{It's very muggy.}}$$
$$\overline{\text{SO, It's going to rain today.}}$$

Presumably not. That it hasn't rained in a week does not in any way make the connection between the mugginess and the expectation of rain any tighter. Suppose it had been raining every day this week. Would this make the connection between the mugginess and the rain any weaker? No. So, we conclude that we have two independent lines of reasoning here. The passage exhibits a convergent structure.

EXERCISES

9.4:1   For each of the following passages, indicate whether you think the structure is convergent or conjoined, and explain your reasons.

a.   John paid the rent on time because if he didn't, then he would be evicted, and he certainly didn't want to be evicted.

b.   John didn't pay the rent on time because he wanted his landlord to stew a bit and because he also wanted to use the money to buy a bicycle.

c.   The landlord turned off the heat in the building because he wanted some of the tenants to move out and also because he wanted to save money.

d. Because the patient had a temperature and a sore throat, the doctor guessed that she had a strep throat.

e. Either the Democrats win or the Republicans win. If either one of them wins, taxes will go up. So, it's pretty evident that taxes will go up.

Study Vocabulary: convergent structure
conjoined structure

9.5   MORE COMPLICATED EXAMPLES

We have been dealing in this chapter with relatively simple examples of argument structures; in each passage, we found only one of the structures we have identified. Frequently, however, we find combinations of these structures, especially when we look at longer passages. In this section, we will discuss how to deal with such complex passages.

When faced with a complex passage, the best thing to do is to work with a pencil and mark the text. Begin by looking for argument indicators. These are your signposts, and there is no better way to feel your way around a text than by finding your signposts. Circle the argument indicators. Then, bracket the sentences occurring in the passage, keeping the argument indicators visible, and assign numbers to the individual sentences. Next, using your knowledge of the argument indicators, identify the flow of the argument, using your conclusion(s) as your main guide(s). Then, using the arrow notation, try to re-create the flow of reasoning. If you seem to find independent arguments, try to connect them so that there is a main point in the passage that is the ultimate point being argued for.

Let us practice this technique with a simple example:

I can't go to the movie with you tonight because I have a final examination tomorrow.

First, circle the argument indicator *because*:

I can't go to the movie with you tonight (because) I have a final examination tomorrow.

Second, bracket the individual statements in the passage and assign each a number:

(1)   (2)
[I can't go to the movie with you tonight] (because) [I have a final examination tomorrow].

Third, using your knowledge of the argument indicator *because,* structure the argument, using our arrow notation:

$$(2)$$
$$\downarrow$$
$$(1)$$

Now let's tackle a slightly more complicated example:

Either John or Mary stole the cookies. But Mary has an alibi. Therefore John did it.

First, circle the argument indicators. There is only one in this passage, *therefore:*

Either John or Mary stole the cookies. But Mary has an alibi. (Therefore) John did it.

Second, bracket the premiss(es) and conclusion, and assign a number to each:

(1)   (2)
[Either John or Mary stole the cookies.] [But Mary has an alibi.]
            (3)
(Therefore) [John did it].

Third, determine the structure of the passage. Since *therefore* precedes the conclusion, (3) must be the conclusion and (1) and (2) the premisses. And, since we have two premisses, we need to determine whether the passage contains two arguments in a convergent structure or a single argument in a conjoined structure. Which do you think it is? We suggest that it is conjoined:

$$(1) +$$
$$(2)$$
$$\downarrow$$
$$(3)$$

Now that we understand how to attack a complex passage, let us begin to consider the sorts of circumstances in which complex structures come up. Here's one. Someone might be arguing for a particular point, developing a sequence of reasons that lead to the desired conclusion, but diverging at one point to draw another conclusion, one that is not further developed.

The structure of such a passage would, in broad outline, look like this (where (6) is the main point of the passage):

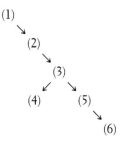

Here is an example of a paragraph having such a structure:

John had no money for school. He was laid off at the factory because the firm lost a big government contract. So he ran downtown first thing in the morning to the employment agency—which is why he missed class yesterday. And because he was there early, he got the job at the supermarket. So he will be able to complete the term.

Let's go through an analysis of this passage and see that it is, essentially, like the structure described above. First, we circle the argument indicators:

John had no money for school. He was laid off at the factory(because) the firm lost a big government contract. (So) he ran downtown first thing in the morning to the employment agency—(which is why) he missed class yesterday. And(because) he was there early, he got the job at the supermarket.(So) he will be able to complete the term.

Next, we bracket the sentences and assign numbers to them:

   (1)   (2)
[John had no money for school.] [He was laid off at the factory]
        (3)   (4)
(because)[the firm lost a big government contract.](So)[he ran down-

town first thing in the morning to the employment agency]—(which
      (5)   (6)
is why)[he missed class yesterday.] And(because)[he was there early],
(7)   (8)
[he got the job at the supermarket].(So)[he will be able to complete

the term].

What do you think the structure of the argument is? We think it looks like this:

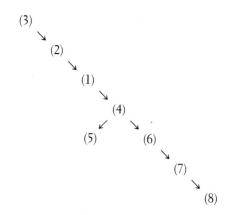

Note that the order of exposition in the passage does not coincide with the order of the reasoning. The author starts off his paragraph with the information that John had no money. But this is not the starting point in the argument, since the author gives us the reason why John had no money in the second sentence. Can you tell why he did this? We think that the author believed that the fact that John had no money was the important point that led to the ensuing events, and so he mentioned it first.

Here is a slightly different type of complex structure we frequently run into. Someone argues for a particular point, and, in the middle, provides an argument for one of the premisses she is using. The passage might look like this:

(6) is the main point of the passage. The author is joining (1), (2), and (5) to get (6). But, since she believes (2) requires support, she suddenly supplies an argument for (2) in the middle of the argument for (6).

The following passage exhibits this type of structure:

> Since anyone over thirty is untrustworthy, and anyone who is untrustworthy is a bad friend, and since Harry is over thirty—because his hair is gray and also because he no longer has to carry a draft card—it follows that Harry is a bad friend.

First, we circle the argument indicators:

> (Since) anyone over thirty is untrustworthy, and anyone who is untrustworthy is a bad friend, and (since) Harry is over thirty—(because)

his hair is gray and also(because) he no longer has to carry a draft card—(it follows that)Harry is a bad friend.

Next, we number the sentences and bracket them:

(1)   (2)
(Since)[anyone over thirty is untrustworthy], and [anyone who is un-
                                             (3)
trustworthy is a bad friend], and(since)[Harry is over thirty]—because
(4)   (5)
[his hair is gray] and also(because)[he no longer has to carry a draft
                                              (6)
card]—(it follows that)[Harry is a bad friend].

The pattern here is slightly different from the one used for illustrative purposes above. What we have is

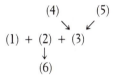

That is, the author is trying to establish (6). She has a tight argument for (6) with premises (1), (2), and (3). However, she believes that (3) needs support, and so, in the middle of her argument, she inserts her reasons for believing (3).

Here is another type of complex structure we run across. Frequently, an essay will have a main point (expressed right at the beginning of the essay, we would hope, so the reader will know what the point of the essay is), which is argued for throughout the essay. The paragraphs will begin with *First*, *Second*, *Third*, and so on, and then *Finally*, each containing a reason (which might then be argued for in the paragraph) supporting the conclusion. In such a case, the whole essay can be structured as follows:

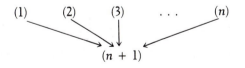

That is, it can take the form of a huge convergent structure for the conclusion $(n + 1)$.

There are, of course, many combinations of these structures. It is impossible to re-create them all. You must recognize that these structures follow the patterns of thought of the author, and to identify the structures, you must try to enter the author's way of thinking.

EXERCISES

9.5:1   For each of the following passages, circle the argument indicators, number the sentences, and exhibit the structure of the argument. If you have any doubts about your choice of structure, explain why you decided to take it one way rather than another.

a. Harry is a math major. He didn't major in physics because he couldn't pass the language requirement. And he didn't major in biology because he couldn't stand the smell of formaldehyde. (It made him sneeze.) And there wasn't anything else he was good at.

b. Because of the influence of the women's movement, not only are women responsible for the home and for the children, but now they must have a career too. So, instead of having one difficult job, they now have two. The women's movement is the worst thing that ever happened to women.

c. There is no need to require on-site inspection in a nuclear test-ban treaty with the Soviets. Since we already have the capabilities in our new spy satellites to discriminate an atomic explosion anywhere on the globe, and since everybody knows that we have these capabilities, the Soviets could never presume that they could test nuclear weapons without our knowledge.

d. Whether or not Mr. Tolstoy and Mr. Gorky manage to form a government in Russia, Americans should have no illusions about the fate of Afghanistan. The hard-line expansionist record of Mr. Tolstoy's faction is known to all, and Mr. Gorky—in a coalition or governing alone— can offer little alternative, for he is sure to find upon assuming office that his policy for the return of the occupied country to its people is bankrupt and impossible to realize.

REVIEW

Frequently, there is more than one argument in a paragraph. However complex the paragraph, the flow of reasoning will be one, or some combination, of the following four types of structures:

  1. *Sequential structure:* statement (1) is put forward as a premiss to support statement (2), and then statement (2), in turn, serves as a premiss to support the conclusion, (3):

2. *Divergent structure:* statement (1) is put forward as a premiss to support two independent conclusions, statements (2) and (3):

3. *Convergent structure:* a conclusion, statement (3), is supported by two independent lines of reasoning, statements (1) and (2):

$$
\begin{array}{ccc}
(1) & & (2) \\
& \searrow \quad \swarrow & \\
& (3) &
\end{array}
$$

4. *Conjoined structure:* two reasons, statements (1) and (2), must be put together to derive the conclusion, statement (3):

$$
\begin{array}{c}
(1) + \\
(2) \\
\downarrow \\
(3)
\end{array}
$$

10

NATURAL DEDUCTION

10.1 NATURAL DEDUCTION

The arrows that we introduced in the last chapter to show the flow of reasoning in a paragraph suggest the image of a path. It is helpful to think of an argument in this way, as leading an individual across the difficult and complex territory of thoughts, one thought at a time. In presenting an argument, one claims to find a path from a starting point (the premisses) to an end point (the conclusion). A good argument, like a good path, helps you get smoothly from one point to the other.

Like a good path, a good argument goes step by step, with no leaps or gaps, so that an individual can easily follow it. The smallest steps in the argument will be those allowed by the elementary valid inference patterns that we isolated in Chapters 1–7 of this text. So, if a person puts forward an argument, then, if it is a valid argument, we should be able to fill in the steps so that each point in the argument will be seen to be one of the following:

(1)   a premiss,
(2)   a tautology (which is true on logical grounds alone),
(3)   a step that follows from previous steps by one or another of our valid inference patterns, or
(4)   a rephrasing (that is, a logically equivalent way of saying the same thing) of an earlier step in the argument.

An argument that has this form is called a **natural deduction**.

Let us first review some of the valid inference patterns that we discussed in the first seven chapters of this textbook. We will group the patterns according to the most important logical connective occurring in them. Note that we use X, Y, and Z in these patterns to stand for any statements (or formulas) whatsoever, however complex they may be.

The Conditional

Modus ponens
$$\frac{\begin{array}{l} X \rightarrow Y \\ X \end{array}}{SO,\ Y}$$

Modus tollens
$$\frac{\begin{array}{l} X \rightarrow Y \\ -Y \end{array}}{SO,\ -X}$$

Chain argument
$$\frac{\begin{array}{l} X \rightarrow Y \\ Y \rightarrow Z \end{array}}{SO,\ X \rightarrow Z}$$

Disjunction

Addition
$$\frac{X}{SO,\ X \vee Y}$$

Disjunctive
syllogism
$$\frac{\begin{array}{l} X \vee Y \\ -X \end{array}}{SO,\ Y}$$

Simple
dilemma
$$\frac{\begin{array}{l} X \vee Y \\ X \rightarrow Z \\ Y \rightarrow Z \end{array}}{SO,\ Z}$$

Complex
dilemma
$$\frac{\begin{array}{l} X \vee Y \\ X \rightarrow Z \\ Y \rightarrow W \end{array}}{SO,\ Z \vee W}$$

Conjunction

Simplification
$$\frac{X \& Y}{SO,\ X}$$

Principle of
conjunction
$$\frac{\begin{array}{l} X \\ Y \end{array}}{SO,\ X \& Y}$$

Exclusion
$$\frac{\begin{array}{l} -(X \& Y) \\ X \end{array}}{SO,\ -Y}$$

Negation

Double negation	$\dfrac{--X}{\text{SO, } X}$ or $\dfrac{X}{\text{SO, } --X}$

Each of these elementary valid inference patterns is simple and for the most part obvious. However, when combined they constitute extraordinarily powerful tools for developing and for evaluating arguments.

The arguments involving the *conditional* are straightforward, and should be intuitively evident by now. **Modus ponens** and **modus tollens** are among the most fundamental inference patterns that we use. **Chain argument** is also a familiar pattern for us. If X is a sufficient condition for Y and Y is a sufficient condition for Z, then X must be a sufficient condition for Z.

The arguments involving *disjunction* are also familiar. **Addition** is simply an application of the truth-table definition of 'v': a disjunction containing a true disjunct must be true. **Disjunction syllogism** also comes directly from the truth tables: if a disjunction is true and one disjunct is false, then the other disjunct must be true. The two **dilemma** arguments have not yet been explicitly introduced, but both forms, **simple** and **complex**, are among our most useful ways of arguing. You can verify that each is valid by using truth tables. But, we can intuitively see that simple dilemma is valid. If one or the other of X and Y is true, and, moreover, if Z is true when either of them is true, then you know that Z must be true.

Consider next the arguments involving *conjunction*. Both **simplification** and **principle of conjunction** come directly from the truth-table definition of '&'. In the case of simplification, if a conjunction is true, then each conjunct is true; in the case of the principle of conjunction, if both conjuncts are true, the conjunction is true. **Exclusion** is a pattern we studied carefully in Chapters 1–7: if X and Y are not both true, and one is true, the other has to be false.

Finally we have **double negation**: idiomatically, two negatives make a positive.

It is helpful also to list some equivalences that we might use in a deduction. The list is not meant to be exhaustive; it is only meant to remind you of some frequently encountered equivalences. If you have doubts about any one of them, check it out on a truth table.

$P \rightarrow Q$	is equivalent to	$-P \vee Q,\ -(P \ \& \ -Q),\ -Q \rightarrow -P$
$P \vee Q$	is equivalent to	$Q \vee P,\ -(-P \ \& \ -Q),\ -P \rightarrow Q$
$P \ \& \ Q$	is equivalent to	$Q \ \& \ P,\ -(-P \vee -Q),\ -(P \rightarrow -Q)$
$(P \ \& \ Q) \rightarrow R$	is equivalent to	$(P \rightarrow Q) \rightarrow R$
$P \ \& \ (Q \vee R)$	is equivalent to	$(P \ \& \ Q) \vee (P \ \& \ R)$
$P \vee (Q \ \& \ R)$	is equivalent to	$(P \vee Q) \ \& \ (P \vee R)$

Often, because these elementary inference patterns are so obvious—which is why they are called elementary—writers don't bother to spell them out. They assume the reader will be able to fill in the steps according to the elementary patterns. Of course, the reader cannot always follow such a fast mover on the turf of thought. Sometimes, moreover, it turns out that the writer is mistaken and there are no legitimate steps to fill the gap in the argument. Trying to fill in the gaps is one of the ways readers can assure themselves that the conclusion the writer intends to support does in fact follow from the premisses.

Each step in a natural deduction proof must be (1) a premiss, or (2) a tautology, or (3) a step that follows from previous steps by one of our valid inference patterns, or (4) a formula that is logically equivalent to an earlier step. The deduction is set up with the step listed on the left, and the justification for that step on the right.

Here is an example of how a deduction is set up. Consider the following argument:

$$P \rightarrow R$$
$$\underline{P \,\&\, Q}$$
$$\text{SO, } R$$

We want to show that the argument is valid—that the conclusion follows from the premisses—by natural deduction. The deduction is set up as follows:

(1)	$P \rightarrow R$	Premiss
(2)	$P \,\&\, Q$	Premiss
(3)	P	Simplification, (2)
(4)	R	Modus ponens, (1), (3)

We begin the deduction by listing the premisses. We then derive step (3) from step (2) by using simplification. Finally, once we have obtained (3), we can use modus ponens on (1) and (3) to derive our conclusion, R. The conclusion of the argument is the last step in the deduction.

Here is another example. Consider the following argument:

$$(P \,\&\, Q) \lor R$$
$$(P \,\&\, Q) \rightarrow S$$
$$\underline{R \rightarrow S}$$
$$\text{SO, } S$$

This is a straightforward instance of simple dilemma. For, we have a disjunction, with each disjunct being sufficient for S, and so S follows. That is, we take $P \,\&\, Q$ to be X, R to be Y, and S to be Z. The deduction looks like this:

(1)	$(P \\& Q) \lor R$	Premiss
(2)	$(P \\& Q) \to S$	Premiss
(3)	$R \to S$	Premiss
(4)	S	Simple dilemma, (1), (2), (3)

(Note that you must become familiar with the ways in which complex formulas can fall into these valid inference patterns.)

   When faced with a difficult deduction, work from the two ends to the middle. Write down the premisses, write down the conclusion, and leave a space in the middle. The strategy is to let the inference patterns be your guide. See which logical connectives occur in the premisses, and use the patterns governing those connectives to give you ideas as to how to proceed.

   Here is an example of this strategy. We want to show that the following argument is valid:

$$P$$
$$P \to Q$$
$$\underline{Q \to -R}$$
$$\text{SO, } -R$$

First, let's set up the deduction by listing the premisses, leaving some space, and then putting down the conclusion:

(1)	P	Premiss
(2)	$P \to Q$	Premiss
(3)	$Q \to -R$	Premiss
(4)	. . . .	
(5)	. . . .	
(6)	$-R$	

We have to fill in the middle steps. We look to the premisses, and we note that we have two conditionals. Clearly, we will have to use the inference patterns governing the conditional. We have modus ponens, modus tollens, and chain argument. Are any of these applicable? Let's try modus ponens. In order to use modus ponens, we must have a conditional on one line and the antecedent of the conditional on another line. Do we have that? Yes. The first two lines of the deduction are of that form. So, we can use modus ponens to deduce Q:

(1)	P	Premiss
(2)	$P \to Q$	Premiss

(3)	$Q \to -R$	Premiss
(4)	Q	Modus ponens, (1), (2)
(5)	. . . .	
(6)	$-R$	

We have already used the first two premisses of the argument, (1) and (2). We could, of course, always use them again, but we should at this point go on to see whether we can use the third premiss. We have Q, and we want now to get $-R$. Is there any line in the deduction that connects up the two? Yes, (3). We can use modus ponens again, this time on (3) and (4), and we now have our deduction:

(1)	P	Premiss
(2)	$P \to Q$	Premiss
(3)	$Q \to -R$	Premiss
(4)	Q	Modus ponens, (1), (2)
(5)	$-R$	Modus ponens, (3), (4)

So, the conclusion follows from the premisses by two applications of modus ponens.

Here is another example.

$$P \to Q$$
$$\underline{-P \to Q}$$
$$\text{SO, } Q$$

We begin by writing down the premisses, leaving a space, and then writing down the conclusion:

(1)	$P \to Q$	Premiss
(2)	$-P \to Q$	Premiss
(3)	. . . .	
(4)	. . . .	
(5)	Q	

The two conditionals should lead us to consider simple dilemma. But we have no line on which we find the disjunction that will enable us to complete the pattern. What is the disjunction that is needed? $P \lor -P$. But this is a tautology, and we can always add a tautology to the deduction. Hence we can fill in all the steps now:

(1)	$P \to Q$	Premiss
(2)	$-P \to Q$	Premiss

(3)	$P \lor -P$	Tautology
(4)	Q	Simple dilemma, (1), (2), (3)

Here is another example. We want to show the following argument to be valid:

$$\frac{-(P \lor Q)}{\text{SO}, \ -P}$$

Let's set up the deduction:

(1)	$-(P \lor Q)$	Premiss
(2)	. . . .	
(3)	. . . .	
(4)	$-P$	

We look to the valid patterns to see how to proceed. But, when we look to the patterns governing disjunction, none gives us any guide. We cannot use addition or disjunctive syllogism, or either of the two dilemmas. What do we do in this case? We try to rephrase the premiss. We try to state it in a different but logically equivalent form, in the hope that, when stated in a different way, we will be able to apply our patterns to it. What's another way of saying $-(P \lor Q)$? $-P \ \& \ -Q$. That's De Morgan's Law. Let's try it:

(1)	$-(P \lor Q)$	Premiss
(2)	$-P \ \& \ -Q$	De Morgan's Law, (1)
(3)	. . . .	
(4)	$-P$	

Does this rephrasing of (1) help us? We now have to look at the patterns governing conjunction to see if we can work on (2). Are any of the patterns applicable? Yes, simplification. If a conjunction is true, each conjunct is true. So, we ought to be able to pull $-P$ out of $-P \ \& \ -Q$. And that completes the deduction:

(1)	$-(P \lor Q)$	Premiss
(2)	$-P \ \& \ -Q$	De Morgan's Law, (1)
(3)	$-P$	Simplification, (2)

So, if you are unable to continue with a deduction, try rephrasing one of the premisses using a logically equivalent formulation. Sometimes saying something in a different way helps to make the connection we need.

One final example. Let us create a deduction for the following argument:

$$-(P \vee Q)$$
$$\underline{R \rightarrow (P \vee Q)}$$
$$\text{SO, } -R \vee -Q$$

First, we set up the deduction:

(1)	$-(P \vee Q)$	Premiss
(2)	$R \rightarrow (P \vee Q)$	Premiss
(3)	. . . .	
(4)	. . . .	
(5)	$-R \vee -Q$	

Let's look at this deduction for a moment. We want to derive a disjunction. Since this disjunction does not appear in any of the premisses, it's quite likely that we shall need to derive this disjunction by using addition or complex dilemma. (Check down the patterns and try to figure out which patterns have disjunctions as conclusions.) Now, let's look at the premisses. We have the negation of a disjunction as one premiss, and a conditional as the other. Which patterns would you check? We suggest the conditional patterns. We can't use chain argument, because we do not have two conditionals to work with. We cannot use modus ponens because, although we have a conditional, we do not have the antecedent on a separate line. How about modus tollens? Yes. We have a conditional, and, on another line, the negation of the consequent. So, from (1) and (2), we can derive $-R$.

(1)	$-(P \vee Q)$	Premiss
(2)	$R \rightarrow (P \vee Q)$	Premiss
(3)	$-R$	Modus tollens, (1), (2)
(4)	. . . .	
(5)	$-R \vee -Q$	

How can we get $-R \vee -Q$ from $-R$? Addition!

(1)	$-(P \vee Q)$	Premiss
(2)	$R \rightarrow (P \vee Q)$	Premiss
(3)	$-R$	Modus tollens, (1), (2)
(4)	$-R \vee -Q$	Addition, (3)

Our deduction is complete.

EXERCISES

10.1:1   Each of the following arguments is an instance of one of the elementary valid patterns we isolated in the text. Identify which pattern it is an instance of, explaining what X, Y, and Z are.

a. $-(P \vee Q) \vee -R$
   $--R$
   SO, $-(P \vee Q)$

b. $-(P \,\&\, Q) \rightarrow R$
   $-R$
   SO, $--(P \,\&\, Q)$

c. $-((P \vee -Q) \,\&\, -R)$
   $P \vee -Q$
   SO, $--R$

d. $P \rightarrow -(Q \,\&\, -R)$
   $-(Q \,\&\, -R) \rightarrow -P$
   SO, $P \rightarrow -P$

e. $-(R \vee Q)$
   $-(P \rightarrow Q)$
   SO, $-(R \vee Q) \,\&\, -(P \rightarrow Q)$

f. $-(P \,\&\, Q) \vee (P \,\&\, -Q)$
   $-(P \,\&\, Q) \rightarrow (-P \rightarrow (P \,\&\, Q))$
   $(P \,\&\, -Q) \rightarrow (-P \rightarrow (P \,\&\, Q))$
   SO, $-P \rightarrow (P \,\&\, Q)$

10.1:2   For each of the following deductions, fill in the justification for each step.

a.   (1) $--(P \,\&\, Q)$ Premiss
   (2) P Premiss
   (3) $-Q$
   (4) $-Q \vee R$

b.   (1) $-Q$ Premiss
   (2) $P \rightarrow Q$ Premiss
   (3) $-P$
   (4) $-P \,\&\, -Q$

c.   (1) $P \rightarrow Q$ Premiss
   (2) $-(P \,\&\, Q)$ Premiss
   (3) P Premiss
   (4) Q

(5) $-Q$
(6) $Q \& -Q$

d. (1) $-P \lor Q$ Premiss
    (2) $Q \to R$ Premiss
    (3) $-P \to S$ Premiss
    (4) $-S$ Premiss
    (5) $R \lor S$
    (6) R

10.1:3 Construct a natural deduction for each of the following arguments.

a. $P \& Q$
    $P \to R$
    _____
    SO, R

b. $-(P \& Q)$
        P
     $R \to Q$
    _____
      SO, R

c. $-(P \lor Q)$
    $-P \to R$
    _____
    SO, $-R$

d. $-P$
    _____
    SO, $-(P \& Q)$

e. $-(P \lor Q)$
    _____
    SO, $-P$

f. $-(P \lor -Q)$
     $Q \to -R$
    _____
    SO, $-R$

g. $P \lor (Q \& R)$
        $P \to S$
        $Q \to S$
    _____
      SO, S

h. $-(P \lor Q)$
     $R \to Q$
    _____
    SO, $-R \lor T$

i. $-P$
    _____
    SO, $P \to Q$

Study Vocabulary: **natural deduction**
                           modus ponens

modus tollens
chain argument
addition
disjunctive syllogism
dilemma
simple dilemma
complex dilemma
simplification
principle of conjunction
exclusion
double negation

10.2   ARGUMENTS IN ENGLISH

Let us turn to some simple examples of combinations of these inference patterns as they occur in English.

There are three steps to follow in working on an English argument. First, we must *structure the argument*, identifying the premisses and the conclusion. Second, we must *symbolize the argument*, replacing atomic statements (statements containing no logical connectives) with atomic letters, and the logical connectives with the symbols '$-$', '$\&$', '$\vee$', '$\rightarrow$'. Third, we must *develop the proof.*

Let us see how this works with the following argument:

If either Harry or Sam calls today, then we got the contract. Harry called today. So, we got the contract.

Step 1: Structure the argument.   It is clear that this argument consists of two conjoined premisses and a conclusion, which is announced by *So:*

> If either Harry or Sam calls today, then we got the contract.
> Harry called.
> ―――――――――――――――――――――――――
> SO, We got the contract.

Step 2: Symbolize the argument.   Replace each atomic statement with a letter, leaving the logical particles visible.

The first premiss is a conditional. The antecedent is

Either Harry or Sam calls today.

The consequent is

We got the contract.

The consequent is an atomic statement: it contains no logical particles. But the antecedent is complex. It is a disjunction:

Either *Harry calls today* or *Sam calls today.*

Each of these disjuncts is atomic. Since the argument contains no other atomic statements, we are now in position to assign letters to the atomic statements:

H: Harry calls today.

S: Sam calls today.

W: We got the contract.

Our argument may be symbolized as follows:

$$(H \vee S) \rightarrow W$$
$$\frac{H}{\text{SO, } W}$$

Step 3: Develop the proof.   We try to figure out how the conclusion, *W*, can be derived from the premisses. When we look to the premisses, we see that *W* is the consequent of the first premiss, $(H \vee S) \rightarrow W$. We immediately think of the patterns governing the conditional, and we remember that modus ponens will allow us to detach the consequent if we have another premiss identical with the antecedent, $H \vee S$. But the only other premiss is *H*. Can we infer $H \vee S$ from *H*? Again, we go back to our patterns, this time to those governing disjunction. Addition allows us to make the inference: if one disjunct is true, then the disjunction must be true.

Now we can fill in all the steps in the argument. We do so as follows. On the left we list the step; on the right we list the justification. As we have said, each step in the argument must be (1) a premiss, (2) a tautology, (3) a step that follows from previous steps by one of our valid inference patterns, or (4) a rephrasing of an earlier step in the argument. The completed proof looks like this:

(1)	$(H \vee S) \rightarrow W$	Premiss
(2)	H	Premiss
(3)	$H \vee S$	Addition, (2)
(4)	W	Modus Ponens, (1), (3)

We can now see explicitly what is going on in the argument. The step that was left out (presumably because it was obvious) is (3): the inference, by addition, from "Harry called" to "Harry or Sam called."

Here's another example.

It's clear that John didn't pass logic, because if he passed logic then he wouldn't have to take both math and reading, and he does.

Let's go over how we analyze this argument, step by step.

Step 1: Structure the argument (identify the premisses and conclusion). The word *because* tells us that the premiss is coming, so the very first sentence must be the conclusion of the argument. We can also see that we have a conjoined structure, the premisses being as follows:

> If he passed logic then he wouldn't have had to take both math and reading.
>
> He does [have to take both math and reading].

The conclusion is

> John didn't pass logic.

Step 2: Symbolize the argument (replace atomic statements with letters). The first premiss is a conditional whose antecedent is

> He passed logic.

This is an atomic statement. The consequent is

> He wouldn't have to take both math and reading,

which is a complex statement. Can you figure out how this complex is built up? We suggest:

> It is not the case both that he has to take math and that he has to take reading.

Since there are no other atomic statements in the argument, we may proceed to assign letters to each statement:

> L: He passed logic.
> M: He has to take math.
> R: He has to take reading.

Symbolized, the argument is

$$L \rightarrow -(M \ \& \ R)$$
$$\frac{M \ \& \ R}{\text{SO, } -L}$$

Step 3: Develop the proof. Our conclusion is $-L$. How do we get this from the premisses? We find L is the antecedent of the conditional on top. We check our elementary inference patterns for the conditional. Since we are deriving the negation of the antecedent, we immediately think of modus tollens. But, to use modus tollens, we need the negation of the consequent, which would be $--(M \ \& \ R)$. How can we get this? By double-negating the second premiss.

Now we have re-created the reasoning, filling in all the steps along the way so that there are no gaps:

(1)	$L \to -(M \ \& \ R)$	Premiss
(2)	$M \ \& \ R$	Premiss
(3)	$--(M \ \& \ R)$	Double negation, (2)
(4)	$-L$	Modus tollens, (1), (3)

In this way, we have shown how the author is logically able to get from his premisses—his starting point—to his conclusion—his end point.

One final example. Consider the following argument:

Taxes will go up. For, either the Republicans will get in or the Democrats will get in, and whoever gets in, taxes will go up.

The conclusion in this case is "Taxes will go up." The tip-off is the argument indicator *for*. The premisses are conjoined to draw the conclusion. This completes step 1. What are our atomic statements? We suggest:

T: Taxes will go up.
R: The Republicans will get in.
D: The Democrats will get in.

Then, the first premiss is

$$R \vee D.$$

But what about the second premiss,

Whoever gets in, taxes will go up.

What's being claimed (in the context of this argument) is that taxes will go up if the Democrats get in; also, that taxes will go up if the Republicans get in. That is,

$$D \to T$$
$$R \to T$$

So, the whole argument looks like this:

$$R \vee D$$
$$D \to T$$
$$\underline{R \to T}$$
$$\text{SO, } T$$

This completes step 2. For step 3, we recognize this to be an instance of simple dilemma. That is,

(1)	$R \lor D$	Premiss
(2)	$D \rightarrow T$	Premiss
(3)	$R \rightarrow T$	Premiss
(4)	T	Simple dilemma, (1), (2), (3)

EXERCISES

10.2:1   For each of the elementary inference patterns listed in this section, construct an argument in everyday English that exhibits the pattern.

10.2:2   Symbolize each of the following arguments and identify which of the elementary patterns listed in this section is exemplified.

a.   Mary will come to the party if Sally comes to the party. And Sally will come to the party if Nancy stays home. So, Mary will come to the party if Nancy stays home.

b.   Mary speaks either French or German. But, she doesn't speak German, so she must speak French.

c.   Mary would have taken conversational French if she had taken French literature. So, since she didn't take conversational French, she didn't take French literature.

d.   If Mary gave the tenant a new refrigerator, then she was going to raise the rent. She gave the tenant a new refrigerator. So, she was going to raise the rent.

e.   Sam didn't get both a new refrigerator and a new stove from his landlord. But he did get a new stove. So, he didn't get a new refrigerator.

10.2:3   Symbolize each of the following arguments and set up the argument as a natural deduction.

a.   The landlord was going to raise Harry's rent if he gave him either a new stove or a new refrigerator. The landlord gave Harry a new stove. So, the landlord was going to raise Harry's rent.

b.   Mary will come to the party if Sally comes to the party. And Sally will come to the party if Nancy stays home. Nancy will definitely stay home. So, Mary will come to the party.

c.   If John didn't take French then he didn't take German. But he took German. So, he took French.

d.   If either Harry or Sam comes to the party, then both Nancy and Sally will walk out. Harry came to the party. So, Sally walked out.

10.3   A WORKED-OUT EXAMPLE

Here is a very complex example. We will work through it slowly:

> Since doing well in mathematics is a necessary condition for getting into medical school, and Sally wants to be a doctor, she should finish her language requirement this summer. If she doesn't, then she won't have enough time next year to study mathematics, and if she doesn't have enough time next year to study mathematics, then she won't do well in it.

Here's how the marked text looks:

> (1)
> Since [doing well in mathematics is a necessary condition for getting
>   (2)   (3)
> into medical school], and [Sally wants to be a doctor], [she should
>   (4)
> finish her language requirement this summer]. [If she doesn't, then
>
> she won't have enough time next year to study mathematics], and
> (5)
> [if she doesn't have enough time next year to study mathematics, then
>
> she won't do well in it].

There is only one argument indicator here, *since*. The first sentence has the form

Since PREMISS and PREMISS, CONCLUSION.

In our arrow notation, the structure of the first sentence looks like this:

(1)   Doing well in mathematics is a necessary condition for getting into medical school. +

(2)   Sally wants to study medicine.
                                       ↓
(3)   Sally should finish her language requirement this summer.

The second sentence in the passage conjoins two statements; although there is no explicit indication whether either is a premiss or a conclusion, it is quite likely that they are conjoined premisses. In our arrow notation:

(4)   If she doesn't finish her language requirement this summer, then she won't have enough time next year to study mathematics.

                                       +

(5)   If she doesn't have enough time next year to study mathematics, then she won't do well in [mathematics].

We can therefore picture the argument, as we have analyzed it so far, like this:

$$(1) + (2) \qquad\qquad (4) + (5)$$
$$\downarrow$$
$$(3)$$

Now, we have to put these two parts together so that there is one main point in the paragraph that the author is arguing for.

The main point of this passage appears to be (3), that Sally will be better off if she takes her language requirement this summer. For, the argument appears designed to help Sally determine how she should structure her program, and especially, when she should take care of her language requirement.

Let us adopt the following abbreviations:

S: Sally finishes language requirement this summer.
T: Sally will have enough time next year to study mathematics.
D: Sally will do well in mathematics.
M: Sally gets into medical school.

Then,

(1) {Doing well in mathematics} is a necessary condition for {getting into medical school}

will be symbolized as the conditional

$$M \rightarrow D.$$

And

(2) Sally wants to study medicine

will be symbolized simply as

$$M$$

because, to suppose that she wants to get into medical school is to suppose that she wants M to be true. And, finally,

(3) Sally should finish her language requirement this summer

will be symbolized as

$$S.$$

The argument here, then, is

$$M \rightarrow D$$
$$\frac{M}{\text{SO, } S}$$

Now, this argument is not, as it stands, valid. There is no way to derive the conclusion from these two premises. And it is highly unlikely that the person putting forward the argument supposes that the conclusion follows from these two premises alone. Clearly, some other premises must be provided, and that is quite likely the role of (4) and (5). So, we will proceed on the assumption—unless it turns out to lead us astray—that these two additional premises are to support the conclusion by being conjoined with the premises already identified. (Note that we sometimes need to figure out what the inference is in order to re-create the structure of an argument.) And, the picture of the argument is this:

$$(1) + (2) \quad + \quad (4) + (5)$$
$$\downarrow$$
$$(3)$$

Let us continue, then, with the symbolization. We will take

(4) [{*If* she doesn't take her language requirement this summer}, *then* {she won't have enough time next year to study mathematics}]

to be

$$-S \rightarrow -T$$

and

(5) If {she doesn't have time next year to study mathematics}, then {she won't do well in [mathematics]}

to be

$$-T \rightarrow -D$$

The full argument now looks like this:

$$-S \rightarrow -T$$
$$-T \rightarrow -D$$
$$M \rightarrow D$$
$$\frac{M}{\text{SO, } S}$$

Let us now try to fill in all the steps in a deduction. First, let's set up the deduction, listing the premisses, leaving space, and, finally, listing the conclusion:

(1)	$-S \rightarrow -T$	Premiss
(2)	$-T \rightarrow -D$	Premiss
(3)	$M \rightarrow D$	Premiss
(4)	M	Premiss
(5)	. . . .	
(6)	. . . .	
(7)	S	

Let us make a mental note, as we look over the argument, that we want to derive S, and that the only place S occurs is in the first premiss. Since we find $-S$ there as the antecedent of a conditional, and we want to pull out S, it's quite likely that at some point in the derivation we will have to apply modus tollens. Having noted this, let's try to fill in the middle. We have a number of conditionals to start with, so we look to the conditional patterns. Chain argument appears applicable to (1) and (2):

(1)	$-S \rightarrow -T$	Premiss
(2)	$-T \rightarrow -D$	Premiss
(3)	$M \rightarrow D$	Premiss
(4)	M	Premiss
(5)	$-S \rightarrow -D$	Chain argument, (1), (2)
(6)	. . . .	
(7)	S	

Modus ponens will now allow us to derive D from (3) and (4):

(1)	$-S \rightarrow -T$	Premiss
(2)	$-T \rightarrow -D$	Premiss
(3)	$M \rightarrow D$	Premiss
(4)	M	Premiss
(5)	$-S \rightarrow -D$	Chain argument, (1), (2)
(6)	D	Modus ponens, (3), (4)
(7)	S	

Now that we have derived (5) and (6), do you see any way to get S from them? Remember the fact we noted when we first looked at the argument. We cannot use modus tollens directly here, because we don't have $--D$. But that's easily obtained from (6). The deduction now falls into place:

(1)	$-S \rightarrow -T$	Premiss
(2)	$-T \rightarrow -D$	Premiss
(3)	$M \rightarrow D$	Premiss
(4)	M	Premiss
(5)	$-S \rightarrow -D$	Chain argument, (1), (2)
(6)	D	Modus ponens, (3), (4)
(7)	$--D$	Double negation, (6)
(8)	$--S$	Modus tollens, (5), (7)
(9)	S	Double negation, (8)

EXERCISES

10.3:1   Work out each of the following arguments as we did in the example this section.

a. John must have taken German in college, for if he didn't, he had to have taken French. But he didn't take French, since if he had, he would never have taken Spanish; and we know he took Spanish.

b. Harry is always complaining. If it rains, he's unhappy, and if it doesn't rain, he's unhappy. Moreover, whenever he's unhappy, he complains.

c. Mary and John don't both have to watch the store. If the school is closed on Lincoln's birthday—as it always is—then John will watch the store. That means that Mary will be able to take the day off.

d. John had no money for school. He was laid off at the factory because the firm lost a big government contract. So he ran downtown first thing in the morning to the employment agency—which is why he missed class yesterday. And because he was there early, he got the job at the supermarket. So he will be able to complete the term. (Hint: Treat each *so* as an *if, then*.)

e. Since anyone over thirty is untrustworthy, and anyone who is untrustworthy is a bad friend, and since Harry is over thirty—because his hair is gray and also because he no longer has to carry a draft card—it follows that Harry is a bad friend.

f. Whether or not Mr. Tolstoy and Mr. Gorky manage to form a government in Russia, Americans should have no illusions about the fate of Afghanistan. The hard-line expansionist record of Mr. Tolstoy's faction is known to all, and Mr. Gorky—in a coalition or governing alone— can offer little alternative, for he is sure to find upon assuming office that his policy for the return of the occupied country to its people is bankrupt and impossible to realize.

REVIEW

The object of a natural deduction is to identify all the steps in the argument, leaving no gaps. So, each step in a natural deduction is a premiss, a tautology, a rephrasing of a previous step, or an elementary inference from previous steps. The list of elementary inference patterns and logical equivalences is given in Section 10.1.

11

ARGUMENT ANALYSIS

11.1 EVALUATING ARGUMENTS

In evaluating arguments, there are three distinct considerations:

(1)   Is the argument **valid**?
(2)   Is the argument **sound**?
(3)   Is the argument **useful**?

Good arguments must pass all three tests. If an argument fails any one of them, it is unsatisfactory. To this point in the text, we have focused primarily on validity. In this chapter, we will turn to the other two criteria.

Validity.   If an argument is valid, the premisses imply the conclusion. It is impossible to get all of the premisses true and the conclusion false. If, on the other hand, an argument is invalid, the premisses do not imply the conclusion. It is possible to get all of the premisses true and the conclusion false.

When we are concerned with the validity of an argument, we are not interested in whether the premisses are actually true (or whether we actually believe them). We are interested only in determining the logical consequences of the premisses—what would have to be true if the premisses are true. So, valid arguments may have false premisses, and valid arguments may have a false conclusion. To accept the validity of an argument is to commit oneself only to the claim that the conclusion *follows from* the premisses. False claims have consequences, just as well as true claims.

The following is a valid argument:

> Jack Kennedy was a Republican.
> If Jack Kennedy was a Republican, then Richard Nixon was a Democrat.
> _____
> SO, Richard Nixon was a Democrat.

This is an instance of modus ponens. The conclusion is, as a matter of fact, false; so is one of the premisses. But the argument is valid; *if* the premisses *were* both true, the conclusion would *have to be* true.

A valid argument can have true premisses and a true conclusion; it can have false premisses and a true conclusion; it can have false premisses and a false conclusion. The only case ruled out by validity is this: true premisses and a false conclusion.

An invalid argument, on the other hand, can have every combination of truth values for premisses and conclusion. Here is an example of an invalid argument with a true premiss and a true conclusion:

> Jack Kennedy was not a resident of both Michigan and Ohio.
> _____
> SO, Jack Kennedy was not a resident of Michigan.

The premiss is true, and so is the conclusion. But the argument is not valid. From the fact that Jack Kennedy was not a resident of both of those states, it does not follow that he was not a resident of Michigan. To be sure, Jack Kennedy was not a resident of Michigan. We have no quarrel with the truth of the claim. We quarrel with the reason put forward to support it: it doesn't. If someone challenged you to produce evidence to support the claim that he was not a resident of Michigan, you wouldn't say that he wasn't a resident of both of those states. And you wouldn't give that as your reason, because it is insufficient evidence.

The argument has the form

$$-(P \ \& \ Q)$$
$$\text{SO, } -P,$$

where P abbreviates "Jack Kennedy was a resident of Michigan" and Q abbreviates "Jack Kennedy was a resident of Ohio." And you can easily check on the truth table that it is possible to get the premiss true and conclusion false. When stated abstractly, with Ps and Qs instead of actual statements, you have no difficulty seeing that the argument is invalid.

To determine validity, not only do we ignore the actual truth values of the statements making up the argument, we are not even interested in what the statements mean. The following argument is valid:

> Geometry is undecidable.
> If geometry is undecidable then there is no computer program to
> decide whether a geometric statement is a theorem.
> ___
> SO, there is no computer program to decide whether a geometric
> statement is a theorem.

You know that the conclusion follows from the premisses, because the argument is an instance of modus ponens. It is hardly likely that you know whether the premisses are true; it is hardly likely that you know whether the conclusion is true. Indeed, it is hardly likely that you even *understand* the premisses or conclusion. But even so, you can determine with certainty that the argument is valid.

By the same token, you know the following argument is invalid:

> There is no computer program to decide whether a geometric
> statement is a theorem.
> If geometry is undecidable then there is no computer program to
> decide whether a geometric statement is a theorem.
> ___
> SO, Geometry is undecidable.

You don't know whether the premisses are true or false; you don't even understand what the argument is all about. But you know it is invalid because it has the form of the fallacy of affirming the consequent.

Using symbols, then, forces us to look solely at the form of the argument, which is what its validity depends upon. All the information for deriving the conclusion from the premisses is provided right up front. Because we're looking at symbols, our knowledge of the subject matter cannot fool us into importing information into the argument that is not explicitly stated. Indeed, using symbols helps us to uncover unstated assumptions in an argument, as we will come to see later in this chapter.

Soundness.   Validity assures us that if an argument is valid *and* the premisses are all true, then the conclusion must be true. (By the same token, validity also assures us that if the conclusion is false, then at least one premiss must be false.) An argument based on false premisses, even if its conclusion follows from those premisses, does not assure us of the truth of the conclusion. Since in everyday life we are interested in the truth of the conclusion, we need to consider not merely the validity of an argument but its soundness as well:

An argument is sound if it is valid and all its premisses are true.

Much of what constitutes argument analysis in everyday life turns on considering the truth of the premisses. There are, for example, many valid arguments for the existence of God. Here's one:

> Either Washington, D.C., is the capital of the United States or God exists.
> Washington, D.C., is not the capital of the United States.
> _____
> SO, God exists.

This argument has the form of a disjunctive syllogism. It is valid. But it is not sound. To be sure, *if* the premisses were all true, the conclusion would have to be true. But the premisses are not all true: the second premiss is false. So, even though the argument is valid, since one of the premisses is clearly false, the argument gives us no assurance that the conclusion is true—it might be or it might not be. An unsound argument provides no good reason for believing either that its conclusion is true or that it is false.

Usefulness.   Even if an argument is valid and all of its premisses are true, the argument might still not be a good one. For, the persons participating in the argument might not accept the truth of the premisses.

We have already seen that validity only assures that the conclusion follows from the premisses. If the premisses were true, the conclusion would have to be true. But to the extent that someone has doubts about the truth of even one premiss, that person will equally doubt the truth of the conclusion. The confidence one has in the conclusion of an argument cannot be any stronger than the confidence one has in the weakest premiss of that argument.

The most blatant example of an argument that exhibits a lack of usefulness is one that **begs the question**. Consider the following example:

$$\frac{E = MC^2}{SO, E = MC^2}$$

This argument is trivially valid: if the premiss is true, then the conclusion must be true as well. Moreover, the premiss is true; so, the conclusion is also true. Nevertheless, from a practical point of view, the argument is unsatisfactory. There is a perfectly good everyday sense in which one can say that *no* reason has been given for the conclusion. It's like answering a *why* with a *because*:

Harry: Why does $E = MC^2$?
Sam: Because it does.

What's wrong here, of course, is that the argument assumes the very point it sets out to prove: it begs the question. Anyone who doubts the premiss will equally doubt the conclusion. Conversely, anyone who doubts the conclusion will equally doubt the premiss.

Here is a more complicated example of an argument that begs the question:

> God exists because the Bible tells us so. And we know that what the Bible tells us is true because it is the revealed word of God.

This is an argument for God's existence. The flow of the reasoning looks like this:

The Bible is the revealed word of God.
$$\downarrow$$
Whatever the Bible says is true. + The Bible says God exists.
$$\downarrow$$
God exists.

But, clearly, anyone who has doubts about the conclusion would be equally troubled about the claim that the Bible is the revealed word of God. For how could it be the revealed word of God unless God exists? This is a good example of what people have called **circular argument**. It begs the question, although not explicitly. God exists. Why? Because the Bible says so. But why should I believe the Bible? Because everything it says is true. But what makes the Bible so different from other books? How come it contains no errors? Because the Bible is the revealed word of God. Aha! That assumes God exists, and that was the point one wondered about at the beginning.

For an argument to be useful, it must start with premises that the participants in the argument will *accept* as true. An argument that begs the question obviously is not useful. But, that is the most blatant case. Here is a more subtle example of an argument that is not useful. Again, we have a valid argument for God's existence:

> The United States of America is the most powerful country in the world.
> If the United States of America is the most powerful country in the world, then God exists.
> _____
> SO, God exists.

This is a modus ponens argument. It is therefore valid. But does the argument establish its conclusion? Do you now, as a result of this argument, believe that God exists? It's hardly likely. For, although you might be willing to grant that the first premise is true, you will, no doubt, hesitate about the second. To the extent that you find the second premise doubtful, you will not be willing to accept the conclusion. So, although it is a valid argument, it is not particularly useful unless one can allay doubts about that second premiss.

In sum, then, when faced with the problem of evaluating an argument, we ask,

First: Is it valid?

If the answer to this question is "Yes," we then ask,

Second: Is it sound?

If the answer to this question is "Yes," we then ask,

Third: Is the argument useful?

If the answer to all three questions is "Yes," the argument is a good one. That is, an argument is a good one if it (1) is valid, (2) employs true premisses, and (3) employs premisses that are accepted by the participants in the argument.

EXERCISES

11.1:1   Which of the following are true?

a.   Valid arguments may have false premisses.
b.   Valid arguments may have false conclusions.
c.   Invalid arguments may have true conclusions.
d.   Invalid arguments must have false conclusions.
e.   Invalid arguments with true premisses must have a false conclusion.
f.   Sound arguments may not be useful.
g.   Any statement follows from inconsistent premisses.
h.   Every argument with inconsistent premisses is valid.
i.   Every argument with inconsistent premisses is unsound.
j.   A valid argument with a false conclusion must have at least one false premiss.
k.   An unsound argument must have a false conclusion.
l.   Arguments that beg the question are unsound.
m.   Arguments that beg the question may be valid.

11.1:2   Construct a valid argument for a position with which you disagree.

11.1:3   Construct an invalid argument for a position with which you disagree.

11.1:4   Construct a sound argument for a position with which you agree.

11.1:5   Construct an unsound argument for a position with which you agree.

11.1:6   Can you construct a sound argument for a position with which you disagree? Explain your answer.

11.1:7   In each of the following passages, indicate whether Harry is attacking the validity or the soundness of the argument.

a.   Sam: Sally didn't take both French and German in high school, and she took French, so she couldn't have taken German.

   Harry: What do you mean she didn't take both French and German in high school?

b.   Sam: Sally didn't take both French and German in high school, and she took French, so she couldn't have taken German.

   Harry: She never took French!

c.   Sam: Sally didn't take both French and German in high school, and she didn't take French, so she must have taken German.

   Harry: She did so take French.

d.   Sam: Sally didn't take both French and German in high school, and she didn't take French, so she must have taken German.

   Harry: She might have taken neither.

e.   Sam: If John didn't take French in high school, then he didn't take German. He took German, however, so he must have taken French.

   Harry: Taking German has nothing to do with taking French.

Study Vocabulary: valid
                      sound
                      useful
                      begging the question
                      circular argument

11.2   ENTHYMEMES

An **enthymeme** is an argument in which the author leaves out a premiss needed to derive the conclusion. (An argument in which the author fails to mention the conclusion is also considered enthymematic.) The premiss omitted is called a *suppressed premiss*. In this section, we will explore enthymematic arguments.

Here is a simple example of an enthymeme:

John left at 2:00 P.M. So, he got there on time.

The structure of the argument is obvious:

John left at 2:00 P.M.
$$\downarrow$$
He got there on time.

Let us now symbolize it. Since premiss and conclusion are both atomic, we need only assign letters:

    L: John left at 2:00 P.M.
    G: He got there on time.

Our argument, then, looks like this:

$$L$$
$$SO, G$$

Now, let's develop the proof. But here we are stopped. There is no elementary valid argument pattern that allows us to derive *G* from *L*. Nor is *G* logically equivalent to *L*. So, as it stands, the argument is invalid.

Should we reject the argument? No. In this case, it seems fair to suppose that the author is assuming something he is not stating in the argument, something that he believes enables him to infer *G* from *L*. What do you think he is assuming? What would be the simplest and most obvious premiss that would get him *G* from *L*? Most likely,

If John left at 2:00 P.M., then he got there on time.

This connects up premiss and conclusion immediately, and we impute to the author the most obvious inference pattern, modus ponens:

$$L \rightarrow G$$
$$L$$
$$SO, G$$

When we find that an argument is formally invalid, we have a choice of ways to proceed. One alternative is to reject the argument. Since the premisses do not support the conclusion, we may decide that we have not been given a good reason to believe the conclusion. On the other hand, we may look to see whether the argument can be repaired. Perhaps, as in the present case, the argument is invalid not because the reasoning is wrong, but rather because a premiss has not been explicitly stated. (In this respect, reasoning is no different from any other activity. When a course of action is not working, one must choose whether to drop it or to try to modify it. When a car gets old and needs repairs, one must decide whether to junk it or to try to repair it. There are many delicate considerations that go into such a choice).

Sometimes the missing premiss is one that you'll accept, and sometimes it will be one that you doubt. Supplying the missing premiss does not commit you to accepting its truth. Nevertheless, being able to recognize and supply missing premisses often enables us to uncover assumptions an author is making—assumptions she might or might not be aware she is making. Indeed, sometimes, having had the missing assumption pointed out to her, she will be led to retract her argument, acknowledging that the missing premiss is false or, at least, doubtful.

Repairing an argument means identifying the suppressed premiss. How do we determine what the suppressed premiss is? We choose a premiss having the least information needed to make the argument valid in accordance with one of the elementary valid argument patterns we identified in Chapter 10. The principle of charity tells us to try to make it a premiss that the author most likely believes, one that is consistent with the rest of his view.

With this in mind, let's consider another example:

If it's hot, John is uncomfortable, and if it's cold, John is uncomfortable. So, John is uncomfortable.

Step 1.   We need to structure the argument. The word *So* tells us that "John is uncomfortable" is our conclusion. The preceding sentence must therefore express the premiss.

Step 2.   We now symbolize the argument. The conclusion is atomic, but the premiss is a conjunction of two conditionals:

If it's hot, John is uncomfortable.

If it's cold, John is uncomfortable.

Our atomic statements, then, with the symbols we will replace them with, are:

H: It's hot.

C: It's cold.

U: John is uncomfortable.

The argument may be symbolized as follows:

$$\frac{(H \rightarrow U) \,\&\, (C \rightarrow U)}{SO,\ U}$$

Step 3. We now move on to develop the proof. We start the proof by listing our first step as the premiss and our last step as the conclusion:

(1)	$(H \rightarrow U) \,\&\, (C \rightarrow U)$	Premiss
$\vdots$		
(n)	U	???????

How can we get from the premiss to the conclusion? What inference patterns can we draw on? Since our premiss is a conjunction, we look to our conjunction patterns and alight on simplification. This allows us to make a beginning:

(1)	$(H \rightarrow U) \,\&\, (C \rightarrow U)$	Premiss
(2)	$H \rightarrow U$	Simplification, (1)
(3)	$C \rightarrow U$	Simplification, (2)
$\vdots$		
(n)	U	???????

But now we are stopped: there is nothing more we can do using our elementary inference patterns. The argument is apparently invalid as it stands. (Work it out on the truth table and you will see that it is possible to get the premisses true and the conclusion false.)

Step 4. Consider whether the argument can be repaired. The conclusion must somehow be obtained from the conditionals, (2) and (3). So, the author is most likely using one of the conditional patterns to do this. Could it be modus tollens? This is unlikely because there are no negations in the argument. Could it be chain argument? This too seems unlikely, because the two conditionals do not follow that pattern.

How about modus ponens? This might work. For, if we suppose the author had been assuming H, then U would follow from (2) by modus ponens. Then the argument would be formally valid:

	(1)	$(H \rightarrow U) \,\&\, (C \rightarrow U)$	Premiss
	(2)	$H \rightarrow U$	Simplification, (1)
	(3)	$C \rightarrow U$	Simplification, (2)
$\Rightarrow$	(4)	H	Assumption $\Leftarrow$
	(5)	U	Modus Ponens, (2), (4)

Is this the proper reconstruction of the argument? To be sure, the argument is now formally valid. Nevertheless, it does not appear to do justice to the argument, since, in our reconstruction, (3) is never used. Remember, the original premiss was

> If it's hot, John is uncomfortable, and if it's cold, John is uncomfortable.

Why would our author have distinguished two cases, the case when it's hot and the case when it's cold, if he were using only one of them in the argument? The principle of charity leads us to suppose that both cases are relevant.

Perhaps, then, two assumptions were made: the author assumed H, but he also assumed C. This would certainly make the argument valid:

	(1)	$(H \rightarrow U) \,\&\, (C \rightarrow U)$	Premiss	
	(2)	$H \rightarrow U$	Simplification, (1)	
	(3)	$C \rightarrow U$	Simplification, (2)	
$\Rightarrow$	(4)	H	Assumption	$\Leftarrow$
$\Rightarrow$	(5)	C	Assumption	$\Leftarrow$
	(6)	U	Modus Ponens, (2), (4)	

But this reconstruction also leaves something to be desired. For one thing, although we add on the second assumption, (5), it is never used to derive (6). But, even more important, we are imputing to the author two inconsistent assumptions: that it's hot and also that it's cold. Surely he is not making such a blatant error.

Modus ponens, then, does not seem to be a likely candidate. This leaves only simple dilemma. For the argument to be a simple dilemma, we must suppose that the author is assuming $H \lor C$: either it's hot or it's cold. The argument would then look like this:

	(1)	$(H \rightarrow U) \,\&\, (C \rightarrow U)$	Premiss	
	(2)	$H \rightarrow U$	Simpification, (1)	
	(3)	$C \rightarrow U$	Simplification, (2)	
$\Rightarrow$	(4)	$H \lor C$	Assumption	$\Leftarrow$
	(5)	U	Simple Dilemma, (2), (3), (4)	

This seems to be right. The pattern of reasoning is straightforward, and the assumption imputed to the author seems to be the minimal one that allows him to get his conclusion without our supposing that he is using unnecessary or inconsistent premises.

Of course, we are not committed to the truth of the suppressed premiss. Far from it. Recall our discussion back in Chapter 2: *hot* and *cold* are contraries; they do not exhaust all the possibilities. So, the premiss exhibits the mistake people frequently fall into of confusing contraries with contradictories. But we attribute this premiss to the author because, within the context of the argument, it is the minimal premiss needed to get the conclusion.

Filling in the unstated premiss brings to view just the questionable assumption the author is making. We can now understand precisely what our author is thinking. We have all of his reasons right in front of us so that we can inspect them. We are in a good position to consider the truth of each of the premises and evaluate the soundness of the argument.

It is in analyzing enthymemes that you can understand most clearly the virtues of our using abstract symbols and our emphasizing formal validity. We can use logic to fill in all the premisses, all the assumptions the author is relying on, so that they are right in front for us to see. Insisting on formal validity give us a means by which we can identify the unstated assumptions.

EXERCISES

11.2:1   Each of the following is an enthymeme. Identify in each the premiss that is assumed but not explicitly stated.

a.   She is an accountant. So she must make a lot of money.

b.   John didn't say hello to me today, so he must be angry at me.

c.   The milkman isn't a man. So the milkman must be a woman.

d.   If it rains, the party will be canceled, so we won't have any fun if it rains.

e.   Harry won't pass French because he won't pass both French and mathematics.

11.2:2   Each of the following is an enthymeme. Symbolize the argument and identify the premiss that is assumed but not explicitly stated.

a.   Death is nothing terrible, else it would have appeared so to Socrates.

b.   Any beings of advanced intelligence on another planet should be able to do mathematics. Therefore, we can communicate with them by a number code.

c.   A politician running for office always needs campaign funds, and anyone needing campaign funds will be responsive to special-interest groups. [Hint: the conclusion is not stated in this argument.]

d.   At this writing, the legal propriety of Harrison's book is before the courts and is accordingly not an appropriate subject for discussion.

11.2:3   Many of the arguments we discussed in Chapter 9 are enthymemes. For each of the following exercises, identify the logical structure of the argument and fill in any suppressed premisses.

   9.2:1 (c), (e)
   9.3:1 (a), (b), (c)
   9.4:1 (b), (c), (d)

Study Vocabulary: **enthymeme**

11.3   IDENTIFYING INVALID INFERENCE PATTERNS

It is as important for us to recognize invalid inference patterns as it is for us to recognize the valid ones. People frequently reason incorrectly, and the mistakes that they make are for the most part predictable. As we have seen, an argument might be invalid only because it is enthymematic. In such cases, we can repair it. But, on the other hand, an argument might exhibit *bad reasoning*, in which case we should reject it outright. In this section, we will review some of the commonly occurring invalid patterns.

Consider the following example. It is one of our favorite examples of bad reasoning. Some years ago, Abe Beame was running for mayor of New York City. He wanted to emphasize his experience as comptroller of the city's finances, so he used the following slogan in an effort to portray himself as the most qualified person for the job:

> If you don't know the buck, you don't know the job. And Abe Beame knows the buck.

Now, this is an argument. It is also an enthymeme, for the conclusion is unstated. What conclusion are you to draw? We think it is

Abe Beame knows the job.

It is a very clever advertisement, for it does not *tell* you that Abe Beame knows the job; it allows *you* to make the inference, as if you had made up your own mind about the subject.

But although this is clearly the inference that the advertisers wish you to draw, it is an *invalid inference.* For if you look at the argument with the conclusion filled in, you will see that essentially it is a case of the fallacy of denying the antecedent:

> If Abe Beame doesn't know the buck, then he doesn't know the job.
> Abe Beame knows the buck.
> _____
> SO, Abe Beame knows the job.

We adopt the following symbols:

B: Abe Beame knows the buck.

J: Abe Beame knows the job.

The "proof," then, will look like this:

(1)	$-B \rightarrow -J$	Premiss
(2)	B	Premiss
(3)	$--B$	Double Negation, (2)

(4)	$--J$	(?) Fallacy of Denying
		the Antecedent, (1), (3)
(5)	J	Double Negation, (4)

It is quite clear that just this fallacious inference pattern is at work here. The advertisers assume we will make this inference, and we (almost) inevitably do make the inference. Nevertheless, it is an invalid inference. From the premisses laid down, it does not follow that Abe Beame knows the job.

But what about the principle of charity discussed earlier? After all, you might say, if we were to rewrite the first premiss to read

(1) If you know the buck, then you know the job,

then the argument would be valid. It would be an instance of Modus ponens.

It's true, of course, that replacing the original premiss with (1) would make the argument valid. But (1) is very different from the premiss actually used in the argument, and those who created the advertisement were most certainly aware of the difference. (1) claims that knowing the buck is a *sufficient* condition for knowing the job. The original premiss, on the other hand, claims only that knowing the buck is a *necessary* condition for knowing the job.

Many of us are likely to accept the original premiss, not (1). For, although we would agree that a person who cannot manage money isn't qualified to be mayor, we would not agree that that's all there is to the job. Being a good mayor certainly involves being able to manage money, but it involves a good deal more than just that. So, although the argument using (1) is valid, the premiss is doubtful. On the other hand, the argument that uses the less doubtful original premiss is invalid. So, either way, the argument is *unsound*.

Here is another example:

A person who wears an American flag on his lapel is loyal. But John doesn't wear an American flag on his lapel. So he isn't loyal.

We can spell the argument out as follows:

> If John wears a flag on his lapel, then he is loyal.
> John doesn't wear a flag on his lapel.
> _____
> SO, John is not loyal.

It is hardly necessary to symbolize the argument to recognize this as another instance of the fallacy of denying the antecedent.

Here is another example of bad reasoning. Imagine that you have written to your landlord explaining that you need a new stove. He comes to your apartment and tells you that if he gives you a new stove, he will raise your rent. You agree to the terms. The next month, your rent goes up, even though you have not yet received a new stove. So, you write to your landlord, explaining that you won't pay the increase because he hasn't given you a new stove. A few days later, the landlord comes knocking at your door. He's angry and threatening. "Look," he says, "I told you that if I gave you a new stove, I would raise the rent, right?" "Right," you agree. "And I raised the rent, right?" Again, you agree. "Well, then," he concludes, "I *must* have given you that new stove." Well, you are totally dumbfounded by the man's logic. "Look at this stove here. This isn't a new stove," you cry. But nothing can stop the inevitable logic of this landlord. "Sure," he says, "you must be an incredible slob. You took this perfectly good new stove I just gave you and turned it into a piece of garbage just like the old one."

What has happened here? How can you avoid the relentless logic of this landlord? Well, the landlord's logic is not so good. If you consider that he claims to have given you a new stove, and his evidence is that he raised the rent, why he is simply affirming the consequent. That is, his argument is:

> If I give you a new stove, then I will raise the rent.
> $\underline{\text{I raised the rent.}}$
> SO, I gave you a new stove.

The landlord is trying to make raising the rent, not a necessary condition for giving you a new stove—the condition you had agreed to—but a sufficient condition for giving you a new stove, something that is far from true.

There are a number of other fallacies people frequently fall into. We have already come across them during our investigation of the connectives in Chapters 1–7 of this textbook. We list them here.

The Conditional

Fallacy of affirming the consequent	$X \rightarrow Y$ $\underline{Y}$ SO, X
Fallacy of denying the antecedent	$X \rightarrow Y$ $\underline{-X}$ SO, $-Y$

Disjunction

Invalid pattern	$X \vee Y$ $\underline{X}$ SO, $-Y$

Conjunction

Invalid pattern
$$\frac{-(X \,\&\, Y)}{-X}$$
$$\overline{\text{SO, } Y}$$

These do not exhaust all the invalid patterns. Don't forget that if you should find yourself unsure whether a particular pattern is invalid, you can always go back to your truth tables.

EXERCISES

11.3:1   Determine whether any of the following arguments is valid.

a.   Dickens didn't write both *Oliver Twist* and *Jane Eyre*. Now that I think of it, he didn't write *Jane Eyre*. So he must have written *Oliver Twist*.

b.   If Dickens wrote *Oliver Twist*, then he didn't write *Jane Eyre*. However, he didn't write *Jane Eyre*. So he must have written *Oliver Twist*.

c.   Student: "The professor said, 'If you don't hand in the assignments on time, you'll flunk the course.' But I did hand in my assignments on time. So I won't flunk the course."

d.   We'll be safer if we hire more guards. I will hire more guards. So we'll be safer.

e.   If what he said is true, then John did it. Since John did it, what he said must have been true.

f.   It will either rain or snow. It's going to rain. So it won't snow.

11.4   INFORMAL FALLACIES

In this section, we will discuss a number of **informal fallacies**, as they are called. This is a loosely defined group of patterns that have been compiled over many years, including some of the most common errors in reasoning that people are prone to. Although there is no common thread, the techniques we have developed in this text will aid in understanding and exposing them.

First, we will discuss some patterns that trade on a faulty logical treatment of one of the statements in the argument.

The Black and White Fallacy.   The black and white fallacy gets its name from the supposition that it is a tautology that a thing is either black or white. It's not a tautology; it's not even true. There are many other possibilities besides black and white. Indeed, there is the whole spectrum of colors in between. The mistake here is to confuse contraries with contradictories. Black and white are contraries; black and nonblack are contradictories.

Here is a common example of the black and white fallacy:

> You're either for us or against us.
> <u>You're not for us.</u>
> SO, you must be against us.

The argument is valid. But are the premisses true? The first premiss is presented as if it were a tautology. But it is not a tautology, and it ought not be confused with

> You're either for us or not for us,

which is a tautology. The original premiss implicitly assumes not only that

> If someone is against us, then he is not for us,

which is true, but also that

> If someone is not for us, then he is against us,

which is highly doubtful. Can't someone sit on the sidelines, being neither for nor against someone? A referee, for example, is not (or, at least, should not be) either for your side or against your side.

Again, there used to be a popular slogan

> You're either part of the problem or part of the solution.

Although this is a nice, catchy slogan, it's hardly plausible.

> You're either part of the problem or not part of the problem,

on the other hand, is a tautology. Why should anyone assume that if someone is not part of the problem, she is therefore part of the solution? Maybe she's just not part of the problem! Would you say the same about the parts of a broken car? Your car makes a terrible grinding noise and burns oil. If the valve lifters are not part of the problem, are they therefore part of the solution?

What do you have to say about the following argument?

> John is either a Communist or supports American policy.
> <u>John is not a Communist.</u>
> SO, he supports American policy.

Hasty Generalization.   Here are some examples of hasty generalization:

John ate dinner in that diner, and he got sick. So, it's dangerous to eat in that diner.

Candidate X lied; so, all candidates are liars.

Jogging often causes shin splints; so people should never jog.

In each of these cases, the reasoner is generalizing uncritically—and hastily—from one case to all cases of that sort. Recall our discussion of generalizations in Chapters 2 and 3. A generalization can be regarded as a conjunction with many conjuncts. But just because one conjunct is true, it does not follow that all conjuncts are true. The argument pattern

$$\frac{P}{SO, P \& Q \& R \& S \& \ldots Z}$$

is clearly invalid.

To be sure, we are rarely in a position to check all the conjuncts implicit in a generalization, but we should try to check as large a number as we can before we accept the generalization—and even then, only if we have independent reason to believe it. When generalizing from one instance, or even a few instances, we run a very large risk of being mistaken, as in the examples above. And this is especially true if the case from which we generalize is special or unusual.

Accident. This is the converse of hasty generalization. It consists of applying a generalization blindly, without paying attention to special circumstances or characteristics. For example:

> Since I should always tell the truth, I should tell Mary, who is playing hide-and-seek with the children, where the children are hiding.

Or, again, and more seriously,

> Since smoking is bad for you, and I shouldn't contribute to people's doing what's bad for them, I therefore shouldn't get my ninety-year-old grandfather the cigarettes he asked for.

Or, again,

> Milk is good for us; so milk is good for John.

In each of these cases the reasoner is moving uncritically from a generalization to a specific case to which the generalization does not necessarily apply. Is it true that one should always tell the truth? Clearly not. We needn't tell the truth when we are playing a game. So, the generalization does not apply necessarily to such cases. Similarly for the second example. It might well be foolish to refuse cigarettes to an older person even though we should not, generally speaking, contribute to people's harming themselves. And suppose John has an illness that requires him to limit his calcium intake.

The moral is: be careful when using generalizations in arguments. A generalization is true when and only when every instance of it is true. Loosely stated generalizations are often false, so when they are used as premisses in arguments, the arguments are often unsound. In each of the preceding cases, for example, it is at least as reasonable to reject the generalization as to apply it to the specific case.

False Cause.   This pattern, also known as *post hoc, ergo propter hoc*, occurs when someone mistakes a regularity for a cause. Here's an example:

> John is fat and drinks diet soda.
> _____
> SO, drinking diet soda makes John fat.

To be sure, it is a difficult problem to specify when two events are causally related. But it is clear that the fact that two events regularly occur together is not, by itself, sufficient.

Perhaps the easiest way of seeing the weakness of this kind of argument is to realize that both of the following arguments are valid.

$$P \ \& \ Q$$
$$\text{SO, } P \rightarrow Q$$

$$P \ \& \ Q$$
$$\text{SO, } Q \rightarrow P$$

Let P be "John is fat" and let Q be "John drinks diet soda." The conjunction supports both conditionals: "If John is fat, then he drinks diet soda" and "If John drinks diet soda, then he is fat." But the causal claim is meant to go in *only one way*. This is a good example of the difference between *if,then* and *cause*.

The Fallacies of Composition and Division.   Consider the following argument:

> The orchestra played badly; so the first violinist must have played badly.

Does the premiss imply the conclusion? No. Can't a person in the orchestra have played well even if the orchestra as a whole played badly? This kind of reasoning is called the fallacy of **division**. There is a suppressed premiss in the argument that is simply false: whatever is true of a group is true of each individual in that group. Here is another example of the fallacy:

> Men are stronger than women. So, John is stronger than Mary.

The fallacy of **composition** assumes the converse premiss: what is true of each individual is true of the whole group to which the individual belongs. For example:

> Each part of a car engine is light; so the car engine itself is light.

Here is a more disturbing example:

> Officials of the Freedonia government were implicated in illegal drug deals. So, the Freedonia government is implicated in illegal drug deals.

Both of these, composition and division, are good examples of enthymemes. Once the suppressed premiss is spelled out, you can see the argument is unsound.

Argumentum ad Ignorantiam.   The name means, literally, "arguing from ignorance." From the fact that a statement has not been proved false (or true), it is inferred that the statement is true (or false). Here is an example:

> No one has proved that Christopher Columbus did not have eggs on the morning he discovered America; so he must have had eggs that morning.

Clearly, you won't find this pattern convincing. But just what has gone wrong? The answer is that the reasoner has confused "true" with "proved" and "false" with "disproved." But, whereas the two statements

> P is true
> P is false

are contradictories, the two statements

> P has been proved true
> P has been proved false

are not contradictories; they are contraries. So are

> P has been proved false
> P is true.

In the case of contraries, as we have seen, we may not infer from the fact that one of them is false, that the other must be true.

It might appear as if there are exceptions to this. In a law court, for instance, we do accept the following argument:

The prisoner has not been proved guilty; so the prisoner is innocent.

But this is not really an exception. For, in a court of law, to be guilty *is* to be proved guilty, and to be innocent is to be not proved guilty.

There are other cases, however, where we consider a closely related pattern to be cogent. Assuming that scientists have made many attempts to find a bird that doesn't have wings, the following argument is persuasive:

Nobody has ever found a counterexample to the claim that all
birds have wings.
_____
SO, it's probably true that all birds have wings.

Note, however, that the claim that all birds have wings is only said to be *probable*. Moreover, the conclusion is strengthened by the fact that there is an independent, theoretical reason, based on the anatomy and physiology of the family of birds, to think that all birds have wings. Because of our independent belief that the conclusion is probably true, the fact that, after so many attempts, no one has come up with a counterexample, only strengthens our belief in it. In such cases, the burden of proof shifts to showing the conclusion to be false.

One must always keep careful track of where the burden of proof lies in an argument to avoid falling into error. There is no independent reason to think that Columbus had eggs the morning he discovered America; so the failure to show otherwise does not strengthen our belief that he did. By the same token, if I have grave doubts about the existence of God, the following will be *ad ignorantiam*:

No one has ever succeeded in proving that God doesn't exist.
_____
SO, God must exist.

On the other hand, if I firmly believe that God exists, and I have *independent reason* for believing in God's existence, then this argument will not be *ad ignorantiam* at all, but will actually strengthen my belief.

Again, each of these arguments can be conceived of as enthymematic, the suppressed premiss identifying where the burden of proof lies. The argument will be *ad ignorantiam* when the suppressed premiss is false—that is, when the burden of proof is incorrectly stated.

Fallacies that trade on authority.   Because we rely so much on the authority of others, there are many ways in which we can be fooled. A number of fallacies trade on this reliance. The argument pattern

John said that *P*.
_____
SO, *P*.

is certainly not valid. Just because someone says something, it does not follow that it is true. On the other hand, the pattern

> John is reliable in what he says.
> John said that P.
> _____
> SO, it is likely that P.

is a good one. With the difference between these two argument patterns clearly in mind, let us turn to some fallacies.

Often we make the error of supposing that an authority in one field is equally an authority in all. This gives rise to the fallacy of **false authority**. Here's an example:

> (My physics professor is an authority.)
> My physics professor said the president made a bad decision.
> _____
> SO, it is quite likely that the president made a bad decision.

Physics professors are, no doubt, authorities on physics. But that is no reason to think that their beliefs about politics are any more informed than anyone else's. If, indeed, they were experts on politics, something that was never expressed in the premisses, then the conclusion might be warranted. As it stands, however, it is highly suspect. Here's another example:

> (Senator Smith is an authority.)
> Senator Smith says the war is morally unjustifiable.
> _____
> SO, it's quite likely that it is morally unjustifiable.

Although Senator Smith is no doubt privy to much inside information, it is not clear what makes her an authority on this particular issue. On the other hand,

> (General Smith is the commander of the armed services.)
> General Smith says that the war is unwinnable.
> _____
> SO, it is quite likely that the war is unwinnable.

is extremely cogent. General Smith is an authority on this particular issue, so if he says that the war is unwinnable (and we have no reason to suppose that he is lying or in any way trying to deceive us), then it is *likely* that it is unwinnable.

Closely related is the **ad populum** fallacy:

Everyone believes that P; so, you should too.

Of course, just because everyone believes P, it does not follow that P *is* true. Everyone can be wrong. On the other hand, if everyone does believe

P, then it's quite likely that *P* is true. So, where's the fallacy? Consider the following argument:

> Most Americans believe that Kennedy was a good president.
> SO, it's likely he was a good president.

Are you persuaded by this argument? Suppose you had doubts about whether Kennedy was a good president. Would this reasoning set your doubts to rest? Actually not. Most likely it would make you even more doubtful about the conclusion. And the reason is quite clear. If the belief is so widespread that he was a good president, then the reasons justifying the belief must be well known to all. And since the reasons are well known to all, one would expect those reasons to be put forward in support of the claim. The fact that they are not leads one to suppose that they are not particularly good reasons, and that the appeal to what "most Americans" believe is an emotional one designed to get you on the bandwagon.

So, although the form of the argument is not particularly bad, implicit in the argument is that a better one could be put forward. The fact that the better one is not put forward vitiates the argument itself.

Ad Hominem. *Ad hominem* means, literally, "to the person." One argues *ad hominem* if one attacks the person putting forward the claim, not the claim itself. This is a particularly interesting tactic because, although it is sometimes bad, it is sometimes precisely the right way to proceed. Consider the following example:

> Of course Lenin's claims that economic justice is possible only if the workers destroy the bourgeoisie is false. He was a Communist, wasn't he?

The structure of the argument is:

> Lenin was a Communist.
> SO, Lenin's claims that economic justice is possible only if
> the workers destroy the bourgeoisie is likely false.

Obviously, the argument is enthymematic. What is being assumed is the conditional

> If Lenin was a Communist, then Lenin's claim that . . . is likely false.

So, the pattern here is simply modus ponens. If you believe both premisses, then you will accept the conclusion. If you don't, you'll deny that the argument is sound.

Notice that the argument does not focus directly on the *claim* that economic justice is possible only if the workers destroy the bourgeoisie; it focuses on its being *Lenin's* claim. The focus of the argument is on who said it, not on the claim itself.

Is this a bad argument? That depends upon what we think of the suppressed premiss. We don't find this premiss especially convincing; so we don't believe that the conclusion has been warranted. Is it true that everything said by Communists is false? The overall strategy of the argument, however, appears to be basically sound. The arguer is trying to show that something is likely false by damaging the veracity of the witness.

Here's another example of this technique:

> Jim's claim that the earth is spinning at 6000 miles per second is probably false. Jim knows nothing about astronomy.

If, indeed, our only reason for believing that the earth is spinning at 6000 miles per second is Jim's say-so, and Jim is so unreliable, then we are not likely to believe it.

What makes an argument *ad hominem*, however, is that instead of addressing the issue itself, where that is possible, the arguer attacks those who believe or propose the view. Consider, again, the question about economic justice for the workers. The conditions under which they have economic justice should be determined by reasons that speak directly to the issue, not by what others have said about it. For in this context, authorities are not invited, but only reasons relevant to the issue. To argue *ad hominem* is to shift this focus.

Here's a variant of the *ad hominem* argument. It is called **tu quoque**— literally, "you're another."

> My counselor says that it's bad to be late. But what he says is false. He's always late.

Presumably, the counselor does not practice what he preaches. And clearly, then, since there is a discrepancy between what he says and what he does, he is not believable. That does not mean that what he says is false. More likely, it means that he does not really believe what he is saying.

Fallacies arising from nonparticipation. Finally, we mention some fallacies in which the participant chooses not to engage in argument at all. That is, she chooses, not to give reasons to support her claim.

Ad misericordiam is, literally, an appeal "to pity." Here's an example:

> Attorney (to the jury): "My client is not guilty of theft. She's had a hard time of it. She's poor, uneducated, and unhappy."

The lawyer is not giving reasons to support the claim that his client is not guilty. Instead, he is appealing to the jury to take pity on his client and not apply the rules of the game in her case.

Ad baculum is, literally, an appeal "to force." Here's an example:

> Child (after a close play at first base): "I was safe. If you call me out, I'll quit and take my ball with me."

The child's threat to quit is irrelevant to the issue of whether she was safe. The threat is not a reason at all, but an attempt to influence the decision without playing by the rules.

The examples in this section should make it clear that what is required to evaluate an argument is careful formulation of the statements that compose it, careful attention to the steps undertaken to reach its conclusion, and careful attention to the issue that is under discussion.

EXERCISES

11.4:1   Structure the following arguments and identify the fallacy committed. (We have included some cases of begging the question.)

a.   You're either a winner or a loser. You're not a winner. So you must be a loser.

b.   This event has a cause, and that cause has a cause, and that cause has a cause, etc. So, the whole chain of events must have a cause.

c.   The teacher shouldn't have sent me out of class just because I wouldn't stop talking out loud. It's unconstitutional. Freedom of speech is guaranteed, isn't it?

d.   You can either buy good clothes or buy cheap clothes. I couldn't afford good clothes; so I bought cheap ones.

e.   You shouldn't trust doctors. Just the other day my friend's doctor sent her to the hospital for tests, and nothing was wrong.

f.   Since police cars may go through red lights, so may I.

g.   Since my friend doesn't wear English Leather, he must wear nothing at all.

h.   You have a father; I have a father; every person has a father. So it is reasonable to think that humanity has a father.

i.   Educated people have good vocabularies; so I'm getting myself a vocabulary book.

j.   Don't pay any attention to psychoanalysis. After all, Freud was neurotic himself.

k.   Brut must be good cologne. Joe Namath uses it.

l.   The faculty at this school is awful. My teacher never gives back the papers I write.

m. Child to parents: "What do you mean, I shouldn't stay out late. You did just last night."

n. I know I could have saved his life. But I didn't stop to help him because I had promised to meet my friend at the movies. One should always keep one's promises.

o. When we had got to this point in the argument, and every one saw that the definition of justice had been completely upset, Thrasyma-chus, instead of replying to me, said: "Tell me, Socrates, have you got a wetnurse?" "Why do you ask such a question," I said, "when you ought rather to be answering?" "Because she leaves you to snivel, and never wipes your nose; she has not even taught you to know the shep-herd from the sheep."

> Plato, *The Republic*, trans. B. Jowett, in *The Dialogues of Plato*, vol. I (New York: Random House, 1937), p. 608.

p. More people buy this cereal than any other cereal. So, it must be good.

q. It is pathetic to see John criticize the political situation in Philadelphia when Boston is itself so corrupt.

r. Student to teacher: "You shouldn't fail me. I worked hard, very hard, for this course."

s. You should agree that capital punishment is proper. If you don't, we'll vote you out of office.

t. Prosecutor to the jury: "You should find the defendant guilty. It is every citizen's responsibility to show that crime doesn't pay."

u. Since I can tear each page of the phone book in two, I can tear the phone book in two.

Study Vocabulary: informal fallacy
black and white fallacy
hasty generalization
accident
false cause
division
composition
ad ignorantiam
false authority
ad populum
ad hominem
tu quoque
ad misericordiam
ad baculum

11.5 DEFINITION

How many of you have engaged in argument and at some point been chal-lenged to *define your terms?* Sometimes this is merely a debater's point. It is difficult to define words—try defining such a simple word as *chair* or *car* or *home*—and your opponent is simply placing a difficult task on you, shifting the focus away from the main point of the argument. You don't have to define all your terms when you argue. You can very well know the meaning of words, even though you are unable to define them—as in the cases just mentioned. It is useful to define one's terms only if doing so directly affects the argument you are engaged in—for example, in order to avoid fallacies of ambiguity, such as that exhibited here:

> All men are rational.
> No woman is a man.
> _____
> SO, no woman is rational.

The error here is easy to spot. In the first premiss, the term *man* is used to refer to the class of human beings. In the second premiss, however, it is used to refer to the class of males.

In this section, we will discuss some of the main points about meaning and definition. A definition has two parts: the word being defined and the words being used to define it. Here is an example of a definition of the word *bachelor*:

> Bachelor: unmarried male.

The word being defined (in this case, *bachelor*) is called the **definiendum**; the words being used to define *bachelor* (in this case, "unmarried male") are called the **definiens**.

A definition relates one word (the definiendum) to others (the definiens) that, taken together, mean the same thing. The word being defined can be conceived of as an *abbreviation* of the definiens. So, a definition sets up a substitution rule, allowing you to replace the definiens in any sentence by its abbreviation, the definiendum. Defining *bachelor* allows us to replace the definiens "unmarried male" with the definiendum *bachelor*, without changing the meaning of the sentence in which the terms are used. The two statements

> John is a bachelor
>
> John is an unmarried male

mean the very same thing.

Philosophers and linguists have traditionally distinguished two aspects of meaning: the denotation of a word and the connotation of a word.

> *The denotation of a word is the thing or things to which the word truly applies.*

> *The connotation of a word is the attributes a thing must have in order to be truly called by that word.*

The denotation of *bachelor* is simply all the bachelors there are, have been, and will be. At that time of our writing this text, *bachelor* denotes Ed Koch, George Hamilton, Wilt Chamberlain, and so forth. The connotation of *bachelor* is the set of properties a thing must have in order to be properly called by that word. What are the characteristics of a thing that makes it a bachelor? We have already seen from the definition given previously: it must be a male, and it must be unmarried. *Bachelor* connotes these properties.

Since there are two aspects to meaning, there are two ways of giving the meaning of a word, two types of definition. One type of definition gives the connotation of the word; the other gives the denotation of the word. Classically, the type of definition that is most highly prized, and the one dictionaries often strive for, is that which gives the connotation of the word. This is called an **explicit** or **lexical definition**:

> *An explicit definition gives the connotation of the word, the set of attributes a thing must have in order to be called by that word.*

An explicit definition gives you a general rule for determining whether the word applies to a given thing. The other type of definition gives you the denotation of the word by giving you examples of things to which the word applies. This is called **ostensive definition**:

> *An ostensive definition gives the denotation of the word, examples of things to which the word applies.*

Dictionaries frequently incorporate both types of definition: you will be given a general rule for picking out things of that sort, and then some examples.

If two words have the same connotation, then they must have the same denotation. If the characteristics a thing must possess in order to be called by one of them are exactly the same as the characteristics a thing must have to be called by the other, then the two words must apply to exactly the same things.

But if two words have the same denotation, it does not follow that they have the same connotation. Let's introduce two words explicitly:

Renate: creature with a kidney.

Cordate: creature with a heart.

These two words do not have the same connotation. In order for something to be a *renate*, it must have a kidney; it is not part of the connotation of the word that the creature must have a heart. Similarly, in order for something to be a *cordate*, it must have a heart; it is not part of the connotation of the word that the creature must have a kidney. However, it turns out, as a matter of biology, that the two terms have the same denotation. Every creature with a heart has a kidney, and every creature with a kidney has a heart. Nevertheless, the two do not have the same connotation. We determine that something is a cordate by seeing whether it has a heart; that is the deciding characteristic. The fact that it has a kidney is irrelevant. So, although the two words coincide in denotation, they differ in connotation.

Let us summarize what we have learned so far. We have identified two aspects of meaning—connotation and denotation—and, correspondingly, two types of definition—explicit and ostensive. Explicit definition is the one more highly prized, but ostensive definitions are sometimes more practical, and in some cases even necessary. For an explicit definition of X meaning Y to be correct,

(1)   every X must be a Y,

(2)   every Y must be an X, and

(3)   having the characteristic Y must be the deciding factor for something to be X.

So, in order to have a *good* explicit definition, the definition must be neither too narrow nor too broad. Furthermore, the definiendum and definiens must coincide in connotation as well as in denotation. These are the fundamental criteria for good definitions.

Another important ingredient of giving good definitions is to limit the definiens to terms that are familiar to the person for whom you are defining the expression. Suppose you are learning French in college. You come across the word *neige* and you don't know what it means. So, you look it up in a dictionary. What kind of dictionary are you going to use? Most likely a French/English dictionary, for, to learn what this French word means, you are going to try to see what the English equivalent is. You wouldn't use a French/French dictionary, because in that case, all you will get is a French equivalent to the word *neige*. A definition in French won't help you because you won't understand the French words being used to define *neige*.

Indeed, there are a wide variety of English/English dictionaries. Most likely, as you gained greater knowledge and maturity, you changed the dictionary you use. A dictionary that you used in grammar school is no longer good for you in high school. And even your high school dictionary will not be good enough for sophisticated college work. It is not that one dictionary is better than another. It is that, at different stages in your intellectual development, different dictionaries have been more or less appropriate to your needs.

This aspect of giving a good definition points to one of the most important features of good definitions. If a definition is to be of any value, it must not be *circular*. Since a good definition must contain only words that are already understood, you cannot include the definiendum in the definiens. One of the most frustrating experiences in using a dictionary occurs when you look up a word, X, and see its definition, Y. You don't know what Y means, so you look it up and you see its definition, Z. You don't know what this means, and when you look up Z, you get X. Unfortunately, you have gotten into a closed loop. You cannot figure out what X means because, as you work your way through the dictionary, you find that in order to know what X means, you will already have had to know what X means. This is a circle.

It is important at this point to recognize that not all words can be explicitly defined without the definer ultimately falling into a circle. This follows immediately from our notion of definitions as abbreviations. If we eliminated from the language all defined words—that is, all words that are abbreviations for others—then we would eventually come to some words that are not abbreviations of others. We cannot give explicit definitions of these words. So, how can we learn their meaning? Only by breaking out of the sphere of *words* and reaching the things to which they apply. Ultimately these words would have to be learned by ostension. Indeed, possibly the first dictionary you ever used was a picture dictionary. Since you did not have a vast vocabulary and you could barely read, instead of giving verbal clues to the meaning of a word, the dictionary provided pictures of the thing to which the word applies. So, for example, next to the word *bell* would be a picture of a bell, and next to the word *clown* would be a picture of a clown. To avoid circularity, a good dictionary therefore does not give only lexical definitions; it also provides ostensive definitions of some words, examples of the things to which the words apply.

There is one more refinement to this idea of limiting the definiens. Because ordinary usage is vague or ambiguous, we frequently want to limit what we are willing to include in the definiens. Psychologists, for example, have tried to make the word *intelligent* more precise by pinning its meaning to results on an IQ test. So,

John is intelligent

means

John scored at least n on an IQ test.

In so doing, psychologists severely restrict the elements of the definiens to characteristics that are objectively measurable. And in so doing, they give the word a precise meaning. Such *technical* definitions will be good only to the extent that the denotation of the scientifically defined term corresponds in the main with the term's ordinary use.

EXERCISES

11.5:1   Give two definitions, one lexical and one ostensive, for each of the following.

a.   *skyscraper*

b. *color*

c. *animal*

d. *representative*

e. *noise*

f. *chair*

Study Vocabulary: definiendum
definiens
detonation
connotation
explicit (*lexical*) definition
ostensive definition

REVIEW

1.   To evaluate an argument, we need to know whether it is valid—that is, whether the premisses imply the conclusion. We need to know whether it is sound—whether it is valid *and* all of the premisses are true. And we need to know whether it is useful—whether the premisses are acceptable to the participants. (And, in particular, we need to know that it does not beg the question.)

2.   If an argument is formally valid, then we can show it to be valid by using natural deduction. If it is not formally valid, we can show it to be invalid by using truth tables. But if an argument is formally invalid, then it might be an enthymeme—an argument with a suppressed premiss or conclusion—or it might be an example of bad reasoning. We can use natural deduction techniques to identify suppressed premisses, choosing the minimal premiss consistent with the patterns that enables the author to get her conclusion. In the case of bad reasoning, however, the argument must simply be rejected. We identified a number of commonly occurring invalid argument patterns.

3.   We also identified a number of informal fallacies, and discussed what the main error was in each case. The black and white fallacy mistakes a disjunction of contraries for a disjunction of contradictories. In hasty generalization, one generalizes too quickly from a single or special case. In converse accident, one applies a loosely stated generalization to a situation it was not meant to be applied to. In false cause, one mistakes a regularity for a causal connection. In composition one supposes that whatever is true of the parts is true of the whole. In division, one supposes that whatever is true of the whole is true of the parts. One argues *ad ignorantiam* when one mistakes where the burden of proof lies. In the fallacy of false authority, one mistakes an authority in one field for an authority in another. To argue *ad populum* is to appeal to an individual to get on the bandwagon and believe

P since everybody else does. To argue *ad hominem* is to attack the person and not the claim put forth. To argue *tu quoque* is to identify a conflict between what an individual preaches and what he practices, taking this to be a refutation of what he preaches. Finally, in *ad misericordiam* (appealing to pity) and *ad baculum* (appealing to force), one gives up reasons entirely in order to get one's way.

4.   There are two aspects to meaning. The connotation of a word is the properties a thing must have to be properly called by the word; the denotation of the word is the thing or things to which it properly applies. Corresponding to these two aspects of meaning are two types of definition. Explicit or lexical definition gives the connotation of a word; ostensive definition gives examples of things to which the word applies. The word being defined is called the definiendum; the words used in the definition are the definiens. For a definition to be good, not only must definiendum and definiens coincide in meaning, but the definiens must contain words one is already familiar with.

APPENDIXES

We have already seen that the context in which you speak or write can, to a great extent, determine what your words say. We want to consider now some other factors that are involved in successful communication.

Communicating with another human being often requires a great deal of information and a great deal of work. When you are talking with a friend, for example, you engage in a give and take: she speaks a bit, then you speak a bit, and so on. You can ask questions, ask your friend to repeat what she has said, ask for evidence, ask why your friend is saying what she is saying, say something with a smile, or a groan, or a wink. If she's a close friend, you will have a relatively deep understanding of her. You will know what she likes and what she dislikes, you will know when she is happy, when she is sad, and when she is angry. Often, you will know these things when other people do not. Often, you will know so much that you probably do not have to speak in complete sentences; a single word will drum up a host of imagery, of shared experiences, of reactions in her that you will be fully aware of. Usually you will not have to fill her in on the background of your remarks. You don't have to speak in precise, clear, complete sentences. Moreover, speaking in front of her, you can see immediately her reaction to what you are saying, whether she is interested or not, whether she is following what you are saying or not, whether she approves or disapproves, and you can make adjustments accordingly.

We all like to speak with our friends and close family; we're comfortable with them. Communication with them is often easy, and little formality is necessary. They often know what we mean to say even before we've said it, and they often make sympathetic interpretations of what we do say. They—our audience, so to speak—are familiar and comfortable. The further away we get from our audience, however, the more fragile and difficult is the communication. For, the further away we get from our audience, the less we can rely on shared experiences, values, and vocabulary, and the less we can be sure that our message is getting across.

There are a number of ways in which we can be distant from our audience. We will discuss here two of particular importance. First, we can be distant from our audience with respect to common beliefs, values, and experiences. Second, we can be distant from our audience with respect to the actual physical channel of communication. Let us explore these two dimensions of communication.

When we speak with someone unfamiliar, the way we speak is rather different from the way we speak with someone closer. We tend to be much more careful. And this does not mean simply that we are more polite and formal. Not knowing what is going on inside the stranger's head, we are not sure what reaction our words will have on him and we therefore face a greater risk of being misunderstood.

Suppose, for example, that you happened to meet someone from a faraway place—say, Uzbekistan in Central Asia. This person comes from a very different culture, he holds beliefs that are very different from yours, his way of life is vastly different from yours, and the sorts of things he knows and has experienced are unlike the sorts of things you know and have experienced. How could you communicate to him things with which you are familiar? Would that person know who Joe DiMaggio is? Would he know what break-dancing is? Would he know the difference between Greyhound and Trailways? Would he even know what Trailways is? Probably not. So, if, for example, in speaking with him, you were to say

> Greyhound is faster than Trailways,

it's quite likely that he wouldn't have any idea what you are talking about. Or, even worse, he might be guessing to himself, thinking that he knows, and guessing incorrectly. For all we know, he might suppose you to be talking about dogs. And then, everything you say subsequently will be thoroughly misunderstood because he thinks that you are talking about dogs when you are really talking about buses. Since you cannot suppose that he shares your knowledge about the two big nationwide bus companies, then, in order to communicate with him, you are going to have to inform him about what these companies are.

The less information you share in common with your audience, the more you have to supply to get your message across. And if you are unsure about what your audience knows, and especially if it is important that you be understood, you will tend to say more rather than less. So, too, when the person with whom you are speaking is possibly hostile and a potential adversary, you make sure that nothing is left unsaid: the *i*'s are dotted and the *t*'s crossed. This, after all, is a large part of what goes into writing a good legal contract. Nothing is left to chance. Assuming that another person will like what we like and know what we know frequently gets us into trouble. What you might think is completely obvious might not be obvious to others. The failure to recognize this leads to breakdowns in communication.

Let's now consider the role of the actual channel of communication. In ordinary, face-to-face conversation, there are a large number of clues we can give other than the words we explicitly say to get our message across. For example, we might rely on facial expressions, tones of voice, and other sorts of body language. Equally important, in face-to-face communication, we get immediate responses from our audience as to whether our message is getting across, and we can accordingly adjust what we are saying.

Now, consider what happens when we speak over the telephone. We cannot gesture; the other person will not see it. So we have to rely more on the inflection in our voices, the tone with which we speak, and the words we choose, in order to make the other party understand us. Also, on the telephone, we cannot see the other person's face, and so we do not have quite as good an idea as to whether our message is being understood. Nevertheless, we still have some interaction with our audience: we can question and be questioned, and in that way increase the chances of our being understood.

But when we write, we get no immediate feedback from our audience. We cannot see or hear them, and so we cannot tell whether our message is getting across properly. We have, so to speak, only one shot: we must be sure that our message is phrased just right so that it is understandable. On the other hand, writing has a dimension that both face-to-face conversation and telephone conversation lack. The written word lasts in a way that the spoken word does not. A written text can be referred to over and over, compared, say, with a telephone conversation, which only goes by once. This allows the writer to be much more explicit, much more complicated, and much more precise, for the reader can go over the passage several times until she gets the message.

In many respects, the optimum channel of communication is face-to-face conversation, where the interaction between speaker and hearer is greatest. And the optimum condition of communication is where speaker and hearer have knowledge and values in common. To a large extent, as you get further and further from your audience, you adjust the nature of what you say, to try to re-create or capture as much as possible of this optimum situation. So, when writing, you will tend to avoid slang, idioms, and ungrammatical sequences and rely on as much standard, formal language as possible to facilitate communication. You will tend to be clear and precise, and to supply as much information as is necessary to enable the reader to understand the message you are sending; this is particularly true when writing for what would be essentially an anonymous audience.

Conversely, when reading a written piece, we try to re-create many of the virtues of face-to-face conversation. We must recognize that behind all the prose on a printed page stands another person, another human being, who is liable to error and prejudice and other sorts of human failings, just like the rest of us. We must bring to our reading the same sort of consciousness that we bring to conversations with our friends. We have to train ourselves to ask (sympathetic) questions of the text, so that we will be able to dig deeply into what is being said. In the absence of bodily gestures and tones of voice, we must use other clues—and the good writer will give plenty of other clues. This is the point of being an active participant in the reading process. We have to figure out what an individual is saying, and that means constantly asking questions of the text before us, and trying out answers. Reading and writing thus turn out to be a slightly different way of carrying on a dialogue.

That is, perhaps, one reason why some students find it so difficult to make the adjustment to the demands of college. To a large extent, one is entering an environment that is unfriendly and anonymous. All of a sudden, things become more formal. Writing is expected to be more explicit. Teachers talk about grammar, about precision of expression, and you cannot get away with the sloppier forms of expression that you have become used to with family and friends. The reason teachers demand conformity to these standards is basically to train students to cross the many cultural gaps that exist within the world. Standard language and standard grammar are aids to getting our thoughts across to widely divergent audiences. They enable us each to say what we think is true, and for a wider group of people than our immediate family and friends. Also, since standard, formal English is the conventional medium by which information is disseminated across the English-speaking world, it is only by becoming familiar with this particular style of English that the vast body of knowledge stored by our culture over the centuries will become available to you.

EXERCISES

A.1:1   Use a tape recorder to tape a face-to-face conversation you have with a friend. Tell your friend about, say, the last movie you saw. Now, tape-record a telephone conversation with a friend about the same subject. Listen to the two tapes. What differences do you recognize between the face-to-face conversation and the telephone conversation?

A.1:2   Write a paragraph describing your neighborhood. Whom do you think would understand what you have said?

A.1:3 For each of the following audiences, write a short paragraph describing your neighborhood.

a. your closest friend
b. your grandfather
c. a Bedouin tribesman
d. a member of the United States Congress

What differences do you recognize in the way in which you describe your neighborhood to the four different audiences?

APPENDIX 2:   LANGUAGE AND GRAMMAR

Acknowledging the difficulties of communication we discussed in Appendix 1 helps us appreciate the strong desire for a standardized language to serve as a vehicle for communication. A standardized language makes for reliability and predictability, and these are some of the most highly valued commodities that civilization has handed down to us.

Languages are human creations. Because communication is so important and yet so fragile, speakers in a community tacitly agree to certain conventions about how to talk with one another. Just as it is in each driver's interest to abide by the convention of, say, driving on the right-hand side of the road, so it is in each speaker's interest to abide by these conventions of language. If people are going to drive cars on the road, we need some convention about which side of the road to drive on. Otherwise there would be chaos on the roads. It doesn't matter *which* convention we choose, whether we drive on the right or on the left. What *is* important is that we choose one side. Standardizing the rules of language is thus like other conventions. It doesn't matter, by and large, which conventions we choose. But it matters greatly that we choose some and that we abide by them.

On the other hand, it would be a mistake to think that these conventional standards of language and grammar are written in stone. They are constantly shifting and changing. The standards belong to the whole community. We are the ones who preserve them; we are the ones who change them; we are the ones who pass them on to our children.

For many of us, grammar is something that has been foisted upon us by English teachers: we have to mind our grammar. Speaking grammatically is speaking properly and acceptably. We must mind our grammar in school and, perhaps, at work, but otherwise grammar is a face we put on to the hostile world and not something we need mind when we speak to people close to us. To some extent, this is exactly the correct attitude toward grammar. Grammar is a tool that we need in order to speak to others in an unfamiliar environment.

There are two important aspects to the standardization of language:

vocabulary and grammar. It is fairly obvious why we have a vocabulary, and why we have a standardized vocabulary. Grammar, however, requires some discussion.

Let us begin with a simple example. Consider the sentence

John hit Mary.

This is a grammatically correct English sentence. Looking at the sentence, we understand that John is the one who is doing the hitting and Mary is the one who has been hit. How do we know this? Because *John* goes before the verb *hit*, and *Mary* goes after the verb. If we switched the positions of *John* and *Mary* we would get an entirely different message:

Mary hit John.

With this sentence, we are being informed that Mary did the hitting and that John was hit. So, the position of the expressions in the sentence determines what has been said: the noun in front of the verb stands for the thing doing the action described by the verb, and the noun after the verb stands for the thing to which the action is being done. This is a grammatical rule. It is a convention. If there were no such convention, our words would be hopelessly ambiguous. It would be impossible to determine, apart from context, who was doing what to whom. This is precisely what happens when grammatical rules are violated. Consider

John Mary hit,

an ungrammatical sequence of English words. Can you figure out who did what to whom? We doubt it.

From this example, we can see that one of the primary functions of grammar is to *disambiguate*: the rules are adopted to ensure that a given sequence of words will have a unique, clear interpretation. In English, this function is served in large measure by strict rules concerning the ordering of words. Suppose, for example, that an adjective were added to this sentence:

Old John hit Mary.

Clearly, it is John who is old, not Mary. And we know that it is John who is old because the adjective *old* immediately precedes the noun *John*. If, on the other hand, we had placed *old* in front of *Mary* to get

John hit old Mary,

then it would be Mary who is said to be old and not John. Again, without some such convention, it would not be clear who is the one said to be old. On the other hand, we can modify the verb with an adverb and let that adverb float around the sentence, because, since there is only one verb in the sentence, there is little chance of ambiguity. Any of the following are acceptable:

John forcefully hit Mary.

John hit Mary forcefully.

Forcefully, John hit Mary.

In English, we primarily rely on word ordering to disambiguate, and a large part of learning English grammar is learning the rules of ordering words in a sentence. Other languages use other devices to the same end. For example, one might add particles to the nouns in a sentence, particles that specify which noun stands for the party doing the action described by the verb and which noun stands for the party to whom the action is being done. Just to illustrate this concept, let's suppose that we add a subscript A to the noun standing for the party doing the action, and a subscript B to the noun standing for the party to whom the action is being done. In this case, strict word ordering would no longer be necessary. We could unambiguously express that John hit Mary by using any of the following:

$John_A$ hit $Mary_B$.

$John_A$ $Mary_B$ hit.

$Mary_B$ hit $John_A$.

Once we add on the particles, we can place the nouns anywhere in the sentence and the message will be clear. And if we were also to add these particles onto adjectives, then these too could be placed anywhere in the sentence without ambiguity. Just for fun, try to figure out what this says:

Old_A $Mary_B$ $John_A$ hit.

German and Latin use this concept: the particles are called *case endings*. But whether we use case endings or word order, the point of the grammatical distinction is to help make the message clear. It is to communicate an unambiguous message.

Grammatical rules frequently serve another purpose, and that is to introduce *redundancy* into the message. Redundancy is evident in our conjugation of verbs. In English, the verb *to be* is conjugated as follows:

I am	we are
you are	you are
he/she is	they are

If you go down the list, you will note that redundancy has been introduced, primarily with the singular pronouns. We have different pronouns *and* different forms of the verb. The sequence

am happy

is unambiguously clear. Adding on the pronoun *I* to get

I am happy

is simply redundant: nothing more has been added to the message. It would appear, actually, to be more efficient either to drop the pronoun and use just the special form of the verb, as in the preceding example, or to keep the pronouns but have a uniform verb—for example:

I is	we is
you is	you is
he/she is	they is

Another example of redundancy can be seen in the way we distinguish indicative, interrogative, and imperative sentences. Compare

> The door is shut.
> Is the door shut?
> Shut the door!

Not only do we change the word order for the different forms, but we also change the punctuation. The same information for distinguishing the three types of sentence is given twice. Either we could change the word order, keeping the punctuation constant:

> The door is shut.
> Is the door shut.
> Shut the door.

Or, we could keep the word order constant and simply change the punctuation:

> The door is shut.
> The door is shut?
> The door is shut!

Although it would be more efficient to do without redundancies, they often are of great value. When you speak with someone, it is important to you that your message comes across to him. This entails something as simple as speaking loudly enough so that he can hear you. If the person you are speaking to is across the room, you might even have to shout. Sometimes, in order to make sure that you are understood, you will repeat the message: "Stop," I said. "Stop what you are doing right now!" Giving the message more than once helps assure you that it is received.

There is, then, a trade-off between redundancy and efficiency in a language. Languages shift and change as the members of the language-using community try to find an optimal solution to current problems of communication, incorporating the advantages both of redundancy and of efficiency.

It is worth noting that a great deal of what is called "bad grammar" consists in not getting the redundancies of the language matched up correctly. And the price of using "bad grammar" in this way is that you increase the risk of your message not getting through to the audience. If, for example, you wrote

Is the door shut!

you would be giving your readers a mixed message, making it harder for them to understand you. You have the word order of an interrogative sentence but the punctuation of an imperative. Are you asking a question or issuing a command? Or, again, if you were to write

I likes the way he cooks,

or

I eats everything on the table,

your reader is going to stumble because the pronoun is mismatched with the verb form. To be sure, these sentences would most likely be understood, but in a more complicated case, such a mismatch can introduce problems. For example,

I likes the way he cooks and eats everything on the table

is ambiguous. It can be understood either as

I like the way he cooks and eat everything on the table.

or as

I like the way he cooks and eats everything on the table.

Undertstood the first way, *I* eat everything on the table; understood the second way, *he*, the cook, eats everything on the table. This illustrates, incidentally, some of the complexities of the trade-off between redundancy and efficiency. Although the redundancy introduced by matching a pronoun with a specific verb form seems inefficient in simple sentences, it actually increases the efficiency with which we can build complex sentences.

The main point of grammar, then, is to facilitate communication. We often find ourselves relying on grammatical cues both to make ourselves understood and to help us to understand others.

EXERCISES

A.2:1 Try to work out a different grammatical device for distinguishing among statements, questions, and commands. In what ways is the device you worked out better than the one we use? In what ways is the device you worked out worse than the one we use?

A.2:2 We mark the distinction among indicative, interrogative, and imperative sentences in two ways: word order and punctuation. Does this duplication of effort in the language enhance the expressive powers of the language at all? Or is it simply redundant and unnecessary?

APPENDIX 3: *P* AND *IT IS TRUE THAT P*

For any statement *P*,

>   *P*

and

>   *It is true that P*

are essentially the same statement. Compare, for example, the following two claims:

(1)   The earth is round.
(2)   It is true that the earth is round.

If (1) is true, then so is (2), and if (2) is true, then so is (1). Equally, if (1) is false, then so is (2), and if (2) is false, then so is (1). That is, to say that a statement is true is to make another statement, and the truth of this latter statement will depend upon the truth of the original. What is being claimed is that a given statement is true, and this claim will be true if and only if the given statement is true. Nothing has really been added to a statement by putting *It is true that* in front of it.

  This makes it look as though truth is meaningless, as though it is all a matter of opinion. But it isn't. Suppose we said to you,

>   The earth is flat.

This, we all know, is false. Now, suppose we said to you,

>   It's true that the earth is flat.

Does this make it true that the earth is flat? Clearly not! Just as the first claim is false, so is the second. Since *P* and *It is true that P* are the same claim, anyone who says *P* says it is true that *P*, and anyone who believes *P* believes that it is true that *P*. So, whenever we make a statement, whenever we claim something, we claim it to be true. And, whenever we believe something, we believe it to be true. But in neither case does this mean that it *is* true.

  Try the following experiment. Take some statement that you happen to believe—for example, the statement that the earth is round. Now, try to believe

>   The earth is round

and, at the same time, try to believe

It is false that the earth is round.

If you really worked at this experiment, you will have found that you cannot do what was asked. You cannot really believe both of these statements. Had you succeeded, you would be believing both that it is true and also that it is false that the earth is round. And, clearly, it cannot be *both* true and false that the earth is round; it must be *either* true or false. The point, again, is that to believe a statement *is* to believe that it is true.

It is perfectly possible for someone to believe a statement that happens to be false. There is, after all, a great difference between truth and belief. It doesn't follow from the fact that someone believes something that it is true. We all make mistakes. Indeed, we make mistakes all the time. Most likely, some of the beliefs we now have are false ones. We do not, of course, know which ones they are, for if we did, we would change our minds about them. And this is no reflection on us in particular. This doesn't make us dumb or weak or silly. *All people make mistakes.* Even the smartest people can be wrong. Just because Albert Einstein believed something to be true, it doesn't mean that it is true. Albert Einstein made mistakes too. Everybody makes mistakes. So, even if everybody believes that a certain statement is true (supposing that you could get everyone to agree on anything), that would still not ensure that the statement *is* true. *Everybody* might be wrong. Nevertheless, at any given time, what we believe, we believe to be true.

There is one complication that must be noted here. Unless a person is lying, there is no difference between his saying, for example,

Peanuts grow in the ground

and his saying

I believe that peanuts grow in the ground.

It doesn't make any sense for someone to say

Peanuts grow in the ground, but I don't believe it.

There is a direct connection between making a statement and saying what we take to be true: when we make statements, we give our audience reason to think that we believe them. It is the fact of our making the statement, not the statement itself, that entitles them to infer that we believe it. So to make a statement and then to say that we don't believe the statement we have just made is to speak nonsense.

It would be tedious, however, to have to preface every statement we make with the expression "In my opinion" or with "I believe that." It would also, to a large extent, be redundant. To be sure, we sometimes preface our statements with expressions such as "In my opinion" or "I think" in order to indicate that we do not have complete confidence in the statement we are making, or that perhaps there is no general agreement with the claim we are making. And, it is sometimes important to note this. But, for the most part, such warnings are unnecessary. The point, however, that we wish to underscore is this: unless you are lying, everything you say is your opinion. Unless you are lying, whatever you say is what you believe. This holds true for everyone, including the authors of this textbook: everything stated in this book is what we believe, what we think to be true, our opinion.

We said before that it is very easy to confuse truth with belief. The issues that we have been discussing just now are precisely the issues that lead people to confuse truth with belief. Let's see if you are confused. Consider the following three statements:

(1) *Carmen* is a beautiful opera.

(2) It's true that *Carmen* is a beautiful opera.

(3) I believe that *Carmen* is a beautiful opera.

Do (1), (2), and (3) express the same statement? Do (1), (2), and (3) express different statements? Or do two of (1), (2), and (3) express the same statement, and the third, a different statement? Read back over this section. What answer do you give?

If you think that (1), (2), and (3) express the same statement, then you are confused: you are collapsing the distinction between truth and belief. The reason is this. Since, in your view, (2) and (3) express the very same statement, then they are either both true or both false. They stand or fall together. So, in your view, your beliefs coincide with truths: whatever you believe is true and whatever you don't believe is false.

If you think that (1), (2), and (3) all express different statements, then, again, you are confused. (1) and (2) express the very same statement. For, (1) and (2) are related to each other in the abstract manner described as *P* and *It is true that P*: to get (2), all you need do is insert *It is true that* in front of (1).

The correct answer is that two of (1), (2), and (3) express the same statement and the other does not.

The reason that this is difficult to see is that we have actually made two different but closely related points in this appendix. First, we said that there is no difference between believing a statement and believing that it is true. And the reason is this. Since *P* and *It is true that P* are the same statement, there is no difference whether we use one or the other. So, if

John believes that *P*,

where *P* is any statement, then we can replace *P* with *it is true that P* to get the equivalent statement:

John believes that it is true that *P*.

In this sense, whatever you believe you believe to be true. By the same token, whatever you claim, you claim to be true.

John claims that *P*,

is equivalent to

John claims that it is true that *P*.

But, of course, none of these four statements is equivalent to

P,

or to

It is true that P.

For, just because John believes that *P* is true and John claims that *P* is true, it doesn't follow that it *is* true. John, after all, might be wrong.

The second point we made, however, is that unless you are lying, whatever you say, you believe. What this means is that, if

John claims that *P*,

then, assuming that John is not trying to deceive us, it is reasonable to infer that

John believes that *P*.

Let's turn back to (1)–(3), and try to figure out where the confusion might have come in. We know that they do not all express the same statement. For, while (1) and (2) do express the same statement, both differ from (3): it is perfectly possible that (3) is false when (1) and (2) are both true; it is perfectly possible that (3) is true when (1) and (2) are both false. On the other hand, and this is the tricky point, anyone who *honestly says* (1) has, in her very saying of it, given us reason to infer that she believes it. So, although the three statements are not all the same, anyone who *asserts* one of them, effectively asserts all three. Put a slightly different way, although we cannot infer

It is true that the earth is round

from

I believe that the earth is round,

these being very different and independent claims, we can infer

John claimed that it is true that the earth is round

from

John claimed that he believed that the earth is round,

if we suppose John not to be trying to deceive us.

So, although there is a difference between a statement's being *true* and that statement's being *believed* by anyone, there is no difference among someone's saying what he believes, his saying what he thinks is true, and his just plain saying it.

EXERCISES

A.3:1   Show that the following two statements say the same thing.

It is true that John believes that seawater is salty.

John believes that it is true that seawater is salty.

A.3:2   Show that the following two statements do not say the same thing.

It is true that seawater is salty.

John believes that it is true that seawater is salty.

A.3:3   Consider the sentence

It is false that John believes that seawater is salty.

Which of the following say the same thing as this sentence?

a.   John does not believe that seawater is salty.
b.   John believes that it is false that seawater is salty.
c.   John believes that seawater is not salty.

APPENDIX 4:   TRUE-FOR-ME

Sometimes people say that a given statement is "true-for-me" but "not-true-for-you" (that is, "false-for-you"). But what does this mean? Does it mean that there is no such thing as *truth, per se,* but only what might be called a relativized notion of *truth-for-someone*? We don't think so. Indeed, we think that the idea of a relativized truth-for-someone makes no sense at all. Rather, "true-for-me" just seems to be another way of saying, "I believe it." If I believe a certain claim—for example, that John is a liar—then I will act as if it were true. I will hesitate to ask him any questions, and I will tend to discount any statements he makes. In this sense, the claim that John is a liar is true-for-me. That is, I believe that he is a liar. Of course, I might be mistaken. It might not be true that John is a liar. So, although I believe it, I might be wrong.

Some people believe that the idea of true-for-me is stronger than the idea of belief, that it means something more than just the fact that I believe it. Suppose that Alice believes that God exists and Jane does not believe that God exists. Then it is true-for-Alice that God exists but not-true-for-Jane. On our view, this means nothing more than that Alice believes that

God exists and Jane does not. On their view, it means something more. But, what else could it mean? Does it mean that there really is a God in Alice's world but not in Jane's? How could it? There is only one world. Alice's world *is* Jane's world. And certainly they don't think that each of us has such power over God that by bringing ourselves to believe that God exists, we can bring him into existence in our world, and by bringing ourselves to disbelieve that God exists, we can knock him out of our world? Such a view makes little sense to us. If there is a God, we surely do not have the power to make him not exist in our world by changing our beliefs.

Perhaps these people mean to suggest that if one believes in God, then God will act on that person's behalf and that God will not act to support those who do not believe that he exists. This, of course, might be true. But it does not mean that God does not exist for Alice. It means what it says, that God will not act for Alice. If those are the conditions under which God acts, then God exists. But then God exists for both Alice and Jane.

Suppose we asked you to believe that the earth is round. How do you do it? Do you grit your teeth, furrow your brow, and b-e-l-i-e-v-e it? Do you think that performing the act of believing is like performing the act of jumping, only you do it inside your head, privately? Is it like holding your breath? Is it like not blinking your eyes for a certain length of time? Perhaps you repeat to yourself (silently, of course): I believe that the earth is round, I believe that the earth is round, I believe that the earth is round. . . . Or, perhaps you repeat to yourself over and over: the earth is round, the earth is round, the earth is round. . . . It's as if you were trying to memorize the claim, etch it into your brain by repeating it over and over again, until you were able to spit it back to someone who asked you the question, "Is the earth round?"

But this is a very unhelpful view of what believing is. In order for you to be said to believe something, you must be willing to act on it. Just spitting back the right answer does not mean that you believe it. It must somehow be integrated into the rest of your life. Suppose, for example, that you want a motorcycle. What do you do? Do you sit down and repeat to yourself over and over again: I want a motorcycle, I want a motorcycle? That's crazy. If you want a motorcycle, you do something about it. Perhaps you get a job or work extra hours at the job you already have. Or you let it be known around the time of your birthday that you want a motorcycle. And so on. If you believe something, it will be incorporated into your actions. So, if you believe that God exists—and we don't mean just giving lip service to the claim that God exists—then you will act in a certain way. In that sense, you see, the notion of belief is perhaps stronger than you had originally thought. It is certainly strong enough to capture the notion of true-for-me. As long as we distinguish believing something from merely giving lip service to it, we will be clear about the close connection between believing something and believing that it is true.

Another comment about the idea of true-for-me is in order. Sometimes people use this phrase to indicate what they think is a deeper philosophical attitude about truth. They want to express a deep sense of tolerance. "Each person is entitled to his or her own beliefs," they might say. Or, "You have your beliefs and I have mine; you look at the world your way and I'll look at it in mine. Who's to say what's true? We're all entitled to our own views. I don't have to believe what you tell me; I believe what I want to believe. This is a democracy." Now that's a fine speech, but what does it mean?

We're told that James Stewart and Henry Fonda were extremely close friends for many years. James Stewart held extremely conservative political views and Henry Fonda was an ardent supporter of extremely liberal causes. The two remained very close friends, in part by agreeing not to discuss politics with each other. Is this what is meant by saying that each person is entitled to his or her own beliefs—that we ought not to discuss our disagreements because otherwise we'll end up fighting? But what has this got to do with truth? This spirit of tolerance seems nothing more than a refusal to discuss issues with each other. "I believe that the Orioles are the best team in the American League, and I don't want to hear about it any further." If this is what true-for-me comes down to, then it amounts to no more than petulance and stubbornness. If you think that this spirit of tolerance means that there is no such thing as truth, but only the relativized notion of true-for-me, then you have given up the idea of there being any genuine disagreement between two individuals. No one denies that each of us has a right to his or her opinion. But it doesn't follow that every person's opinion is right.

Our suggestion, then, is simply to drop these expressions—"true-for-me," "true-for-you"—and use other words to say what we mean. If what you mean by "true-for-me" is "I believe it," then *say* "I believe it." If what you mean by "true-for-me" is "true," then *say* "true." Sticking with these fancy expressions will just lead to trouble.

EXERCISES

A.4:1 Consider the following statement:

There is intelligent life on Mars.

Suppose this statement were true-for-John but false-for-Harry. Do John and Harry disagree? What does their disagreement come to?

A.4:2 Suppose Congress is voting on whether to appropriate money for a new missile system. Congressman Jones claims that passing the bill will lead the Russians to build another system also. Can Congress take a vote on whether Jones's claim is true?

APPENDIX 5:   FACT AND OPINION

We must distinguish the notion of *truth* from both the notion of *proof* and the notion of *knowledge*.

If a particular statement has been proved, then it must have been proved to be true; so if a statement has been proved, it is true. But the converse does not hold. If a statement is true, it does not follow that it must have been proved true. There are many true statements that have never been proved. Consider, for example, the claim

> It rained in New England the morning Christopher Columbus discovered America.

Now, this is a statement; so it must be either true or false. We just don't know which. And it is hardly likely that anyone will ever be able to prove that the statement is true or prove that the statement is false. It's just highly unlikely that we will ever have the information sufficient to either prove it or disprove it. *True*, however, does not mean the same as *proved*, and *false* does not mean the same as *disproved*. For although every statement is either true or false, it is not the case that every statement has been either proved or disproved.

Knowledge is something like proof. For if you know that something is true, then it must be true. You cannot know that a statement is true if it is false. Anyone who says, for example,

> I know that $3 + 3 = 5$

is saying something false because the claim that $3 + 3 = 5$ is false. On the other hand, something might be true without anyone ever knowing that it's true. The example we used for the notion of proof will serve here as well. Either it did rain in New England the morning Christopher Columbus discovered America or it didn't, even though we don't know—and it is highly unlikely that anybody else knows—which.

There is yet another notion that crops up in discussion of truth, and this is the notion of a *fact*. Frequently, facts are contrasted with *opinions*. But the distinction between fact and opinion is not very clear, and its use seems to be more of a hindrance than a help to clear thinking, as we will now explain.

What is a fact? Have you ever seen one? Do they walk down the street? Can you find one in your house? Clearly not. Well, then, what is a fact? The sun is shining, you say. Now that's a fact. But what does this mean? Does it mean that it's true that the sun is shining? This does seem to be one key ingredient in the notion of a fact: to say "It is a fact that" seems to be just another way of saying "It is true that." In other words, a fact is a true statement. Of course, if this is all that there is to the notion of a fact, then it seems perfectly clear that some opinions are facts. Suppose someone were to say to you

   The weather is beautiful.

Is this a fact or an opinion? Well, suppose it's true that the weather is beautiful. Then it must be a fact that the weather is beautiful. But this person, in making the claim, is telling you what he thinks, what he believes to be true—his opinion on the weather. So this very same claim we earlier agreed was a fact turns out also to be an opinion.

   What is an opinion? In simplest terms, a person's opinion is what the person believes is true. But whenever anyone tells you something, if that person is sincere and honest, then she is telling you what she believes. As you read this book, you are reading things that we believe to be true: everything in this book is our opinion! When a scientist reports her research findings in a scientific journal, she is expressing her opinions. So, if this is all that there is to the distinction, there is no distinction: a fact will simply be a true opinion.

   Perhaps there is something else involved in the notion of an opinion. We tend to think that there is a spirit of tolerance about opinions, but the facts are the facts. Opinions are not hard and solid; opinions deal with emotions, likes and dislikes, things that are not easily pinned down. But, suppose I tell you

   I like chocolate-chip cookies.

This is a claim, a claim about what I like, and it will be either true or false depending upon whether I do or do not like chocolate-chip cookies. In this sense, then, since it's true that I do like chocolate-chip cookies, it's a fact that I like chocolate chip cookies. And insofar as I am making a claim about what I like, I am giving you my opinion.

   Suppose you don't like chocolate-chip cookies; you like vanilla cremes. Well, if you say

   I like vanilla cremes,

then you are giving me your opinion. But, of course, if you are being sincere and honest, then you are telling me something that is true, so what you are expressing is a fact. That I like chocolate-chip cookies and you like vanilla cremes is perfectly okay: we're each entitled to like what we like. We're each entitled to our opinions. But what this means—that we are each entitled to our opinions—is that we each have the freedom to express what we believe, as opposed to having to express only what is socially acceptable or legislated by some government. This feature of opinions has nothing to do with logic, nothing to do with truth and falsity. It has to do with the social and political fabric of the society in which we live.

   Are there situations in which you are not entitled to your opinion? That is, are there situations in which you cannot simply say whatever comes into your head or give your advice or express your beliefs? Surely there are. In the army, for example, when the commander gives an order, it is not up for discussion among the members of the company. Or, perhaps, if you are disciplining your child, you do not want somebody coming over to you (a friend, a neighbor, a relative) and telling you their opinion about how to raise a child. It is not their place and it is none of their business. We stress this particular aspect of the discussion because a large part of the notion of an opinion, as it is commonly understood, has to do with the appropriateness of an individual's saying something. Saying to someone "That's your opinion" is actually a nasty comment: you are telling someone that you don't really care what he's saying, and that, perhaps, that person has no authority to say what he is saying.

"That's your opinion" could also be another way of saying, "I don't agree with you," or, perhaps, "Your view is not held by everybody." And this brings up yet another interpretation of the fact/opinion distinction. A fact, one is inclined to say, is not simply a truth, but an indisputable truth. An opinion, on the other hand, is a truth that is still open to doubt. But do you really believe that there are indisputable truths? Do you really believe that you can get each and every human being—who was, is, or will be— to agree on any one thing? That's hardly likely. Everything is up for grabs. So, the problem with this way of marking the distinction is that it makes you think that there is a sharp distinction between disputable and indisputable claims, when in reality there is a continuum of claims that are more reasonable to believe and claims that are less reasonable to believe. To draw a sharp boundary on this continuum between facts and opinions seems arbitrary.

The result of our discussion in this appendix is that there seem to be a number of different distinctions all termed *fact/opinion*, not all of which are coherent. And it is not at all clear that observing any one of these distinctions will in any way help you to think and express yourself more clearly. Our suggestion, then, is to drop the words. We hope we have given you sufficient tools in this textbook to make the necessary distinctions to do the job some have thought the fact/opinion distinction does.

EXERCISES

A.5:1   Do you think that there really is a fact/opinion distinction that has not been treated—or treated fairly—in this text? If so, explain what this distinction is.

A.5:2   Do you think that there really is no fact/opinion distinction and find the discussion in this appendix convincing? Try to explain why you think people have made this distinction. What is the point of making distinctions like this?

GLOSSARY

ad baculum An informal fallacy in which, instead of giving a reason for thinking that something is the right course of action, one threatens the person. (See Chapter 11.)

accident An informal fallacy that consists in applying a loosely stated generalization to an instance it is not meant to apply to. (See Chapter 11.)

addition A valid argument pattern involving disjunction: X; SO, X v Y. (See Chapter 10.)

ad hominem A fallacious argument form in which the arguer attacks the person making the claim instead of the claim itself. (See Chapter 11.)

ad ignorantiam An informal fallacy in which one supposes that since something has not been proved false, it must be true. (See Chapter 11.)

ad misericordiam An informal fallacy in which, instead of giving a good reason for something's being the right thing to do, one appeals to pity. (See Chapter 11.)

ad populum An informal fallacy in which one argues that since everybody believes P, then P must be true. (See Chapter 11.)

affirming the antecedent Another name for **modus ponens**, a valid argument pattern of the form *If P then Q, P, SO Q*. (See Chapter 7.)

affirming the consequent An invalid argument pattern, frequently mistaken for modus ponens, of the form *If P then Q, Q, SO P*. (See Chapter 7.)

ambiguous A sentence is ambiguous if it can be read so as to say something true and can be read so as to say something false. (See Chapter 1.)

antecedent The constituent statement in a conditional that fills the *if* clause. For example, in "If he moves, then he'll be well," the antecedent is "he moves." (See Chapter 7.)

argument A collection of statements, some of which, called **premisses**, are meant to justify or warrant the **conclusion**. (See Chapters 4 and 8.)

argument indicator A word that tells you that a conclusion is coming (such as *therefore*) or that a premiss is coming (such as *because*). (See Chapter 8.)

assignment (of truth values) A choice of either T or F for each of the atomic letters in some complex formula. (See Chapter 3.)

atom, also, **atomic statement** A statement having no significant logical parts—that is, a statement that is not built up from other statements through the use of one or more of the logical connectives. (See Chapter 2.)

atomic letter A letter that represents an atom. (See Chapter 3.)

begging the question A fallacious form of argument in which one assumes the very thing one sets out to prove. Also known as **circular reasoning**. (See Chapter 11.)

black and white fallacy An informal fallacy in which one asserts a disjunction whose disjuncts are not exhaustive, and treats them as if they were. (See Chapter 11.)

chain argument Another name for **hypothetical syllogism**; a valid argument pattern of the form *If P then Q; if Q then R; SO, if P then R.* (See Chapter 10.)

circular reasoning Same as **begging the question**.

command A request or order that someone do something. Usually, one issues a command by using an imperative sentence. (See Chapter 1.)

complex dilemma A valid argument pattern involving disjunction and the conditional: $X \vee Y; X \to Z; Y \to W; SO, Z \vee W.$ (See Chapter 10.)

complex statement A statement that contains one or more statements combined by means of one or more of the logical connectives. (See Chapter 2.)

composition An informal fallacy based on the suppressed premiss that what is true of each part is true of the whole to which the parts belong. (See Chapter 11.)

conclusion The statement in an argument that one is arguing for. An argument can have only one conclusion. (See Chapters 4 and 8.)

conclusion indicator A word that tells you that a conclusion is coming—for example, *therefore.* (See Chapter 8.)

conditional A complex statement formed from *if, then* or an equivalent idiom. For example, "If he moves, then his leg will be fine." (See Chapter 7.)

conjoined structure An argument structure in which two statements work together, not independently, to support a conclusion. (See Chapter 9.)

conjunct A constituent statement in a conjunction. For example, in "John has a stereo and a VCR," the conjuncts are "John has a stereo" and "John has a VCR." (See Chapter 3.)

conjunction A complex statement formed from simpler statements through the use of *and* or one of its logical equivalents. For example, "John went to dinner and the movies." (See Chapter 3.)

connective A particle, such as *not* or *and,* that is attached to one or more statements to create a new statement. (See Chapter 2.)

connotation The connotation of a word is the properties a thing must have to be properly called by that word. (See Chapter 11.)

consequent The constituent statement in a conditional that fills the *then* clause. For example, in "If he walks, then his leg will be fine," the consequent is "his leg will be fine." (See Chapter 7.)

consistent A statement is consistent if it comes out true under at least one interpretation. Two statements are consistent if they can both be true. A group of statements is consistent if it is possible that the statements all are true together. (See Chapters 2 and 7.)

constituent One statement is a constituent of another if the latter is built up from the former by means of one or more of the logical connectives. (See Chapter 3.)

context The circumstances surrounding a person's utterance; for example, the people involved, the time and place of the utterance, and other words used on the occasion. (See Chapter 2.)

contradictory Two statements are contradictory if they cannot both be true and they cannot both be false. The clearest example of a pair of contradictory statements is a statement and its negation. (See Chapter 2.)

contrapositive To form the contrapositive of a conditional, switch antecedent and consequent and negate both. The contrapositive of *If P then Q*, for example, is *If not Q then not P*. A conditional and its contrapositive are logically equivalent. (See Chapter 7.)

contrary Two statements are contrary if they cannot both be true but they can both be false. For example, the statements "John is rich" and "John is poor" are contraries. (See Chapter 2.)

convergent structure An argument structure in which two or more independent lines of reasoning are put forward to support a given conclusion. (See Chapter 9.)

converse To form the converse of a conditional, switch antecedent and consequent. The converse of *If P then Q*, for example, is *If Q then P*. A conditional and its converse are not, in general, logically equivalent. (See Chapter 7.)

counterexample A true statement about a particular case that shows a generalization to be false. (See Chapter 2.)

counterfactual conditional A conditional whose antecedent is contrary to the facts; for example, "If the hostages had been released earlier, Jimmy Carter would have been reelected." (See Chapter 7.)

definiendum In a definition, the word being defined. (See Chapter 11.)

definiens In a definition, the words used to define the term. (See Chapter 11.)

De Morgan's Laws $-(P \vee Q)$ is logically equivalent to $-P \& -Q$. $-(P \& Q)$ is logically equivalent to $-P \vee -Q$. (See Chapter 5.)

denotation The denotation of a word is the thing or things the word properly applies to. (See Chapter 11.)

denying the antecedent An invalid argument pattern, frequently mistaken for modus tollens, having the form *If P then Q, not P, SO, not Q*. (See Chapter 7.)

denying the consequent Another name for **modus tollens**, a valid argument pattern having the form *If P then Q, not Q, SO, not P*. (See Chapter 7.)

dilemma A valid argument pattern that involves disjunction. (See Chapter 10.)

disambiguate To take a sentence that is ambiguous and change it so that it becomes unambiguous. (See Chapters 1 and 5).

disjunct A constituent statement of a disjunction. For example, in the sentence "Either John studied French or John studied Spanish," the two disjuncts are "John studied French" and "John studied Spanish." (See Chapter 5.)

disjunction A complex statement formed by connecting simpler statements with *or* or one of its equivalents. For example, "John went to dinner or to the movies." (See Chapter 5.)

disjunctive syllogism A valid argument pattern involving disjunction: $X \vee Y$; $-X$; SO, Y. (See Chapter 10.)

divergent structure An argument structure in which one statement serves as a premiss from which two distinct conclusions are inferred. (See Chapter 9.)

division An informal fallacy based on the suppressed premiss that what is true of a whole is true of each part of the whole. (See Chapter 11.)

double negation A sentence containing two negative particles that effectively cancel each other out. (See Chapters 2 and 10.)

entails (entailment)   Same as **implies (implication)**. (See Chapter 7.)

enthymeme   An argument in which either a premiss or a conclusion has been left unstated. (See Chapter 11.)

exclusion   A valid argument pattern involving conjunction: $-(X \& Y)$; X; SO, $-Y$. (See Chapter 10.)

exclusive   Two statements are exclusive, or **inconsistent**, if they cannot both be true. (See Chapter 2.)

exclusive *or*   The exclusive *or* means "one or the other but not both," so the truth table for the exclusive *or* is T when and only when the two disjuncts have different truth values. (See Chapter 5.)

exhaustive   Two statements are exhaustive if they cannot both be false. (See Chapter 2.)

explicit definition   A type of definition in which one gives the connotation of a word. Also, **lexical definition**. (See Chapter 11.)

fallacy   An invalid argument that people frequently get tricked into thinking is valid. (See Chapter 7.)

false   A statement is false if what it says is not so. (See Chapter 1.)

false authority   An informal fallacy in which one mistakenly supposes that an authority in one field is an authority in another. (See Chapter 11.)

false cause   An informal fallacy in which one mistakes a regularity for a causal connection. (See Chapter 11.)

generalization   A statement that is supposed to hold true of all things of a given kind (or of no things of a given kind). (See Chapter 2.)

grammatical tree   A way of representing how a complex formula is built up from its atoms. (See Chapter 6.)

hasty generalization   An informal fallacy that consists in generalizing from a single or special instance. (See Chapter 11.)

imperative sentence   A sentence that is used to issue a command. For example, "Open the door!" (See Chapter 1.)

implies (implication)   One statement implies another if it is impossible for the first to be true and the second false. For example, the statement that John is a man implies the statement that John is a human being. (See Chapter 4.)

inclusive *or*   The inclusive *or* means "one or the other or both." This is the sense of the *or* that is symbolized in logic by 'v'. (See Chapter 5.)

inconsistent   Two statements are inconsistent if they cannot both be true. A group of statements is inconsistent if the statements cannot all be true together. (See Chapters 2 and 7.)

indicative sentence   A sentence, ending in a period, that is used to make a claim. (See Chapter 1.)

infer (inference)   To infer is to conclude something on the basis of evidence or reasons. (See Chapter 4.)

informal fallacy   An argument pattern exhibiting an error in reasoning people are commonly prone to make. (See Chapter 11.)

interrogative sentence   A sentence that is used to ask a question. For example, "Did it rain yesterday?" (See Chapter 1.)

lexical definition   See **explicit definition**.   (See Chapter 11.)

logically equivalent   Two statements are logically equivalent if they mutually imply each other, that is, if they always have the same truth value. (See Chapter 2.)

logically independent   Two statements are logically independent if one cannot infer the truth value of the second knowing only the truth value of the first. (See Chapter 2.)

logically related   Two statements are logically related if one can infer something about the truth value of the second knowing only the truth value of the first. (See Chapter 2.)

logical truth, or tautology A statement that cannot possibly be false. For example, "Either it is raining or it is not raining." (See Chapters 2 and 7.)

main connective The main connective of a complex logical formula is the one that is used to construct it from its immediate coherent subclauses. (See Chapter 6.)

material conditional The conditional that is understood to have the following truth-table definition: false when and only when the antecedent is true and the consequent is false; otherwise true. (See Chapter 7.)

modus ponens A valid argument pattern of the form *If P then Q; P; SO Q.* (See Chapters 7 and 10.)

modus tollens A valid argument pattern of the form *If P then Q; not Q; SO not P.* (See Chapters 7 and 10.)

natural deduction A sequence of steps that constitutes an argument for a given conclusion from certain premisses, each step being a premiss, a tautology, an elementary inference from earlier steps in the sequence, or a rephrasing of an earlier step. (See Chapters 5 and 10.)

necessary condition P is a necessary condition for Q if Q wouldn't be true without P's being true. That is, *if Q then P.* (See Chapter 7.)

negation The negation of a statement is the denial of that statement. Usually, it is formed by putting *It is not the case that* in front of the statement or by inserting *not* in the appropriate place. (See Chapter 2.)

ostensive definition A type of definition in which one gives or points to examples of things to which the defined word applies. (See Chapter 11.)

parse To break down a statement into its constituent subclauses. (See Chapter 5.)

premiss A statement in an argument that is put forward to support or justify the conclusion. (See Chapters 4 and 8.)

premiss indicator A word that tells you that a premiss is coming—for example, *because.* (See Chapter 8.)

principle of candor A principle of interpretation, to the effect that an individual should say everything he or she truly believes is relevant to the issue at hand. (See Chapter 9.)

principle of charity A principle of interpretation, to the effect that one should give a text the benefit of the doubt and put the best possible reading on it. (See Chapter 9.)

principle of conjunction A valid argument pattern involving conjunction: X; Y; SO, X & Y. (See Chapter 10.)

question A request for information, usually expressed in an interrogative sentence. (See Chapter 1.)

reason A statement that explains why another statement is true or why a person should believe that another statement is true. (See Chapter 8.)

sequential structure An argument structure in which a statement is the conclusion of one argument and the premiss in another. (See Chapter 9.)

simple dilemma A valid argument pattern having the form *Either P or Q; if P then R; if Q then R; SO R.* (See Chapter 10.)

simplification A valid argument pattern involving conjunction: a conjunction implies each of its conjuncts, or, X & Y; SO, X. (See Chapter 10.)

sound argument An argument is sound if it is valid *and* all the premisses are true. (See Chapters 7 and 11.)

square of opposition A mnemonic device for remembering the logical relations between sentences of the forms: All Fs are Gs; No Fs are Gs; Some Fs are Gs; Some Fs are not Gs. (See Chapter 2.)

statement A claim or assertion that is either true or false but not both. (See Chapter 1.)

statement letter See **atomic letter**.

subcontrary Two statements are subcontrary if they can both be true but they cannot both be false; for example, the statements "John is six feet tall or more" and "John is six feet tall or less" are subcontraries. (See Chapter 2.)

sufficient condition P is a sufficient condition for Q if P's being true is enough to assure Q's being true. That is, *if P then Q*. (See Chapter 7.)

tautology   A tautology is a formula that comes out true for every line in the truth table—that is, a formula that comes out true under every possible circumstance. For example, $P \lor -P$. (See Chapter 7.)

transitive relation   A relation is transitive when if X bears the relation to Y and Y bears the relation to Z, then X bears the relation to Z. For example, implication is transitive: if P implies Q and Q implies R, then P implies R. On the other hand, "being the father of" is not transitive: if A is the father of B and B is the father of C, it does not follow that A is the father of C. (See Chapter 4.)

true   A statement is true if what it says is so. (See Chapter 1.)

truth conditions   The truth conditions of a statement are the circumstances that would make it true and the circumstances that would make it false. (See Chapter 2.)

truth table   A method of both figuring out and representing how the truth value of a complex is determined by the truth values of its atomic statements. (See Chapter 2.)

truth value   There are two truth values, **true** and **false**. (See Chapter 1.)

tu quoque   A version of *ad hominem* in which one attacks the person putting forward a claim for not practicing what he or she preaches. (See Chapter 11.)

unambiguous   A sentence is unambiguous if it does not have two distinct interpretations, on one of which it comes out true and on the other of which it comes out false. (See Chapter 1.)

useful argument   A valid argument whose premises are acceptable to the participants in the discussion. (See Chapters 7 and 11.)

vague   A statement is vague if it does not have a clear enough meaning for us to assign it any truth value. (See Chapter 1.)

valid argument   An argument whose premises imply its conclusion. An argument is valid if it is impossible for all of the premises to be true and the conclusion false. (See Chapters 4 and 11.)

INDEX

Words in bold type are listed in the Glossary.